D0908279

Spies in the Promised Land

ALSO BY MICHEL BAR-ZOHAR

The Hunt for German Scientists
Ben-Gurion: The Armed Prophet
The Avengers
Embassies in Crisis:
Diplomats and Demagogues Behind the Six Day War

Spies in the Promised Land

Iser Harel and the Israeli Secret Service

Michel Bar-Zohar

Translated from the French by
Monroe Stearns

DAVIS-POYNTER

First published in Great Britain in 1972 by
Davis-Poynter Limited Broadwick House Broadwick Street
London W1V 2AH

Copyright © 1972 by Michel Bar-Zohar

ISBN 0 7067 0033 3

Originally published in French in 1971 under the title
J'ai Risqué Ma Vie. Copyright Librairie Arthème Fayard 1971

Printed in Great Britain by
Compton Printing Limited Aylesbury Buckinghamshire

Preface

FOR OVER FIFTEEN YEARS after the State of Israel came into being the identity of one man was a deep and dark secret — Iser Harel, the chief executive of all the agencies of national security. Even after the press, in 1965, publicized his name and made his face familiar to one and all, his achievements, as well as the vast majority of the operations of the secret army he commanded, remained indistinct.

Frequently, to be sure, the newspapers published many stories on the uncovering of subversive networks, on the activities of Israeli secret agents abroad, and on various incidents involving spies and counterspies, but all were fragmentary and superficial. During this time, however, Israel's security department was covering itself with glory. "It is among the world's best," said Allen Dulles, former head of the American Central Intelligence Agency (CIA).

What made it so? What were — and still are — its methods? And how did they originate?

To answer such questions I undertook this biography of Iser Harel up to the time of his resignation on March 25, 1963. Since then he has not been concerned with the inside activities of the Secret Service except for a brief period from 1965 to 1966 when he acted as Prime Minister Levi Eshkol's special adviser on matters of intelligence and security. At present Iser Harel is a member of the Knesset.

Iser's chief claim to fame is his having built with his own skillful hands a secret service that is not only one of the best of our times, but also one of the most unusual. For he imbued his organization with principles of morality and justice unequaled in any similar system and gave it ideals that seem incompatible with undercover work.

The story of Iser Harel's own life and accomplishments is to a great extent also the story of the Israeli Secret Service. I have, naturally, put most of my emphasis on the personality of its chief executive, and have only rarely mentioned his deputies and associates, whom I have seldom called by name. Without those hundreds of brave and single-minded secret agents, however, Iser Harel would never have been able to form that shadowy army that keeps watch over Israel. It is to those nameless soldiers of security that I dedicate this book.

MICHEL BAR-ZOHAR
Tel Aviv

Contents

1 : A Secret Service Is Born   1

2 : Young Iser's Private Wars   4

3 : The Battle in the Barracks   11

4 : The Records of Shai Are Missing   19

5 : Our Man in Amman   31

6 : The Fall of Big Iser   40

7 : The Toubianski Case   47

8 : Ben-Gurion Discovers Iser Harel   55

9 : School for Spies   65

10 : Rebellion   72

11 : The Gallows of Baghdad   83

12 : Iser Reaches the Top   99

13 : Rachel's Chauffeur   104

14 : Dangerous Games   113

15 : Iser Harel's Mikes   125

16 : Three-Act Tragedy   133

17 : *Nasser's Secret Ally*   144

18 : *In Vino Veritas*   156

19 : *Traitors*   164

20 : *Nocturnal Visitors*   173

21 : *Room at the Top*   188

22 : *Secret Mission to Cairo*   211

23 : *Israel Saves de Gaulle*   225

24 : *Where Is Yossele?*   231

25 : *The Mohel and the Arab Prince*   239

26 : *Madeleine's Secret*   248

27 : *Nasser's Secret Weapons*   256

28 : *The Affair of the German Scientists*   267

29 : *Iser Resigns*   273

30 : *"Faithful Guardian of the State's Security,
Its Honor, and Its Secrets"*   286

Spies in the Promised Land

1

A Secret Service Is Born

Sun-drenched Ben-Yehuda Avenue in Tel Aviv was humming with life on the morning of June 30, 1948. For the six weeks since the State of Israel had come into being by proclamation, the War of Independence had been raging on many fronts, and vast numbers of young soldiers in khaki shirts and trousers were streaming along the sidewalks. None of those who were watching them, however, seemed aware of the shadowy figures that kept slipping one by one into Number 85 on the corner of Gordon Street.

It was an undistinguished, gray, three-story house, with a flower shop and a small café in the basement, and a taxi station at the curb. Eminently respectable middle-class families lived on the first two floors, but the third consisted of an unpretentious apartment on whose door a tarnished brass plate read: "Veterans' Counseling Service." Actually it was the headquarters of Shai.

Shai, a syllable always uttered in a whisper, was the mysterious Intelligence Service of Haganah, the underground Jewish army in Palestine.

That morning Shai's high priests were meeting in the apartment's small rear room. The conference had been called by the top executive of Shai, Iser Be'eri, who had summoned to it the heads of the various departments of the agency: Benjamin Gibli, chief of the Jerusalem District; Avraham Kidron, chief of the Northern District; David Karon, chief of the Negev District; Boris Guriel, chief of the British Department"; and Iser Harel, chief of the Tel Aviv District.

Tall, thin, silver-haired Be'eri had the floor. "Now that Israel is a state," he said, "Ben-Gurion has decided that the Security and Intelligence Agencies must be reorganized, and so, as he directed me to do, I submitted to him a new plan which he has just okayed. From now on there will be three divisions of the Secret Service:

"One: The Bureau of Military Intelligence (Aman), of which I myself will take charge, as well as of the Department of Counterespionage (Ran).

"Two: The Foreign Ministry's Political Department, which will collect intelligence abroad. Boris Guriel will be its director.

"Three: The Department of Internal Security, to be called Shin-Bet. Its director will be Iser Harel.

"That's all." Be'eri carefully gathered his papers together.

The Secret Service of the State of Israel had been born.

There were no comments, no questions. As the conference broke up, however, Be'eri asked some of his staff to remain, but not Iser Harel. Iser rose without saying anything and went back to his own command post, which was hidden away in a huge refrigeration plant to the north of Tel Aviv.

A week later the department heads of Shai were given military rank. Wearing his new colonel's uniform, which was too big for him, short, plump, and balding Iser Harel paid a visit to the little barber shop near Haganah headquarters where all the leaders of the Jewish army went to get their mops of hair trimmed.

The barber stared at him in astonishment. "You're a colonel?"

In 1948 a colonelcy was so high a rank that the fellow would never have dreamed his retiring little customer could possibly have achieved it. "Why doesn't anyone ever tell me anything?" he complained. "Here you've been my customer all these years, and you never said a word about being a top army officer!"

Iser did not answer him and merely shrugged his shoulders in embarrassment, being considerably different from most of the patrons who never let a chance slip by for advertising their importance in the military. People said that the Harel family were "different" anyway — taciturn, shy, self-effacing, and stubborn as mules. Gossips added that they might not be very talkative, but were trickier than the Devil himself.

2

Young Iser's Private Wars

BACK IN THE DVINSK of Imperial Russia (now Daugavpils, Latvian S.S.R.) the lavish wedding of vinegar magnate David Levin's youngest daughter Yocheved to Nathan Neta Halperin* was talked about for a long time afterward.

Halperin was the man whom David Levin had gone far into Poland to select for his son-in-law in the local tradition that rich Jewish businessmen married their daughters to brilliant but impoverished young men who were well versed in the Scriptures and the Talmud. Levin had found Halperin at the famous rabbinical college in Volozhin.

The youthful rabbi enjoyed the respect and admiration of his new neighbors. He had, they said, unusual qualities of mind, was uncommonly skillful in analyzing difficult passages of the Talmud, and possessed an astonishing understanding of the abstractions in Jewish mysticism. His family tree stemmed from the legendary Hayyim of Volozhin, who had founded the rabbinate there. On the other hand, they found him reserved and unsocial, and totally without a sense of humor. He had never

---

* Iser Harel's father. After he became a government official in Israel Iser adopted the Hebrew form of the name Halperin — Harel.

surmounted the blow of losing his parents when he was a child, they decided, and it must have been that tragedy which made him so painfully ascetic.

David Levin was so ecstatic over having found such a prize that the young man's social failings bothered him not at all. He made his son-in-law manager of the big vinegar works in Vitebsk and gave the couple a handsome house surrounded by flower beds. Presently Yetta, Hannah, and Shalom made their entry into the world, and in 1912 Iser followed them.

Iser became a small, thin, active child with sharp blue eyes, and ears that fanned out from a round head. Like his father he was not much of a talker and stuck by himself, disliking to play with his brother and sisters. Still, he was by no means spoiled; no one ever saw him cry or run to his mother for comfort. On the contrary, he was stubbornly and aggressively unruly. He could use his fists, got involved in all the neighborhood kids' scuffles, and, naturally, became one of their gang leaders, in which capacity he would frequently mount an offensive against a rival gang. After one of these battles, which generally raged around the steaming tanks of vinegar behind the factory, he would come home in tatters, his knuckles raw and his eyes black, but looking as innocent as the Last of the Just. His parents gave up trying to reason him out of his scrappy disposition and resigned themselves to letting his nature take its course.

While Iser was waging his diminutive campaigns, full-scale wars were raging all around him. World War I had broken out when he was only two years old, and Nathan Halperin's spacious house had become an asylum for several refugees. Grandfather Levin and all his children and grandchildren had fled war-torn Dvinsk for Vitebsk, but they did not complain, for all through the early years of the war the vinegar works were in full operation and brought in plenty of money. The impressive old man, in fact, kept up his business trips to the large Russian cities, from which he always returned laden down with toys and big bars of Bormann Swiss chocolate. Every week

Grandmother Levin went to the theater in her carriage. The house might have been a bit crowded, but life was far from austere.

Iser was five years old on the day his father burst into the house and exclaimed in an anguished voice: "They've overthrown the Czar!"

Their old Russian servant dropped her duster, crossed herself, and wept as she murmured: "Our holy father, the Czar!"

Then began an infernal cycle of Whites and Reds alternatively gaining control of the city and mercilessly slaughtering civilians. Windows were kept shuttered, and doors bolted.

Too young to understand what was going on, Iser roamed the streets on the heels of the soldiers, and once saw Trotsky haranguing a mob in the main square of Vitebsk.

Inevitably disaster struck the Halperins in full force. First, the grandfather, who had been the mainstay of the whole family, succumbed to a heart attack, after which his widow and her sons went back to Dvinsk. Then the Soviets nationalized the vinegar factories. A few weeks later everything the Halperins had was gone — house, fine clothes, entertainment, even their daily bread, for famine was ravaging Russia. The family, who had wanted for nothing, were suddenly paupers. At night the children would creep into the stables of the Red cavalry and steal the horses' oats, and their mother collected potato skins discarded by the Russian soldiers and made knishes from them. Iser's shoes were falling to pieces, and all he had to wear were a faded gray smock and pants too short for him.

Like all children, however, Iser easily adapted himself to the new turn of events. His older brother, along with other teenagers, had considerable admiration for the Bolshevik revolution, which responded to their ideals, had an aura of romance about it, and, especially, changed school programs in their favor. Iser and he would have joined the revolution if it had not been for the strong Zionist traditions of the Halperin household. Their father carefully hid his Zionist books and periodicals, which were forbidden by the authorities, and secretly instructed Iser in his own dedication to Zionism. The boy read the classics of Zionist literature and found himself profoundly stirred by them.

When Iser was ten years old his family decided to leave Russia. New borders had just been set for the U.S.S.R., and since Dvinsk was now in Latvia — the "free world" — most of the family moved there. With help from his friends and relatives Nathan Halperin obtained falsified papers which stated that Iser and his brother were twins, had been born in Dvinsk, and had been only temporarily living in Vitebsk. Early in 1923 the Halperins, loaded down with bundles and suitcases, took the train at the Vitebsk station. But they arrived in Dvinsk empty-handed; all their belongings had been stolen during the journey.

The war had spared Dvinsk's ancient fortress that surveyed from a hilltop the broad valley of the muddy Dvina River, but it had violently ravaged the city itself. Whole neighborhoods had been reduced to piles of rubble with caves and tunnels that gangs of adolescents fortified and defended in bloody battles against all intruders. Bricks and stones served them as shells, and sacks of powdered mortar as hand grenades. Sometimes when the gangs tired of total war they would pit their leaders against each other in single-handed combat. Iser was often the champion of his gang in such duels.

No one at home bothered about him anymore. Every day he helped his father in the vinegar factory, which had been partially rebuilt. Not his mother's darling, he shared almost equally with the other children in the household. But when friends or relatives remarked to his mother that Iser seemed to have fewer clothes than his siblings, Mrs. Halperin would shrug and reply: "He doesn't need them." She knew that her youngest was already quite independent and could look out for himself.

His father tried to get him to go to synagogue, at least on the Sabbath, but Iser firmly refused.

Iser's poker face is discernible even in family photographs taken during the Dvinsk period. Years later his sphinxlike expression became his dominant characteristic. Yet however calm and cold he seemed externally, Iser was, nevertheless, savagely proud, never forgetting an insult and rarely apologizing.

No one, not even his own family, had any idea that this bantam rooster was fundamentally sensitive or that he was secretly writing poems that he published under a pseudonym in Riga's Jewish newspaper. Alone in his double-locked room he used to devour the Russian classics — Pushkin, Dostoevski, Lermontov. There he also discovered the novels of Victor Hugo, which enthralled him. But he was also unconsciously preparing himself for his distant future by earnestly studying detective stories and memorizing all the exploits of Arsène Lupin, Sherlock Holmes, and Nick Carter.

Once a week he would go to the neighborhood movie theater to watch a serial called "The Mysterious Hand" (fifty episodes, two hours a week). Later he adored talking films, especially the masterpieces of Sergei Eisenstein and musical comedies starring Al Jolson. His favorite, however, was an obscure film about the adventures of a French abbé during the Revolution, in which the priest substituted a sword for his cross in order to succor the unfortunate.

As Iser advanced in high school he became conscious of his destiny as a Jew and joined the ranks of Zionist Socialists. When he was sixteen years old he came home from school one day and announced that he was going away. The Zionist movement was sending him for a year's training to a collective farm near Riga. His family tried to persuade him to stay in school for the few months left until he graduated and called in his class teacher and the high school principal to help them reason with him. It was a waste of effort. After a few days Iser's heavy leather boots were trudging down the muddy road toward Riga.

The year Iser spent on the farm was one of the happiest of his whole life. Belonging to a community of young folk and working the soil thrilled him. His vague dreams and hopes began to take form; he would go to Palestine and join a kibbutz. There was no place in his fancies for conquering the Promised Land by force of arms, or even for protecting its early colonists with weapons. He thought only of working with his hands. Such were the reveries of the man who would someday command the secret army of the Jewish State.

He spared no effort to do his best, and he earned a reputation as one of the best workers in the commune, but he still had doubts about his success in Palestine, where he would have to compete for recognition with true pioneers.

In 1929 the call to arms echoed in Zionist gatherings throughout the world. Bloody disorders had broken out in Palestine between the Jews and the Arabs. The Jews were a minority; an organized Arab offensive could crush them completely regardless of the presence of the British army. The Zionist leaders decreed a general mobilization to send reinforcements to the Jews in Palestine. All eligible young Jews were to go together in order to swell the ranks of the threatened community.

The farm where Iser had been working emptied at once. Iser wanted to go too, but he was only seventeen years old. A counterfeiter, however, supplied him with papers certifying that he had just celebrated his eighteenth birthday, and in January 1930 he obtained an immigration visa.

While his parents and friends were seeing him off at the Dvinsk railway station, a militant Zionist whom Iser scarcely knew pulled him aside and, without saying a word, handed him a package. On the moving train Iser opened it and found the traditional parting gift to such as he — a small, well-oiled revolver and a generous supply of bullets.

At Genoa Iser took ship for the long, trying voyage to Palestine. In spite of the heavy seas and the numbing cold he slept on deck like the other immigrants, for he had no money for a berth. He was never to forget the moment he first glimpsed Jaffa, its mosques and minarets glistening in a glorious sunrise.

A representative of the Jewish Immigration Department, an anxious Jew, came on board and kept saying: "Beware of the English. If you have any weapons, throw them overboard. That's what the English are looking for. If they find any on any one of you, all of you will be refused entry."

Some of the immigrants obeyed and threw their guns into the water. Iser, however, cut a big round loaf of bread in two, scooped out the dough and replaced it with his revolver, then stuck the halves together and stowed the reconstituted loaf in the bottom of his knapsack under his soiled clothes. Then he lowered himself into the skiff in which an old Arab fisherman was ferrying the passengers to shore.

The customs official on the dock asked Iser whether he had anything to declare.

"See for yourself."

Iser opened his knapsack and rummaged in it right under the official's eyes. The Englishman looked into the innocent face of the young immigrant, then glanced at the sardine boxes and jam-encrusted spoons in the knapsack.

"Go ahead."

Iser crossed the immigration barrier and disappeared into the throng of Jews and Arabs who were hurrying away from the quayside.

3

The Battle
in the Barracks

ABOUT NINE MILES north of Jaffa, near Herzliya, where there was then a Jewish settlement, rises the sun-baked, wind-eroded, sandy hill of Shefayim. This was the spot where a handful of young pioneers had chosen to pitch their tents.

These lunatics — as the inhabitants of the region called them — were for the most part recent immigrants from Poland; the rest were Sabras — Jews who had been born in Palestine. As they sat around their campfire in the evening they dreamed of some day establishing a true kibbutz where they could till their own land and grow their own fruit trees. In the meantim, in order to survive they had to sign on as field hands with the well-to-do farmers of the region.

Like all other kibbutzim at that time Shefayim was wretchedly poor. Its treasury was always empty, the food was inadequate, and the "public buildings" were one barracks, pretentiously called the "refectory," and one barn used for work during the day and for recreation at night. The area was infested with scorpions and poisonous snakes, and, by a special dispensation of the Almighty, enjoyed stifling heat in summer and violent storms in winter. The English were unfriendly and suspicious; the Arabs kept brandishing their long knives; and the Jewish farmers preferred Arab workers to the young pioneers.

Into this Eden came the newly arrived Iser Harel. He left his thick winter overcoat at the kibbutz storeroom, entrusted his revolver to the local Haganah official, and dragged his knapsack to the bed assigned him in one of the most isolated tents. Night had already fallen, and a cold damp wind was blowing in from the sea.

Iser tucked his blanket around him, but he could not sleep. The test he had wanted so much for so long would confront him early in the morning, when he would set off to work with the others. His diffidence kept him awake until dawn.

Outside the barn a barbarous instrument was thrust into his hands. "That's a pickax," the kibbutz secretary told him.

Iser followed the other pioneers to a barren field where they were to plant an orchard. Someone showed him how to dig holes for the orange trees.

That evening, when, exhausted, he dragged himself to his tent, his hands swollen and his forehead burning, he was the happiest of mortals. He had passed his test. The astonished kibbutz discovered that the little newcomer was an excellent worker. He was earning his place in the sun.

Iser loved working in the kibbutz. He loved the communal life, the talk sessions that sometimes lasted all night long, the vigor of the evening celebrations. On the other hand, he refused to take a leading part in the secret activities of Haganah. He did what he was told to do and no more, for in his eyes it was work that counted most. He became an orthodox "kibbutzer," inflexibly doctrinaire on all questions.

Then one day he met Rivka.

She was a slim Polish girl completely different from Iser. Whereas he was silent and shy, she was extroverted, lively, and cheerful. On evenings when there was a party he would sit on the sidelines as if he were incapable of joining in the others' fun. He did not like to dance, and he did not know how to relax and let himself be drawn into the general carefree atmosphere. Rivka, on the other hand, infected everyone else with her high spirits. They called her "the flame" and said she was utterly mad with the sheer joy of living. She also rode horseback as if she had been born in the saddle.

This ebullient girl and the uncommunicative Stakhanovite who met at Shefayim were drawn together by the law of opposites. They fell in love, and they married. As a couple they were entitled to a separate tent at first, and then to the extraordinary luxury of a tiny room in a newly constructed barracks, where a thin wooden partition was all that separated them from other families.

Those were the years when orange trees were being planted all over Sharon's rich fertile plain. Iser glimpsed an opportunity. He contrived to work his way into the closed circle of those who had a monopoly on the two lucrative occupations of wrapping and packing oranges and of laying irrigation pipes in the orchards as in California. He then organized a squad of workers to whom he taught the jealously guarded secrets of those operations. When winter came they went from orchard to orchard, packing boxes of fruit. They brought back tidy sums to the kibbutz, for while an ordinary worker earned a maximum of twenty piasters a day, an orange packer earned five times more.

Yet in 1935 Iser impulsively quit the kibbutz to which he had been devoted heart and soul. He and Rivka had applied for a leave of absence from the kibbutz in order to earn enough money for their parents' passage to Palestine. Iser toiled day and night as a construction worker, and Rivka got a job as a domestic. In due time they accumulated the necessary sum, and their families landed in Palestine. Both the elders and the young settled at Shefayim and quickly found jobs that would take care of their immediate needs. Iser and Rivka returned to their little room in the kibbutz barracks.

Everything seemed to be going fine until the night Iser came home from work and found Rivka in tears. She told him that during the afternoon she had heard several members of the kibbutz committee talking on the other side of the partition. "Iser is exploiting the kibbutz," one of them said. "He has brought his entire family here, and now the kibbutz has to pay for their passage, and house and feed them." The others agreed with him.

The utter falseness of the charge sent Iser into a towering rage. He could easily have proved it untrue, but he was too proud and sensitive to argue. Instead he burst into the secretary's office, his blood boiling.

"We have heard what you think of us," he shouted. "We're quitting. For good." And he slammed the door behind him.

All night long emissaries kept coming to the Harels' room, trying to explain, apologize, and, above all, to calm Iser down and persuade him to alter his decision. It was no good. The following day he and all his relatives left the kibbutz without a penny and without any possessions other than the clothes on their backs.

In the village of Herzliya Iser had a friend David, a simple unskilled laborer whose financial status provoked no envy from anyone. Yet when he met the whole Harel family on Herzliya's main street he grasped Rivka's hand and led her off to the general store. "Give her whatever she needs," he told the manager, "and charge it all to me."

Rivka bought everyone in her family a spoon, a fork, and a plate. Then she bought a stewpot, cots, mattresses, and blankets. And some oranges for dinner that night.

They lugged everything to the tumble-down shanty Iser had just rented on the village outskirts. Early the next morning the private kibbutz of the Harel family went to work at top speed.

Rivka and her sisters hired themselves out to pick oranges; Iser and his brother packed the fruit; their parents found work in the village itself. A few days later they figured that they could easily earn their own living. At the end of a few months they had built their own house and were prospering. Often an embassy from the kibbutz would visit them and try to persuade them to return. Even one of the top leaders of the kibbutz movement came to work on them.

"It's too late," Iser told him. "Something's snapped between us."

When World War II broke out, Iser was in luck because the British army had a desperate need for fruit and vegetables. The orange orchards were transformed into vegetable gardens, and new pipes were laid. But although Iser was earning more than ever before, he did not feel right. The money burned his fingers.

"It's the war," he said to Rivka. "All my friends are in the army, either the Palmach° or the British, but here I am, healthy and robust, just piling up money."

Iser went to the Haganah official in Herzliya. "I want to enlist in the British army."

"We'll let you know."

Several days later the official sent for Iser. "We would have preferred you to join Haganah," he said. "We need men in Palestine now. The British army can wait." He explained that they were apprehensive about Rommel's forthcoming campaign in North Africa. The Jewish population in the Holy Land had to be organized at once in preparation for a fight to the finish against a possible German invasion.

Iser agreed to attend a secret training school for Haganah officers, which was held in a kibbutz in the middle of the Jordan valley. Military maneuvers were disguised as volunteer trips on the part of young men coming to help with the harvest.

° The striking force, or spearhead, of the Haganah, which the British allowed to function while World War II was on.

After a few weeks Iser returned to Herzliya, where he was entrusted with special missions to procure information for headquarters.

His first assignment was to investigate the strange behavior of a mysterious German who lived in a secluded villa in the hills above Herzliya. "It appears that he is a Nazi spy," the Haganah officer told Iser.

That night Iser slunk through the dark grounds of the villa and managed to creep inside it. He went through the entire house with a fine-toothed comb, but not until he descended into the basement did he find what he was looking for. The whole cellar had been transformed into a plant for counterfeiting small denomination bills. Iser groped his way out through printing presses, vats of colored inks, and piles of freshly minted banknotes.

Some months later Iser was transferred to a coast guard unit that had just been formed owing to Haganah's interest in having several of its members in auxiliary branches of the British army. The Crown would pay them and clothe and feed them all the while they were using their official status to facilitate the secret activities of the Jewish Resistance. Iser donned a khaki uniform, cocked a topee over one ear, and reported for duty at the base near Herzliya.

There he was continually at sword's point with his commanding officer, an Englishman named Meaden, whose palm was constantly greased by both Jews and Arabs. Once a week Captain Meaden came from headquarters in Tel Aviv to inspect the coast guard base, bringing in his car the soldiers' weekly ration of meat. Somehow the choicest joints miraculously disappeared from the shipment and reappeared in the butcher shop windows, while the soldiers got only fatty, second-rate cuts. Everyone knew that Meaden was involved in the black market, but no one dared mention it.

Then one Passover Eve Meaden called Iser into his office. "Did you get your ration of matzo for Passover?" he inquired.

"Not yet."

Meaden grew angry. "That matzo of yours is just one more scheme of your rabbis to play the black market."

Iser saw red. "I am not a practicing Jew," he shouted, "and I don't have to stick up for the rabbis. But any man who steals meat from the army in wartime and sells it on the black market has no right to criticize our rabbis."

Meaden leaped up, his fists clenched, his arms in fighting position. Iser threw himself on the captain and knocked him down.

The officer called for help, but his sergeant, who had witnessed the entire fight, did not dare intervene. Several soldiers had also been watching through the open door. When Iser finally left the office, the captain rushed to the telephone and called Tel Aviv. But it was neither the military police nor any other reinforcements that answered Meaden's call for help. Instead several Haganah representatives descended from the car that entered the base. All they wanted was to hush the fracas up.

"Have you lost your mind?" they screamed at Iser, whom they had taken aside. "Striking an English officer in wartime? That could get you five years in jail. Go and apologize at once. That's an order!"

Iser refused.

They pleaded with him. They threatened him. They commanded him to obey in the name of Haganah, of the Resistance, of the fatherland.

"I will not apologize to anyone," Iser declared. "Why should I? You may be my superiors, but this is a matter of conscience."

The exasperated officials ordered him to leave the base at once. Then they tried to pacify Meaden less with soft words than, apparently, with hard cash. Iser was summoned to give an explanation of his conduct to Porat, the commanding officer of Haganah for that district.

When he had heard Iser's story, Porat said: "You are not to

blame. You were in the right. But you can't ever show your face in the coast guard again. We'll have to find you another job."

A few days later Iser was summoned before Israel Amir, then the omnipotent chief of Shai, the Haganah Intelligence Service, who had met him several times at Herzliya. Amir studied the little pugilist for a long time. Finally he said: "Beginning tomorrow you are going to work for me in Tel Aviv."

4

The Records of Shai
Are Missing

No ONE KNOWS when or how or where the ubiquitous, wraith-like Intelligence Service of the Resistance originated. The British knew it existed, but they could never put their finger on its nerve center, identify its directors, or discover its headquarters in spite of the fact that there were thousands of Shai agents. Nearly all the Jewish police, military officers, and inspectors worked for Shai unbeknownst to their British bosses and their Arab colleagues. The same was true of postal workers, telephone operators, hotel chambermaids, café waiters, newspapermen, secretaries, typists, and the Jewish department heads in the British bureaucratic system. Shai also maintained networks of Arab agents who reported what went on in the headquarters of the Arab tribes and in the secret meetings of influential Palestinians. British officers who either saw rewards forthcoming or were motivated by guilt or remorse regularly supplied Shai with priceless bits of information.

It was seldom that a confidential telephone conversation, an exchange of official correspondence, or a coded telegram escaped detection by the invisible antennae of the Jewish espionage. Jewish postal workers kept their receivers continually plugged in to the telephone lines of the military and civil authorities of the Palestine Mandate. Along Tel Aviv's Keren-Kayemet Boulevard receivers concealed in the furniture of a rich man's apartment daily picked up the coded messages broadcast among the various police stations, the army, and the British Intelligence. Some of these codes had been broken, but the key to most had been stolen from or photographed at the headquarters of the Criminal Investigation Department (CID).

Shai had exhaustive records of the wavelengths and frequencies of the various broadcasting stations, possessed a complete set of police files, and knew the numbers and code names of all the cases under investigation. Shai also had its own radio station, Kol Israel, which took delight in regularly broadcasting the gist of top-secret communications among the different branches of the British administration. Often Kol Israel would disclose the contents of a memorandum before it reached its addressee.

Thanks to this array of informers, listeners, and spies, Shai managed to thwart most of the British attempts to suppress Haganah. Surprise raids on the part of the British to get their hands on an important Resistance figure, a cache of arms or an ammunition factory, or a file of secret documents encountered unexpected obstacles. Haganah had always been tipped off in advance, often by the very officer in charge of the search party, and suspected places were emptied before the police arrived.

When a Haganah official was arrested in 1946 with a notebook full of names and addresses on his person, Shai rushed to the rescue, and that very night the incriminating notebook was replaced in the safe of the CID by one identical in appearance but full of nonexistent addresses entered in it by Shai's best counterfeiter.

Sometimes Shai's achievements were a matter of pure luck, as in the case of the British officer known till this day as "John Smith."

John Smith belonged to the high aristocracy of England, but

he was strongly opposed to his government's policy in Palestine, which he considered anti-Semitic and criminal. While rummaging in a safe he happened on a thick file that the CID had spent years assembling. It contained five thousand names and addresses of the principal Haganah and Palmach officers, and detailed maps showing their training centers and the arms depots of Haganah. In sealed envelopes ready for use were the plans and directives of Operation Broadside, which was intended to shatter Haganah in one nocturnal police and army raid.

Early in May 1945 Smith told his Jewish friends what he had found. A few nights later two Shai agents disguised as British soldiers slipped into the camp near Tel Aviv where British headquarters was. Smith was waiting for them behind a window through which he handed them the heavy file. Half an hour later in a nearby kibbutz a veritable swarm of photographers went to work on the documents. By the first light of dawn their job was done, and the lists, the documents, and the directives for Operation Broadside had been replaced in the file. Fifteen minutes before the CID officials came to work, the file was returned to John Smith, who put it back into the safe.

Morning saw every clothesline in the kibbutz hung with thousands of photocopies drying in the sun. On the following day there was a terrific hubbub in all Haganah centers. At the end of a fortnight the lists and documents that the police had so patiently assembled for the past few years were completely worthless to them.

Israel Amir, who had recruited Iser Harel, directed this phantom army from headquarters in a modest apartment on Tel Aviv's Jabotinski Street, two hundred yards away from the administration center of the British police for the Northern District of Tel Aviv.

Wearing khaki shorts and an open-necked shirt with his old army insignia on its shoulders, Iser Harel reported for duty at that address. It was a new world to him, for he had never worked in an office and had no knowledge whatever of matters of internal security, or of spying on the British and the Arabs and foreigners.

Israel Amir made Iser secretary of the Jewish Division of Shai, the department with the most difficult problems, for Haganah was not the only Resistance organization in Palestine. There were also the dissident groups: Irgun, the extremist right-wing faction, and the Stern Gang of ultranationalists. Haganah and its operations were in sharp conflict with these widely differentiated bodies and for a while attempted to suppress all dissidents by hunting them down, beating them up, and betraying them to the British. It was a period of intense hatred.

On Iser Harel fell the duty of compiling lists and personal histories of dissidents, gathering information about their activities, and keeping records of their organizational structure, their centers, their arms caches, and the minutes of their meetings.

When he first started work for Shai he showed no signs of genius; in fact, his colleagues considered his abilities rather limited. He had trouble communicating orally, finding the right word, and reducing his instructions to orderly, precise terms. His prose was no better, and the style and vocabulary of his memorandums led to friction between him and his associates.

Iser paid no attention to the opinions of his colleagues, but plunged into his work as if there were no one around him. The Jewish Division was located in a small room in the rear of the apartment and consisted of only three persons: the chief, his secretary, and Iser. At the end of every day the Shai employees would clean off their desks and put their papers into secret drawers. These hiding places, called *sliks*, whether for papers, weapons, or radios, were the lifeblood of Haganah. Outside the apartment was the maximum security slik, where the records of the organization were preserved.

The world of utter secrecy that Shai's files revealed to Iser was a source of constant wonder to him. Day and night he would study the documents that came to his desk, sometimes staying away from home until a weekend. All he told his wife was that he was working for Haganah in Tel Aviv. Rivka asked no questions.

Gradually his efforts were rewarded. When he finally took time to think about it, he was astonished to find that he truly understood the meaning of the reports he received. He would go through a file very slowly and before he had come to the end of it knew what steps to take. Now and then remarks circulated in headquarters corridors about Iser's bloodhound "intuition," which could lead him straight to a solution of every matter that came to hand. His memory, however, was selective; he could totally forget the number of his identity card or the name of his next-door neighbor, but he always remembered every detail of an operational file. When a new piece of information was presented to him, he could instantaneously relate it to what he already knew, go into action, and hit the target.

A few months after he joined Shai Iser was appointed head of the Jewish Division.

Iser's first decision in his new capacity was to construct a new slik for his records, for he had discovered that the location of the existing one was known to everyone at headquarters. The files in it contained information that was dynamite — personal histories of British Mandate officials, names of British officers cooperating with Haganah, names and addresses of Jewish informers and traitors who were working hand in hand with the authorities. Iser determined to transfer these records to a safer spot that no one would know about except himself and his secretary. Putting this decision into effect, however, was another matter, for ever since he began his clandestine activities he had had to learn everything by himself.

The first thing he needed was an apartment. After a long search he found a bachelor's establishment in an old building on an alley right in the center of Tel Aviv.

"My name is Regev," Iser told the landlord. "I work for Haganah, but I live outside Tel Aviv, and I need a place like this for the two or three times a week I have to stay in town overnight." The lease was quickly signed, and the landlord gave Iser permission to make "a few alterations" in the bizarre shape of the one-room apartment.

On the following day Iser met a stranger on the platform of the Tel Aviv railway station. The man was an engineer living in Haifa and the Haganah expert in slik construction. That night Iser invited him into his automobile and drove him by a deliberately roundabout route through the dark streets of Tel Aviv to the apartment. The engineer immediately drew up a detailed plan for converting it into a slik.

The next day a truck unloaded a pile of construction materials on the sidewalk opposite the apartment building. As soon as it was dark Iser had these bricks, bags of cement, and an iron door lugged inside. The next night he returned with a construction specialist whom he knew in Herzliya.

"I have a job for you," Iser said.

The man asked no questions, but went to work cutting out a six-foot-wide section of the wall at the rear of the long narrow apartment behind the staircase. He lined this new alcove with brick and built shelves to hold filing cases. Then he sealed it with the iron door, which he disguised with a thick concrete facing. The door could be opened only by a lever operated by a spring concealed in a crack in the wall.

Iser whistled with admiration when he inspected the finished job. No one could possibly suspect that a large part of the room had vanished, or notice that the rear wall was mostly a secret door. The crack hiding the release spring was invisible even at close range, and the same sound came from a knock on the iron door as from the solid walls.

The only person in Shai who knew Iser's new address was his secretary, who would come to work there alone in the early morning and leave late at night.

Iser's private slik was to be of use to him earlier than he had expected.

On the night of Friday, June 28, 1946, while thousands of Jewish families were gathering for their ritual Sabbath-eve meal, the watchman of a kibbutz near Tel Aviv encountered a uniformed British officer.

"Take me to the local Haganah chief," ordered this officer, "and be quick about it."

The Jew was immediately suspicious. "I don't know what you're talking about."

"Listen, I'm a friend of the Jewish nation. I know the head of Shai in Tel Aviv, but I can't go to him now; it's too risky, even though I have an extremely important message for him. Every minute counts."

"Wait here." The watchman vanished into the darkness and ran to warn his superiors. They were unable to determine whether or not this was a trap of the CID, but they thought they should hear the Englishman out just the same.

"Let's say my name is Gordon," said the officer to the Haganah leader at the kibbutz. "I want to warn you of a disaster for the Jewish community. In a few hours the British army is going to mount its biggest operation yet in Palestine. Every town and village and kibbutz will be surrounded and sealed off by military detachments. There's going to be a curfew. Searches will be made, and thousands arrested. The lists are ready. The first to be arrested are the Zionist leaders and the Haganah chiefs. The orders are strict and the raids will be merciless. You must act at once."

Five minutes later the telephone rang in a Tel Aviv apartment. "Kibbutz X here. One of our children is seriously ill. He must be brought to the city in an ambulance."

It was a coded message. An ambulance drove through the night at top speed for the kibbutz.

Everything was ready for its arrival. An eight-year-old named Hanitai, swathed in bandages and covered with white sheets and blankets, was laid on a stretcher, which a white-clad nurse and a doctor lifted into the ambulance. The doctor was no other than the Haganah official who had been interviewing Captain Gordon. Twenty minutes later he was climbing two by two the stairs up to Shai headquarters and making his report to the officer on duty.

That officer was Iser Harel. A few telephone calls and a few whispered code words were enough for him to get confirmation of Gordon's story. All the major British camps had been mysteriously emptied of their garrisons, and army units were on their way to the big towns. The CID's Jewish employees had been sent home early in the evening, but the English inspectors and agents had been ordered to report to their posts at midnight in order to take part in an operation that might last one or two days. There could be no doubt that the great raid which had been feared since the discovery of the plans for Operation Broadside was going to take place that night.

Iser stayed on the telephone calling one after another of his subordinates throughout the country and instructing them in code to activate the alarm system that had been established for emergencies. Hundreds of telephones started ringing in private apartments, offices, cover-addresses, kibbutzim, and secret munitions factories. Dozens of couriers threaded their way through back streets to knock at the doors of persons likely to be arrested. Most of the political leaders of the Jewish community decided to let themselves be arrested, while the Haganah chiefs themselves vanished into the hiding places that had long been kept in readiness.

After putting this vast mechanism into motion Iser hurried to Dr. Moshe Sneh's apartment and warned him personally. Sneh, chief of staff of Haganah, got away seconds before the Tommies arrived. A few days later, thanks to Haganah's network of agents, he was able to leave for Paris to join Ben-Gurion.

After midnight Iser returned to headquarters, where he found a handful of men waiting for him. Together they sorted out the papers that had not been put away and hid most of them in the sliks at hand. Then Iser dumped the most important ones into a suitcase and carried it via back streets and alleys to his private slik. On his way he could see the armored vehicles and the radio-controlled cars of the British massing in the squares. Parachute units had already begun to raid sleeping households.

Iser reached the ground floor of his apartment house on Hoz Street without incident. He opened the iron door and stowed his suitcase in the secret closet. Nothing in the apartment had been disturbed. He was about to leave for one of his other hiding places in Tel Aviv when he heard heavy footsteps in the hallway. The English had come!

Since it was too late for him to escape, he darted into the closet, closed the iron door behind him, and held his breath.

There were knocks on the entrance door and then the sound of a key in the lock. Iser could hear the landlord talking with the British officers, the thud of army boots on the floor of the room, the banging of fists on its walls. What if he had been betrayed? The butts of army rifles pounded on the iron closet door, but it resounded like an ordinary wall, and apparently no one caught sight of the hidden lock.

The British soldiers finally departed, and a few hours later "Mr. Regev" calmly left his private slik and returned to headquarters, suitcase in hand.

June 29, 1946, will always be known in the history of the Jewish Resistance in Palestine as "Black Saturday." Captain Gordon had been correct. Thousands of homes were raided, and several hundred Zionist leaders and other notables were arrested. But it was the British themselves who really suffered on Black Saturday. The arrest of the leaders of the Jewish community, their internment in the Latrun concentration camp, and their proud and dignified attitude aroused a sympathetic world opinion. The English found very few weapons and not a single secret document.

On the day after the raids Iser demanded that greater security measures be taken. The British were growing more and more active, and arrest was following arrest. Someone might say a word too much. The thousands of files that contained the principal records of Shai must be transferred at once to a maximum security location far from Tel Aviv and the raids.

Iser got the reply that Tel Aviv was closely watched by the British and that there were barricades at every exit from the city. How did Iser propose to effect his demand?

"Leave that to me," Iser told his bosses.

In Tel Aviv he met Pinhas Sapir (later finance minister of Israel), who was the chairman of the labor council of Kfar Sava in the Sharon plain. Sapir did not know the silent little man who was drawing him into a corner, but he had a vague notion that he was connected with Haganah and that was enough for him.

"Tell me," Iser said, "is there a public building under construction at Kfar Sava right now?"

"Yes. Several."

"What I must have is a big building outside the town, not in the middle."

Sapir thought a moment. "There is a hospital under construction on the outskirts."

"Can I make use of it?"

"Certainly."

A few days later a big truck piled high with vegetables from Sharon stopped at the barrier the British had put across the road into Tel Aviv. The driver, a boisterous fellow, kept slapping the English soldiers on the back while they were examining his papers and generally making a nuisance of himself. The Tommies had a hard time getting rid of him, and when he stopped at the barrier on his return trip they let him through without inspecting his cargo, which they thought was no more than empty boxes. But if they had taken the trouble to peek inside the truck they would have seen several dozen strong-boxes behind the empty crates — the complete records of Shai.

That evening the truck ended its journey in an isolated farm-yard in Sharon. The strongboxes were shifted to another truck. The garrulous driver went back to his usual daily work without having learned what had really been in the truck or what its final destination was to be.

From within one of the farm buildings Iser watched the transfer. He had never read a treatise on subversive methods, yet he had discovered all by himself its basic principle — sepa-ration of elements and personnel. He could not possibly afford to let more than one or two persons know too much about any operation, for if several were captured and questioned, their interrogators might be able to worm out of each of them enough to piece together the whole affair and its aims.

Late that night the second truck came to a halt at the scaffolding of the hospital under construction in a suburb of Kfar Sava. The strongboxes were unloaded, and the truck went on its way. The Haganah men who had been watching this phase of the operation emerged out of the darkness once the truck was gone and lugged the strongboxes into the basement. On the following day a new crew reported for work on the hospital, for on the previous evening the foreman had given his regular workmen a day off.

The new men, who had never seen the building they were to work on, were told to construct a ceiling over one of the rooms in the cellar — the one where the strongboxes had been stored — and after they had set the concrete blocks in place they left for another job. The former crew came back on the job the next day. None of the workmen had any idea of what was inside the newly sealed chamber, which had neither doors nor windows. Iser sighed with relief.

He had relied on his quite ordinary appearance and his unobtrusive manner to keep him free from suspicion, and he was right. The British searched everywhere for the head of the Jewish Division of Shai, who would have been of inestimable value to them, but although they knew that Iser Harel was an active member of Haganah, they never investigated his activities further. Harel a big wheel? Not a chance.

Not until November 29, 1947, when the United Nations General Assembly authorized the creation of the State of Israel, and the war between the Jews and the Arabs had broken out in Palestine, did Iser go back to Kfar Sava. His most trusted subordinates were with him. With sledgehammers they broke down the concrete casing of the secret room and removed the precious documents, which were urgently needed both for the conduct of the war and for training an Intelligence service for the state that had just been born.

5

Our Man in Amman

WHILE THE BRITISH were evacuating Palestine, a process not completed until May 15, 1948, David Shaltiel succeeded Israel Amir as head of Shai. In spite of his brilliant mind and fertile imagination Shaltiel was not good at organizing data for presenting his programs to his superiors and let Iser Harel do this for him. As Iser thus became better known to the Haganah leaders it began to be rumored that he would be the next head of the Secret Service. Such prognostications, however, were unexpectedly rendered worthless by the arrival on the scene of a new personality, Iser Be'eri.

Be'eri was a tall, thin, curt man with white hair. He was said to be an ascetic, modest, and of unimpeachable integrity, but also a fierce and dangerous megalomaniac. He had been a member of Haganah since 1939 and from 1944 to 1947 had been in charge of a private construction company in Haifa. An unsociable man, he lived with his wife and son in a small, windswept house in the coastal village of Bat Galim.

Be'eri was David Shaltiel's protégé, and Shaltiel told his subordinates that Be'eri would be in charge of "administrative and managerial matters."

Iser Harel was somewhat taken aback by Be'eri's arrival and by the newcomer's first name, for Iser was a rather uncommon name, yet now there were two Isers at headquarters. The staff took to referring to Be'eri as "Big Iser" and to Harel as "Little Iser," a nickname that has stuck to him ever since.

A few weeks after Be'eri's appointment David Shaltiel came into Little Iser's office. "What would you say to my making you chief of the Tel Aviv District?" he asked.

Iser knew that he was indispensable at headquarters, but the offer tempted him, for the greater part of the Jewish population of Palestine lived in that district, and there also were the centers of Haganah activity, of the British authority, and of the Arab organizations. Furthermore, Tel Aviv was one of the principal fronts in the guerrilla war that was going on. In Arab Jaffa, a twin city to Tel Aviv, were the command posts of the Arabs from which issued all directives to the Arab population of Palestine as well as the plans for the bloody campaign against the Jews. To take charge of the Tel Aviv District meant becoming deeply involved in secret operations, which so appealed to Iser that he accepted Shaltiel's proposal.

That very day he left Shai headquarters and installed himself in the Tel Aviv District headquarters, where his office was, to all appearances, merely one of the editorial offices of the workers' newspaper *Davar*, on Allenby Street, right in the heart of the city.

A short time after he assumed his new duties Iser got word from headquarters that David Shaltiel was resigning his position to become commandant of Jerusalem and that his successor would be Iser Be'eri.

The news stupefied Little Iser. If he had stayed at Shai headquarters he would have inherited the vacant post. Clearly Shaltiel had got rid of him so that he could not interfere in the backstage politics that had elevated Be'eri, the favorite of Haganah's left wing.

Several employees at headquarters rebelled against Be'eri's

appointment and disputed his authority because of his igno-
rance of Secret Service methods. But Be'eri managed to survive
and after a while had things well in hand by dint of installing
his partisans in the division that dealt with Jews, dissidents,
and traitors. Iser Harel, being no intriguer, merely buried himself in his new work and said nothing. Besides, he had other
things to occupy his mind, principally the critical situation in
the Arab Division of Shai.

Recruiting Arab informers was one of Shai's major endeavors.
Night after night Shai agents would meet with their Arab
counterparts in deserted orchards, ruined houses, and lonely
spots in the sandy wastes — localities appointed not by some
amateur scene designer but chosen by the Arabs themselves,
who were in terror for their lives, being well aware of what had
happened to compatriots of theirs caught giving information to
the enemy. It had taken Shai a long time and much patient,
hard work to recruit them, and included were several formid-
able traitors, who were either looking for financial rewards or
were prominent leaders or outstanding Arab tribal leaders
who had been ousted from power. A minority were men of integrity who felt sincere friendship for the Jews or were grateful
to them.

Such were, for example, the members of the Latif family.
Ahmed Latif, a rich and highly respected Arab businessman,
had been shot in full daylight on the sidewalk of King George
Boulevard, the principal street of Jaffa. His assassins made no
attempt to conceal their identity from the crowd of bystanders.

The killers were tribesmen of Hassan Salame, a notorious
chieftain who had collaborated with the Nazis during the war
and had been parachuted by them into Palestine in order to
organize sabotage against the British. He had personally given
the order to liquidate Ahmed Latif, who refused to submit to
his authority. He wished to make an example of him.

Hardly had the murdered man fallen to the pavement when
one of his assassins bent down and tied a placard to his neck:

"This traitor got his just reward." Then the killers shouted to the dumfounded crowd: "Anyone who touches Latif will get the same treatment. Let him rot here, and may the dogs eat his corpse!"

For two days no one dared touch the body. The Arab policemen pretended not to see it, and civilians looked the other way. Latif's parents and relatives feared reprisals. On the third day, however, the Latif family decided to act. In the dark of night they carried the body away, and before daylight had buried it in the old Muslim cemetery of Ajami.

Salame, however, did not relent. His men dug up the body and put it back on King George Boulevard. The Latif family buried it a second time, and once again Salame's henchmen disinterred it. This gruesome game went on for a week, and Latif's body decomposed on the street while his grief-stricken family dared not show themselves.

Then Shai stepped in. Through an informer the head of Shai's Arab Division got in touch with the bereft family, and with the help of Haganah workers buried the remains in the Muslim cemetery of Abdul Nabi to the north of Tel Aviv. Here it remained, and for years to come the family showed their deep gratitude.

In these first six months of 1948 — the most critical of the entire War of Independence — Little Iser suddenly had to cope with a ticklish situation. Shai's sources of Arab information were in the process of breaking down, and the operations the British police undertook during the final months of the Mandate forced Shai to curtail its activities. Furthermore, several Arab spies and informers had ceased their services to the Jews either because of the wave of nationalism that swept over the Arab world, or because they feared reprisals.

Iser tried to plug up this drain with all kinds of new strategies but with little success. The anxiety of the chiefs of Shai Arab Division kept increasing. What, they said, are we to do

when the real war begins? So far as Shai was concerned, the
Arab world was vanishing behind a mist that grew thicker and
thicker.

Early in May 1948 a vital question arose to trouble the provisional government of the future state, namely, whether the
Arab Legion of King Abdullah of Transjordan* would attack
Palestine. It was well known that Egypt, Syria, Iraq, and various scattered guerrilla bands intended to invade Jewish territory, but Abdullah's army was the best trained and the best
equipped of all in the Middle East. Haganah's entire campaign
strategy depended on what Abdullah would do. And no one
had the answer.

For many months Abdullah had been holding top-secret conferences with Jewish emissaries, notably with Golda Meir, who
had disguised herself as an Arab and gone to see him in his
Amman palace. A secret agreement for the partition of Palestine was ready for signing, but now at the last moment Abdullah was hesitating under pressure from his "brother states."
Whether or not he would join them and attack Israel was being
hotly discussed at Shai headquarters, Haganah headquarters,
and in civilian assemblies. When Ben-Gurion consulted the
Haganah experts on Arab affairs, their unanimous answer was
that the old King would not attack, but would agree to share
Palestine with the Jews.

Iser followed the debates closely. Thanks to his simple, practical mentality he reached the logical conclusion that in order
to determine whether or not Abdullah would attack, the thing
to do was send someone to Amman who would observe what
was going on in that capital and bring back a well-informed
answer.

A few days later a tanned, lean young man came out of the
forest of Hulda twenty-five miles south of Tel Aviv, slipped
past the positions occupied by Palmach soldiers, who had been

* Since April 26, 1949, the Hashemite Kingdom of Jordan.

ordered not to shoot, and reached the highway. There he was quickly swallowed up in the throng of Arab refugees streaming along the road under the burden of their possessions. A little farther on, this torrent of human beings entered territory under Arab control and completely flooded a crossroad in the Hulda region. There the refugees diverged in two directions, one toward Gaza to the south and the other eastward in order to cross the Jordan River and reach Transjordan.

The young refugee managed to leap on the running board of an ancient truck laden with women and children on their way to Amman, and after forty-eight hours it arrived in the capital of Transjordan. That same night he knocked at the door of a sumptuous villa whose owner held a high position in King Abdullah's government.

Shouts of joy and a rain of kisses greeted him on the part of the entire family, for the unexpected visitor was none other than their beloved and extremely well connected cousin from Jaffa, about whom they had been greatly worried. It was indeed the well-known and highly respected Hassan El Batir. But he also was the personal representative and agent of Iser Harel.

A few days earlier Iser had consulted his experts. "I've got to have an Arab I can trust," he told them, "whom I can send to Amman." Their unanimous answer was Hassan El Batir. "He's a brilliant young man," they said, "well educated and with plenty of ingenuity." Consulting his file on Hassan, Iser found that he was engaged to a Jewish girl and on several occasions had stated that he wished to become a citizen of the new Jewish State and live in it with his wife. He had already accomplished some dangerous missions for Haganah.

Nevertheless, when Iser's experts learned what he intended to do, they were very dubious. "It won't work, Iser," they insisted. "That fellow will never come back. Once he's in Amman and sees the concentration of troops there and gets exposed to all the nationalistic enthusiasm, he'll stay there. Why, for heaven's sake, would he ever want to come back here?"

"I'll talk to him," said Iser.

As soon as it was dark, Iser rang the doorbell of an apartment in central Tel Aviv and soon was being ushered into the room where Hassan was waiting for him. The young man greatly impressed him with his intelligence, his sincerity, and his flawless Hebrew. It was only a moment before Iser said: "You are to go to Amman and find out whether Abdullah will make war on Israel. You must be back here before May fourteenth." Then he added: "It's up to you. I am certain that we will win the war. I know that you sincerely wish to join your destiny with ours. But you are an Arab. You must consider the matter carefully and make your own decision. If you will not go, I shall understand. But if you do go, I want to be absolutely certain that you will return, and you must assure me that you will."

"I will go," said the young man.

Shai agents accompanied him as far as the forest of Hulda on the border. Thereafter Iser could only wait — for the return of someone on whom the fate of the future State of Israel might hang.

About midnight on May 12 the deep silence along the front at Hulda was shattered by the rattle of machine guns and the bark of rifles. From their trenches the Palmach troops had seen a stooping figure zigzagging toward them. "Fire!" ordered their commander, and a hail of bullets greeted the stranger.

The figure then began to shout in Hebrew: "Don't shoot! Stop!"

The soldiers leaped on the young Arab who had jumped over the rampart of their trench and rolled to the bottom.

"Take me to your leader," he panted in Hebrew. "I have a message."

He handed the commander a blank sheet of crumpled, dirty paper. "Dip it in water," he said.

The commander's eyes popped, but he did what he was told. The paper came out of the water covered with Hebrew letters. "To every Palmach commander," it said, "and every Haganah commander: The bearer of this letter has been entrusted with a mission of the highest importance. As soon as he makes contact with you, take him at once to headquarters." It was signed with the code name of a liaison officer.

At dawn Iser met his emissary in a hotel room in Tel Aviv. Hassan told his story. He had stayed two days in Amman, then told his relatives there that he had changed his mind and decided to move on to Gaza. Once more he joined a convoy for Palestine. When he was near Hulda he got off the truck, left the road, and ran to the Jewish lines. The Arabs and the British fired at him from behind, and the Jews shot at him from in front. He had had a very narrow escape.

Before Iser could even frame the question he was dying to ask, Hassan said: "Abdullah is going to go to war. I haven't the slightest doubt of it. I made many good contacts, and that's what everyone told me. His Arab Legion is ready to attack. His tanks are ready to leave for the front. I saw them with my own eyes."

Iser dashed to Ben-Gurion, who listened to him in silence. This new information contradicted the reports of all the Arab experts, but one weighty fact tended to confirm it. Golda Meir had seen Abdullah for the last time on the previous evening. The conference had got nowhere. She too was under the impression that the King of Transjordan, perhaps against his will, would make war on the Jews.

Emergency orders were sent to army headquarters. The same night several units moved forward to check the tanks of the Arab Legion by creating a line of defense along the west bank of the Jordan River.

On May 14, 1948, at the Tel Aviv Museum, Ben-Gurion announced the birth of the State of Israel. Iser did not attend the ceremony; he was too busy with his daily tasks.

The same day the crack divisions of the Arab Legion, coordinated with the Egyptians, the Iraqis, and the Syrians, launched an attack on the Jewish State, but the offensive encountered resistance on every front.

Our man in Amman had told the truth.

6

The Fall of
Big Iser

Six weeks after the proclamation of the State of Israel Shai gave up the ghost and was replaced by the Secret Service of the new nation. Big Iser held a high position among its few directors.

The Secret Service played an important part in the ruthless war that was blazing on Israel's frontiers. It was to be expected that it would make some blunders, but no one could have foreseen that its earliest measures would result in the frightful nightmare known as the Be'eri affair.

In September 1948 the Haifa police were notified that a bullet-riddled corpse had been found in a deep gully at the foot of Mount Carmel. The detectives who hastened to the spot found indications that a murder had been committed, but they had no idea of the victim's identity, much less of the assassin's.

After several weeks of investigation the police established that the body was that of a rich and influential Arab named Ali Kassem, a young, energetic Arab leader with strong nationalistic tendencies who had lived for several years in the pretty village of Sidney Ali overlooking the sea near Tel Aviv. He had long been the center of violent controversies, and Jewish farmers bitterly remembered the time when they had been forced to accept his "protection" in return for liberal donations. Haganah authorities, on the other hand, pretended that he was their secret ally and had rendered invaluable service to the Zionist cause. The truth lay somewhere between these extremes; Ali Kassem had worked for both sides, betraying first one and then the other.

The Arab tribes had sentenced him to death late in 1947, but Haganah had rescued him and he had stayed put in his village even after the Jews took Jaffa. Then in the middle of July 1948 he had suddenly disappeared from his roomy apartment and was not found until two months later — dead in the gully. In their search for Ali Kassem's murderer the police encountered bizarre obstacles and inexplicable delays until suddenly in December 1948 they pierced the wall of silence and came up with a bombshell. The guilty party was none other than Colonel Iser Be'eri.

Be'eri and his men had kidnaped Ali Kassem, taken him to a lonely spot, and shot him without bothering with anything like judicial procedure. Be'eri calmly confessed: "We learned that he was a traitor and was intending to cross the enemy lines and find refuge in Transjordan. So we killed him."

The incident was hushed up because, in the last analysis, Israel was indeed at war with the Arabs and Be'eri must have had good reasons for acting as he did. After all, wasn't Iser Be'eri a dedicated patriot and a man of integrity?

Elsewhere the whole business would have been forgotten, but not in the young State of Israel, which was intent on being a democracy in which the rights of individuals would be respected and the laws upheld. Not even in wartime was a man to be killed before he had been brought to trial and had an opportunity to defend himself. The Secret Service was not to enjoy any special privileges in that respect.

As soon as David Ben-Gurion read the report of the investigation he had Iser Be'eri suspended from all his functions. Attorney General Pinhas Rosen decided to bring Be'eri before a secret court-martial on a charge of homicide.

Be'eri's trial took place in December 1948 in a courtroom to which not even the top command of the army were admitted. The jury consisted of three colonels. Be'eri declined counsel and pleaded his own case. "My position as head of the Secret Service," he told the judges, "entitles me, by definition, to act outside the law and to use extralegal methods. You have no right to try me according to regular procedures."

The unanimous verdict was that Be'eri was guilty. He was removed from office and separated from the Service. But this was only the beginning of the affair. The trial of the extremely powerful head of Aman left Be'eri completely vulnerable. The court-martial had started a snowball downhill.

Two weeks after the trial there appeared in Ben-Gurion's office a stern-faced man of medium height — Shaul Avigur, one of Israel's mystery men. He laid a sheaf of papers on the Prime Minister's desk — the report of the second Be'eri affair. That affair had begun on the very day that Big Iser assumed his duties as administrative director of Shai. On that day he had called Iser Harel into his office. "I've heard about you," he said. "Have you a file on Abba Hushi?"

Little Iser was caught short, even though he knew perfectly well that Abba Hushi was one of the most powerful leaders of Mapai, the Labor Party, a personal friend of David Ben-Gurion, and the beloved and revered leader of tens of thousands of Jewish and Arab workers in the northern part of the country. Hushi was also secretary of the Labor Council in Haifa and, in fact, the strongest man in northern Palestine as well as a big man in the entire Jewish community.

"I do not have a file on him," Little Iser said in astonishment, "and I don't know anything about Abba Hushi."

The behavior of the new administrative director seemed inexplicably strange to Iser Harel. The country was at war and the situation was critical, but this newcomer apparently could not think of anything but the personal history of the Socialist leader. Iser Harel left Be'eri's office in confusion and asked his own secretary to check the files for a dossier on Abba Hushi. She brought it to him, but it contained only a report on the puzzling failure of a Palmach operation in the harbor of Haifa in the spring of 1946.

At that time Jews were entering Palestine illegally in dangerously overloaded skiffs and by night — the only means they had of piercing the British blockade and finding refuge from Nazi persecution. The Royal Navy kept a close watch on the entire coast, and its swift cutters would stop the tiny boats that were trying to reach the shores of the Promised Land. Palmach decided to strike. Its frogmen entered Jaffa harbor and attached magnetic mines to the British coast guard cutters, which presently exploded. Headquarters decided to follow up this success with similar tactics in Haifa harbor, to which the frogmen proceeded by sailboat. Their attack was scheduled for midnight.

During the evening, however, the long ears of Shai intercepted a coded message from CID headquarters in Jerusalem to its member office in Haifa warning of the forthcoming sabotage and instructing it to station soldiers with machine guns around the harbor in order to trap the frogmen.

As soon as Israel Amir, Shai's director at that time, received the decoded message in Tel Aviv, he jumped into his car and speeded to Haifa to warn the commandos. But he could not find them. The sailboat had already left the harbor. Amir commandeered a speedboat and went looking for them. A few minutes before midnight, he succeeded in meeting their boat at sea, on its way to Haifa harbor. The operation was called off. The men were saved, but the operation was a failure. The great question was who had betrayed Palmach's intentions to the British.

The document in Iser's hands did not answer that question, but a few vague references seemed to point to Abba Hushi. His moderate views were well known, as were the close relations he had with the British. It must have been he who had informed them.

Iser Harel put the document back into the file, for it contained no definite proof of Hushi's role. Angrily he decided that the only persons who had a right to demand the file were the high command of Haganah — no one else, least of all the new administrator of Shai. Then Iser hid the file where Be'eri would not be able to find it and dismissed the entire matter from his mind.

The curtain rose on the second act some months later.

In May 1948 a detachment of military police entered the lobby of the Hotel Eden in Haifa, where a group of men had gathered around a table to celebrate the proclamation of the State of Israel.

"Which of you is Jules Amster?" asked the sergeant.

A tall, broad-shouldered man with a disarming smile got to his feet.

"Come with me."

Amster was astonished, but he complied. His friends were not to see him again for seventy-six days, and then they barely recognized him. The Amster who returned to Haifa on August 1, 1948, was a human rag. His teeth were gone, his legs were covered with scars, he was quivering with terror, and he refused to talk. Iser Be'eri's men had beaten him incessantly, even inflicting on him the water torture. He had almost lost his mind and had tried to kill himself.

The only crime Amster had committed was to be an intimate friend of Abba Hushi, who Iser Be'eri was convinced was a traitor. The torture, however, had brought Be'eri no confession and no information, and finally Amster had been set at liberty. Be'eri, however, was not satisfied. He now proceeded to play his ace of trumps. He went to Ben-Gurion and handed him two documents. "We found these," he said triumphantly, "among the British papers in the Haifa telegraph office."

Ben-Gurion was dumfounded, for the papers, which Be'eri said had just come into his possession, were top-secret telegrams of the type used by the British CID to communicate with its various branches. Dated from April 1946, they were incontrovertible evidence that Hushi had indeed been the informer on the frogmen. Big Iser had won his game.

His victory, however, was of short duration. At the end of August a young man appeared at Haganah headquarters, where he was immediately recognized as one Abraham, the master counterfeiter of Shai.

When Abraham was alone with a high-ranking officer, he said: "I have a problem. Iser Be'eri ordered me to do some work I consider highly suspicious. My conscience has bothered me so that I had to come to you." The officer put him at ease, and Abraham recounted that some weeks earlier Big Iser had summoned him and sworn him to secrecy. Then Be'eri had given him two old CID telegrams and directed him to prepare similar copies but with certain sentences inserted. Hence the documentary proof of Abba Hushi's treason with appropriate dates and with expressions borrowed from the British code.

The Haganah officer immediately recognized that he had uncovered a Machiavellian plot against Abba Hushi. "Was it you who forged the telegrams?" he asked Abraham.

"Yes. I gave them to Be'eri. I don't know what he did with them, but ever since I have felt guilty."

Informed at once, Ben-Gurion directed Shaul Avigur to check on Abraham's confession. Military Prosecutor Hoter Ishai appointed a committee of investigation that took evidence from Ben-Gurion, Iser Be'eri, Commander in Chief of the Army Yaakov Dori, the head of Shai in Haifa, and Abraham.

Shaul Avigur made a formal report to Ben-Gurion on January 15, 1949, that the incriminating telegrams were forgeries concocted by Iser Be'eri himself as proofs of the Labor leader's treason.*

Colonel Iser Be'eri was stripped of his rank and dismissed from the army, but the end of the Be'eri affair was yet to come. A third episode, rather like the Dreyfus affair, greatly offended public opinion in Israel. Its unfortunate hero was a young captain named Meir Toubianski.

---

*Abba Hushi later became mayor of Haifa and until his death in 1970 figured in every major decision taken by the leadership of the Israeli Labor party. At one time he was proposed as Prime Minister.

7

The Toubianski Case

IT WAS A CLEAR MORNING in the barren hills of Judea between the villages of El Kubeb and Beth-Giz, which the Arabs had abandoned, and the broiling summer heat had not yet spread its damp heavy blanket on the dried-up wadis and the dusty streets of the deserted hamlets. Around them hundreds of bare-chested Israelis in shorts were digging trenches. They were soldiers of a crack Palmach regiment that had conquered the region in fierce and bloody battles nearly ten days earlier.

Now, on June 30, 1948, a truce with the Arabs had put a temporary end to the fighting, and the soldiers were taking advantage of it to fortify their positions and taste the almost forgotten joys of idleness in the shade of an olive grove near a deep well of cold water.

Then suddenly came the shout: "A traitor! They're going to shoot a traitor!"

The soldiers ran toward Beth-Giz, where the land sloped gently toward a stream. They sat on this hillside facing a shanty and an abandoned orchard enclosed by a stone wall. Out of the cabin came some soldiers guarding a young man dressed in khaki, whom they conducted to the olive grove. They stood him up against the orchard wall. An officer ripped off his stripes while a firing squad of five or six men, not all of whom were in uniform, assembled. Some stood at attention; others kept fidgeting. The officer gave the order. The Palmach soldiers could not hear his words, but the wind brought them the metallic click of rifles being loaded. Everything seemed peaceful and pastoral until the rifles barked and the man fell to the ground.

The soldiers scattered and returned to El Kubeb, saying not a word to one another about what had happened. So a traitor had been shot, so what? The incident was quickly forgotten.

On the same day Colonel Iser Be'eri, the director of Aman, informed the provisional government of Israel that an emergency court-martial had condemned a traitor to death as a spy for the British, and he had been executed by a Palmach detachment. His name was Meir Toubianski.

Early in June 1948 the executives of the Israeli Secret Service in Jerusalem were convinced that the enemy had succeeded in organizing a network of spies who had access to top-secret information. The proof was that for several nights in a row the Arab Legion batteries had been bombarding an Israeli munitions plant with great precision. The factory had not been destroyed, but the high command had decided to transfer the machine tools to another location in order to protect them from the shells. The transfer had been made in deep secrecy. The new factory had been connected with the electrical system for barely four hours, however, when a hail of projectiles fell upon it. The Legion had also directed its fire on a military base and other objectives important to Jerusalem.

Benjamin Gibli, the head of Shai in Jerusalem and a close friend of Iser Be'eri, ordered an investigation. The trail led directly to the Jerusalem Electric Company, for owing to the scarcity of fuel, factories and military bases were given priority in the distribution of electricity. Since the Arabs had bombarded their objectives only a short time after they had been connected to the power lines, it was apparent that spies were at work inside the company.

The United Nations General Assembly had made Jerusalem an international city free from the sovereignty of both Jews and Arabs, but neither paid any attention to that status. The Israeli army had occupied the Jewish section of Jerusalem, and the Arab Legion had taken over the Arab quarter and the Old City. But the city was international in principle, and water, telephone, and electrical services functioned as before, being supplied by the same companies as under the British Mandate. The officially neutral British controlled the telephone and the electricity companies, and even when the fighting was heaviest, an Israeli in the Jewish section could telephone to an Arab.

The directors of the electric company remained in Arab territory, but they sent some of their executives into the Israeli section of the city to see to the distribution of power. These executives — Bryant, Sylvester, and Hawkins — were suspected by Shai of having secretly given their colleagues in the Arab section a list of military targets. The directors had forwarded these to the Arab Legion commanders, who had thereupon aimed their batteries on them.

But how could the British have found out that the Israeli factories and military bases were now hidden unless someone had informed them of the new locations? There must have been an Israeli involved.

Meir Toubianski became the chief suspect. Toubianski was a captain in the Israeli army, but during World War II he had been a major in the British Army Corps of Engineers. His blind devotion to the British apparently dated from that experience. He imitated all their mannerisms, even spoke English to his Jewish friends, and if his British superiors asked him to drink Scotch with them, he was delighted. His idolization of the British antagonized many of his associates.

Deciding to take action, Gibli went to the commandant of

Jerusalem, General David Shaltiel, who himself had once been director of Shai, and informed him of the evidence against Toubianski. Shaltiel said it was inadequate for any purpose other than pursuing the investigation. Gibli then told Iser Be'eri of his suspicions. Big Iser immediately sent his officers after Toubianski.

On June 30, 1948, Meir Toubianski went to visit his brother in Tel Aviv. That afternoon the Shai agents descended upon him.

"General Shaltiel is looking for you," they said. "Come with us."

Meir went along quietly, but instead of taking him to Jerusalem, the jeep turned off in the direction of the hills and set him down at Beth-Giz, where he was kept under guard in the hut. Two hours later Iser Be'eri, Benjamin Gibli, David Karon, and Avraham Kidron arrived, all armed with machine pistols and revolvers.

Toubianski went with them into the courtyard, where they all seated themselves on its big white stones. "We constitute an emergency court-martial," Be'eri informed him.

Toubianski's trial before this extraordinary court lasted only an hour and a half. Then Be'eri sent for Captain Goldmann, the commander of the Palmach troops in the locality.

"He must be shot," Be'eri said.

And he was.

No one told Mrs. Lena Toubianski what had happened to her husband. For three weeks she tried to find some trace of him, but when she went to army headquarters in Jerusalem an officer told her to "get the hell out" if she valued her health. Not until July 20 was a vague official statement published in the Israeli press that "a spy had been executed." Two days later his name was given. That's how Toubianski's family learned of his fate.

A few days later a band of guerrilla fighters stormed the apartment house where the British friends of the dead man were living. They arrested Bryant, Sylvester, and Hawkins. In their apartment they found a walkie-talkie and some coded numbers. Great Britain brought diplomatic pressure to bear, and Bryant was set at liberty. Sylvester and Hawkins were accused of espionage. Hawkins was released for want of evidence, but Sylvester was sentenced to seven years in prison. The Supreme Court of Israel, however, suspended his sentence in the fall, and the last of the alleged British spies left the country.

After the verdict Lena Toubianski wrote to David Ben-Gurion: "Why did those Englishmen accused of spying get the right to a trial according to due process of law whereby they were allowed counsel, whereas the most basic legal rights were denied my husband, who was a loyal ranking officer in Haganah? If Toubianski ever had a trial, where did it take place and when? What law justified the verdict? Why was the condemned man given no opportunity to say farewell to his wife and his young son before he was executed? Even the vilest criminal has that privilege."

Ben-Gurion ordered an investigation of the legality of Toubianski's trial, and on December 27, 1948, replied to the widow: "I have no right to pass judgment on your late husband, but I have checked into his trial and have determined that it was not according to law. Consequently I have ordered the Commander in Chief of the army to review the records of the trial and to appoint a new military tribunal. The government will continue to provide for your child's education whatever the verdict of the new trial. Neither you nor your son need feel the slightest guilt."

On July 1, 1949, after Iser Be'eri had been dismissed from the army, Ben-Gurion sent a second letter to Lena Toubianski:

I wish to inform you that I have just received a detailed report on the investigation conducted by the Military Prosecutor in compliance with the Commander in Chief's orders, as to the trial and execution of your late husband. It has been established that Meir Toubianski was innocent. His death was a tragic mistake.

In order to make such amends as are possible for this terrible miscarriage of justice, the Commander in Chief has decreed, with my approval:

1. To restore to Meir Toubianski posthumously his rank of Captain;
2. To reinter his remains in a military cemetery with all due honors;
3. To pay you and your son appropriate damages.

It is impossible for me to convey to you the anguish that I and all others connected with the affair feel. Such a thing should never have happened. Those responsible will be handed over to justice.

Your late husband, it is true, did make a mistake by sending his British boss a list without presupposing that it might fall into the wrong hands. He admitted his error and regretted it, but he had no wicked intent and no intention whatever of committing treason.

On July 7, 1949, Meir Toubianski's remains were buried with full military honors. On July 19 Big Iser was arrested and charged with the murder of Toubianski. On October 16, 1949, Be'eri's trial began at Rehovot, south of Tel Aviv, with Yaa'cov Shimshon Shapiro (later attorney general) presenting the government's case.

"I plead not guilty" was Iser Be'eri's loud and clear answer to the judge's question. During his testimony, however, he admitted that after Toubianski's execution he had grave doubts as to the legality of the trial: "I wondered whether it was right to burden three of my subordinates with passing judgment on Toubianski. I also wondered whether I myself had acted justly toward him. I have suffered remorse, and I still do."

The trial lasted until November 23. Iser Be'eri was found guilty, but because of his past record he received only a token prison sentence — "one day, from sunrise to sunset." On December 18 Israel's President Chaim Weizmann commuted that sentence "in consideration of the loyal service that Iser Be'eri has rendered Israel."

A broken, bitter man, Be'eri retired to his lonely house in Bat Galim. Never again was he called to the service of his country. On January 30, 1958, alone and friendless, he died of a heart attack. To his relatives he had kept repeating right up to his death: "I had proof of Toubianski's treason."

In 1964 Ben-Gurion wrote to a friend: "Iser Be'eri was a rascal without a shred of conscience."

Big Iser, however, is still a figure of controversy. "My father," his son says, "was an extremely upright and honest man." General Ben-Hur wrote: "He was modest and straightforward, reliable and well-disciplined." One of his associates in Shai, on the other hand, revealed his dislike of Iser Be'eri: "He was a morbid inquisitor, a compulsive avenger, a kind of Dr. Jekyll and Mr. Hyde." Little Iser said of him: "Be'eri was a dangerous megalomaniac."

The Be'eri scandal profoundly shocked the Israeli army, the government, and public opinion, but not so much as Be'eri's own actions and those of his henchmen, which were considered criminal and unworthy of every Jewish tradition. No one doubted Big Iser's devotion to the people and the State of Israel, but his mystical fanaticism compelled him to win regardless of the cost and to crush those he suspected without any scruples about the means he used.

The Be'eri affair left painful scars on the Israeli Secret Service, and without an understanding of it the evolution of the agency would be impossible to comprehend. If, in wartime, the civil leaders had not had the moral courage to condemn and dismiss Be'eri, the Secret Service might well have taken on a different character. It might well have become like the brutal and immoral agencies of some other countries where torture, murder, and the fabrication of false evidence are everyday occurrences.

In the long run Israel profited from the sordid episode. After that bitter experience the Secret Service directors saw to it that such misfortunes would never happen again and that Be'eri's methods would be forever forbidden. The Secret Service itself limited its power, basing its future operations on legal and moral principles that would guarantee the rights of individuals caught in the toils of its shadowy machine.

The rights of an Israeli citizen are well protected. Even if he has betrayed his country, or spied, or informed against its safety, he can be confident that he will not be seized by night and tortured into a confession and that his basic rights before the law will be upheld. The strict observance of these principles constitutes, perhaps, the greatest achievement of Israel's secret services, which have, to be sure, accomplished many other miracles.

8

Ben-Gurion Discovers
Iser Harel

LITTLE ISER, who had played no part in Big Iser's operations or
in the investigations of his conduct, received the news of his
downfall with little emotion and asked no questions, for he did
not like getting involved in matters he considered none of his
business. He was so occupied with his own work that he actually knew nothing of the Ali Kassem, Amster, and Toubianski
cases.

During the War of Independence Iser was conducting a war
of his own against the dissident organizations, a thankless task
and full of pitfalls, for instead of dissolving when the state was
proclaimed, these groups had become a powder keg.

On May 14 Menachem Begin, the "man of a thousand disguises," who as the legendary leader of the Irgun Zvai Leumi
terrorist organization had several times been sentenced to
death by the British, emerged from obscurity and declared over
the underground radio that he was putting his organization at
the service of the provisional government. On June 1 he went
one step further and ordered Irgun to become integrated with
the national army except in Jerusalem, where former Resistance
groups — the Stern Gang, Haganah, Palmach — still operated

owing to the fact that the Holy City had not yet been incorporated with Israel.

For a while it seemed that Begin's announcement would lead to a voluntary disbanding of the various groups, all with conflicting ideologies, but fate decreed that such would not come to pass without the bloody show of force which came to be known as "Altalena."

The *Altalena* was an old LST of the U.S. Marine Force that Irgun had purchased in New York for $75,000. In Europe it had been loaded with rifles, machine guns, cartridges, and hand grenades, part of which Irgun had bought; the remainder was donated by the French. On her decks were some eight hundred members of Irgun who had volunteered to fight in the Israeli army.

On June 11, 1948, the departure of the *Altalena* from Port-de-Bouc near Marseille occasioned a great deal of irresponsible publicity that caused numerous difficulties. When the *Altalena* was already at sea, a secret agreement concerning her cargo was reached between Irgun and the army.

The *Altalena* reached Israel after the first Arab-Israeli truce, the terms of which strictly forbade all importation of arms. Regardless of that injunction, the Israelis were past masters of unloading contraband cargo under the nose, first, of the British, and then of the United Nations observers. In order to fool the U.N. observers the arms had to be unloaded on the beach at Kfar Vitkin, twenty-five miles north of Tel Aviv. Israel Galili, Ben-Gurion's deputy, and Menachem Begin had agreed that twenty percent of the arms would go to the defenders of Jerusalem and the remainder to the regular army.

By June 17, however, while the ship was still at sea, Irgun had changed its policy. Begin told the provisional government's liaison officer: "My associates will not have the arms sent to army depots. First and foremost they must go to the Irgun units that are going to merge with the army. They belong to Irgun, and they are going to be stored in Irgun depots."

On June 20, when the *Altalena* appeared off Kfar Vitkin, Begin ordered a number of Irgun fighters to desert their units, "requisition" trucks in Tel Aviv "for the good of the cause," and help unload the cargo. By morning of the following day the *Altalena* had anchored off the beach and the unloading had begun. Meanwhile the provisional government had met in an emergency session during which the ministers unanimously voted to order Irgun to stop the unloading and deliver both ship and arms to the army, for the government refused to have any organization defying its authority. If Irgun did not comply, the army was to use force.

Some ministers, including David Ben-Gurion, were afraid that Irgun intended to incite a military rebellion against the civil authorities. The arrival of the ship, the broken agreement with the army, the desertion of the Irgun fighters, and the unloading of the arms — all were good evidence of that possibility.

The ultimatum was delivered to Menachem Begin on the beach at Kfar Vitkin. His answer was an unqualified no. Immediately after this reply was received in Tel Aviv, soldiers of the Alexandroni Brigade surrounded the beach and opened fire. The beach, strewn with cases of ammunition and rifles still shiny with grease, became a battlefield.

The Irgun fighters abandoned the arms they had already unloaded, and surrendered, but Menachem Begin and his adjutants, refusing to yield themselves prisoners, boarded the *Altalena*, raised anchor, and headed for the open sea.

The next morning the *Altalena* was proceeding full steam ahead for the beach at Tel Aviv, where it grounded on a sandbar parallel to the boardwalk in front of the luxury hotels where the U.N. observers were staying.

Presently the boardwalk was swarming with pro- and anti-Irgun partisans, and all Tel Aviv was in a frenzy. It appeared that the Irgun leaders were hoping that the presence of so many of their loyal adherents on the one hand, and the dread of a bloody confrontation on the other hand, would prevent the government from enforcing its ultimatum. If so, they were wrong. After another emergency session the government ordered the army to resort to force.

The army units in Tel Aviv, however, were depleted, almost all the soldiers being at the front. Palmach's shock troops had to be summoned. These engaged the Irgun men in a battle that raged on the boardwalk and around the Ritz Hotel, where Palmach headquarters were. Then a young Palmach officer named Yitzhak Rabin* threw a hand grenade out the window of his room, and this stopped the insurgents' attack on the Ritz.

Both sides had lost some men before Ben-Gurion sent for a cannon. Ygal Allon, the Palmach commander, ordered it fired on the *Altalena*. That decided the outcome of the battle. When shells began bursting on the decks, those on board laid down their arms and surrendered.

Ben-Gurion immediately ordered that all Irgun units be disarmed and incorporated into the army, and their members placed under arrest. Iser Harel was designated to carry out this command.

Iser Harel's assignment was an extremely delicate one. The specter of civil war haunted the government, for the nation was not yet fully aware that a state was in existence — the State of Israel, barely one month old. The *Altalena* incident was a defiance of that state's supreme authority. To impress the people with the power of that authority, several members of the government thought Irgun should be dealt with very harshly. The moderates in the government, however, insisted on a more indulgent and liberal policy in order that a compromise might be reached. Two of the religious party were ready to resign after they learned that the battle on the beach had left several Israelis dead or wounded. That Jews should fire on Jews!

Precisely at that critical moment the army and Iser Harel

---

* Later commander in chief of the Israeli army during the Six Day War.

found that they were on the same wavelength. Iser was almost a stranger to Ben-Gurion, who had first heard of him in the spring of 1947, when some of the department heads of Shai had visited the Prime Minister to explain the structure of their agency. When they mentioned Iser Harel as head of the Jewish Division, handling matters relating to internal security, the dissidents, and the communists, Ben-Gurion was disgusted. "Why a 'Jewish Division'?" he asked. "Call it instead the Internal Division." Shai agreed.

Later Ben-Gurion met Iser and approved his nomination as head of Shin-Bet (Department of Internal Security), but he had no idea of Iser's opinions, his thought processes, or his methods. Now, however, during their talks about Irgun, Iser Harel and David Ben-Gurion found that they were of one mind.

"All Irgun members must be required to take an oath of loyalty to the State of Israel and its army," Ben-Gurion declared. "Those who do will be treated like any other soldiers and will have the entire confidence of their superior officers. Those who do not are to be arrested."

That's the way it was done.

Iser pondered the task assigned to him and mapped out the courses he would follow for the rest of his career in dealing with dissidents, terrorists, and underground organizations. He determined not only to crush all subversive actions against the state and its institutions, but also to refrain from branding the guilty with eternal shame. He believed that to ostracize them and force them into impotence was the surest way to make them bitter, inflame their hatred, and thus drive them deeper underground. Once their organizations were disbanded, it was essential that they be allowed to become integrated with the Israeli social order and learn to live according to law.

He applied this principle to Irgun, crushing its organization with a hand of steel so that it could not set up Rightist cells in the army. He searched out and obliterated its resources in Israel and abroad, and raided its caches of weapons. At the same time, however, he arranged conferences with the Irgun leaders and offered them places on the supreme command of the army. Ben-Gurion approved Iser's policy and helped him effect it. It failed in the end only because the Irgun leaders decided to form a political party and become candidates for the Israeli parliament at the next election.

Iser Harel's firm yet patient approach to the Irgun problem seems to have been the first milestone along the way to a mutual understanding between him and Ben-Gurion — an affinity that deepened during the next trial of strength between the authority of the state and the underground organizations.

The United Nations had named a mediator between Israel and the Arabs — the Swedish Count Folke Bernadotte, an aristocrat who promptly aroused the wrath of the Israelis. Without taking into consideration the limits of his jurisdiction Bernadotte, in order to resolve the Jewish-Arab conflict, proposed a plan that differed on several points from the one the United Nations had adopted for the partitioning of Palestine. Bernadotte's scheme was to reinstate the Arab refugees in Israel and transfer the Negev from the Jews to the Arabs, compensating the Jews for that loss of territory by joining Western Galilee to Israel. Furthermore, he recommended demilitarizing Jerusalem and giving it to the Arabs with a provision for the autonomy of its one hundred thousand Jewish inhabitants. These proposals antagonized the extreme Israeli factions in particular.

On September 17, 1948, while a jeep blocked the way of the white automobile in which Bernadotte was riding through the narrow streets of Jerusalem, a masked band armed with machine pistols descended on the vehicle. A hail of bullets killed Bernadotte and also Colonel André P. Serot, a French U.N. observer. The assassins vanished, and in spite of the efforts of all the forces of order their trail was not found. An organization that called itself the National Front assumed responsibility for the assassination, but what in the world was the National Front?

Even today the assassination of Count Folke Bernadotte has not been entirely clarified. No names have been revealed, and many details remain highly classified. But within forty-eight hours of the incident Little Iser had managed to solve the puzzle.

Shortly after the assassination, in fact, Iser went to Ben-Gurion. "I have reliable information," he said, "that Irgun had nothing to do with the murder. It was the Stern Gang. National Front is simply a disguise. In my opinion you must wipe out the Stern Gang at once. There is no time to lose."

Ben-Gurion thought for a moment, then said: "Can it be done?"

He telephoned the young lieutenant colonel in command of the section of Jerusalem where the assassination had taken place, Moshe Dayan. Dayan's answer to Ben-Gurion's question was: "Yes, it can be done."

That night several units of Palmach's Harel Brigade were dispatched to Jerusalem to reinforce the army. Iser Harel got the green light. Squadrons of both civil and military police went into action simultaneously throughout the country. With lightning speed one after another of the Stern Gang leaders was arrested.

While Iser was directing the arrests and the seizure of the printing presses, bases, and arms depots of the Stern Gang, Ben-Gurion was taking constitutional measures. He invited the legal counsel of the government, Yaa'cov Shimshon Shapiro, to draft a law against terrorism that would forbid membership in terrorist organizations and severely penalize acts of terrorism. The Stern Gang was proclaimed such an organization. The Provisional National Council, which took the place of the Legislative Assembly until after the first elections, approved these new regulations.

During this period Iser's teams had arrested over two hundred persons throughout the country, but some of the directors of the Stern Gang and their leader himself, Friedmann Yellin, had disappeared without a trace. Iser, convinced that because Lod Airport had been tightly sealed Friedmann Yellin had been unable to leave the country and was hiding somewhere in Israel, made every effort to lay his hands on the terrorist chief.

Some days after the assassination of Bernadotte, Novik, one of Shin-Bet's best sleuths, was climbing the stairs of an old house on Tel Aviv's Sokolov Street. When he came to the attic door he rapped a few times and gave a password. The door opened. Behind it was hiding one of the principal members of the Stern Gang, Romek Grinberg.

"Let's strike a bargain," he said to Novik. "If you'll guarantee my personal safety and promise not to arrest me, I'll give you detailed information about the Stern Gang leaders and their hiding places."

Once the bargain was made, the weakest link in the terrorists' organizational chain was broken.

Shin-Bet installed Grinberg in room number four of Tel Aviv's Hotel Lampel, where he conscientiously fulfilled his part of the agreement. For six weeks the raids went on, following the leads Grinberg furnished. The Harel Brigade arrested all the key men of the Stern Gang, including the executives of the organization's broadcasting station and the directors of its Intelligence Service. In Jerusalem they uncovered the terrorists' caches of arms and their double agents who had infiltrated the administration and the police. But Grinberg's most important information was also the least accurate. When he was asked about Friedmann Yellin, he said he knew practically nothing, adding only that he should be looked for in the north near Haifa.

That made sense to Iser, for with the Lod Airport closed, Haifa provided the only other means of escape from the country. Determined to capture Yellin, cost what it might, Iser immediately tripled all security measures.

"If we could lay our hands on him," Iser said to a friend, "I know we'd be finished with the Stern Gang once and for all. I don't want any hundred-years' war with those boys, just to smash their organization and then give them a chance to resume a law-abiding life. So long as Yellin is free, the Stern Gang will go on."

Out of the flood of information that regularly deluged Shin-Bet headquarters one rather ordinary-appearing piece nonetheless attracted Iser's attention. In a suspicious house in Haifa strange comings and goings had been reported. This, Iser perceived, jibed with Grinberg's hint. Heading a select squad of detectives, Iser went to Haifa. On the following day he reported to Ben-Gurion: "We have just arrested Yellin."

It was September 30, hardly two weeks after Bernadotte had been shot. The Stern Gang was no more.

Iser's aggressive, efficient program earned him the esteem of the "Old Man," as Ben-Gurion was affectionately called. Their approach to the Stern Gang problem had been identical, and now the two strong, tough, firm personalities mutually agreed to act generously and democratically toward the imprisoned terrorists.

On September 27, 1948, they had met in Ben-Gurion's office with Shapiro, who vigorously demanded that the Stern Gang members be prosecuted. "If not," he said, "then why a law against terrorism?"

Iser and Ben-Gurion disagreed with Shapiro. "It is too soon," said the Old Man. "We haven't arrested all the suspects yet. We might even free some prisoners on the condition that they agree to join the army."

On October 9, 1948, Ben-Gurion and Iser decided on the policy they would adopt toward the Stern Gang. Its members who had joined the army before the assassination or had been arrested after it but against whom there was no evidence of complicity in the murder of Bernadotte would be set free at once. Young members who agreed to join the army or paramilitary formations would also be set at liberty. The only ones who would remain in jail were the leaders and those whose participation in the murder had been proved. These men would be handed over to justice.

By November 1948 most of the prisoners had been liberated. Yellin's trial took place early in January 1949. Sentenced to eight years in prison, he was released after being elected to the Knesset.

After Yellin's trial Iser, with Ben-Gurion's approval, put an end to the pressure on the older members of the Stern Gang; in fact, in his desire to integrate them into Israeli society he even opened the holy of holies to them and employed them in Shin-Bet. One of the most dangerous of the terrorists, whom Iser himself had chased all over the country, was called to his office.

"I want to ask you one question," Iser said to him. "Do you believe that you are morally ready to serve with complete loyalty, forgetting the past?"

"Yes," said the former terrorist.

He was true to his word. In due time he rose through the Shin-Bet echelons to a position of considerable importance and became a personal friend of Iser Harel. He also brought into the service several of his former comrades who have since had many opportunities to demonstrate their devotion to the State of Israel.

The relationship between Iser and Ben-Gurion grew closer. They trusted each other completely. Ben-Gurion rewarded Iser by increasing his responsibilities, opening new fields of action to him, and making him a counselor and confidant.

9

School for Spies

ISER HAREL never breathed a word about his job to Rivka, and she never asked questions about it. The first time he came home wearing a lieutenant colonel's insignia she was just as astonished as the neighbors, and even more so the day he drove up at the wheel of a big new car. But when he acquired a chauffeur, she thought things were going too far. What would the neighbors say? Her point of view and her habits were still those of a kibbutz girl. Her household was simple, and she kept the food budget down by growing vegetables and raising chickens in the back yard.

Little Mira also reproached her father, even though he treated her like a princess and gave her a watch — the first to be owned among any of her school chums. But she did not like being the only one in her class whose father was a "government official" rather than a chauffeur, a tradesman, a doctor, or a laborer or a teacher. What was a "government official" for heaven's sake? Why couldn't her father be a grocer or a laborer like other fathers? Not until much later, when she was called for military service, did she learn what her father really did.

During the War of Independence Iser's headquarters moved from the refrigeration plant in Tel Aviv to Jaffa, from which the Arab inhabitants had fled. Also transferred to Jaffa was the Bureau of Military Intelligence (Aman), which was installed in the Green House, a handsome Arab building on King George Boulevard. Iser's new headquarters were not so splendid, but he was too busy to look for better accommodations.

Once the war was over Iser and his assistants applied themselves to the complicated task of creating and organizing a secret service. Procedures had to be established, departments and secondary services had to be coordinated, rules and principles codified. There was an endless search for answers to these problems, which had to come from the Israelis themselves, for no foreign secret service would dream of giving technical assistance to the Secret Service of the State of Israel.

"Contrary to the army and various ministries and other of the government departments, we have practically no chance of benefiting from the experience of others," Iser Harel explained to his staff. "By their very nature the methods of special services like ours are kept a closely guarded secret. Whatever and wherever those services may be, they are not going to open their headquarters, their files, and their training schools to a young country that wants to learn from their experience. Moreover, why should they do so for Israel especially, since the appearance of our country on the map of the world has not exactly pleased several other nations?"

Hence it was Iser himself who had to lay the foundations of Shin-Bet, define its objectives, and dictate its policies. Consequently its character emerged with the clear imprint of Iser's own.

His first decision was that the agents of the Service were to be under civil service so that their grades, benefits, and salaries would conform to those of all other government employees. Although he knew that in other countries secret service employees enjoyed a special status, he wanted Israel's to be no privileged caste, attracting recruits with higher than average salaries and alluring perquisites. His employees must be sincere and serious.

The personal morality Iser insisted upon was puritanical. From the first he hired many women and was to send some of them on dangerous missions, but he made it an inviolable rule that they were never to use sex to achieve their end. There was to be no Israeli Mata Hari. On the other hand, Iser had no objection to using prostitutes and kept women for certain missions.

He was convinced that a normal, happy family life was essential for his agents, and he systematically fired men whose morality was suspect or who deserted their wives and children. Old-timers still recall that in the early days of Shin-Bet a young agent asked for ten days' leave, told his wife that he was being sent on a mission, and disappeared with his mistress. Some days later his wife telephoned headquarters to ask when he would be back. When his whereabouts and activities were quickly discovered, he was fired.

This uncompromising discipline was the result of Iser's conception of the ideal Israeli secret agent. Every employee of his was to have flawless integrity, morality, and honesty, and an irreproachable past. Firmly rejected were applications from men who had been in trouble with the police, had been convicted of any crime or misdemeanor whatever, or who had bad habits.

The secret service of several other countries would sometimes recruit for certain delicate missions burglars and even murderers, but Shin-Bet never did. Its screening of applicants was meticulous, but in weighing the pros and cons of an application Iser and his assistants would never take into consideration the political background of the candidate, in spite of the fact that party affiliation was a major criterion in weighing any application for other government jobs. The Secret Service was the first of all Israel's administrative departments to cross political barriers and hire former members of Haganah, Palmach, the Stern Gang, and Irgun.

From the very first Iser was fully aware of the enormous power concentrated in his hands. He headed an organization that operated outside the law, was protected by absolute secrecy, was backed by the government, and was beyond the reach of the press. But this supremacy never went to Iser's head. On the contrary, he himself decided to limit his own freedom of action.

In some of the projects submitted for his approval it appeared that his agents would have authority not only to keep a suspect under surveillance but also to arrest him. Iser would have none of that. He decided that his bureau would go no further than gathering evidence on a suspect, and that the arrest would have to be made by the police with a warrant duly signed by a magistrate. Thus Iser established a system of cooperation and coordination with the Special Branch (detectives) of the Israeli police force, similar to that used by the British secret service.

Another innovation of Iser's was requesting the government comptroller, who reported to the Knesset, to audit the operations of the Secret Service every year as he did the ministries and other public services.

Iser's frank explanation of the reasons for his tight regulations was: "The Secret Service is a two-edged sword which could be extremely dangerous if wielded by untrustworthy persons. Because it must often use unconventional methods to achieve its objectives it must respect the letter of international law and the principles of democracy and morality."

So long as he remained director of Shin-Bet, and later of the entire Israeli Secret Service, Iser diligently saw to it that there were no torture chambers in the cellar, that no suspect was beaten while being questioned, and that no one was liquidated under a guise of patriotism.

*

The early years of the new state were far from tranquil. The Arabs continued to threaten its existence, and border incidents increased until renewal of the war seemed imminent. So fresh was the memory of the underground warfare against the British that certain political movements were tempted to resort to subversive means and revive terroristic plots against the government. The Arab minority in Israel constituted another source of danger — a kind of fifth column. The Arab states, thirsting for revenge, were not the only ones attempting to set up sources of information within Israel; several foreign powers were also perhaps a bit too interested in what was going on inside the new little nation situated at the crossroads of Europe, Africa, and Asia. Shin-Bet emerged from the War of Independence burdened with plenty of problems, and it had no time to waste trying to solve them.

Of Shin-Bet's early operations the most important by far was counterespionage against subversive elements. Here it had to grope and stumble like a child in the dark. Its zealous agents were prone to think every foreign correspondent, as well as any Israeli who worked for a foreign newspaper, a spy, and it was difficult to persuade them that Israeli journalists were no less loyal to their country than other citizens. Lack of experience also made the agents hyperemotional; every time they got on the trail of a possible spy, their victim became in their eyes public enemy number one. It required considerable time for the Shin-Bet agents to acquire a sense of proportion and to distinguish a truly maleficent spy from one who could be rendered harmless by a stern warning and a few weeks in jail.

Arab espionage at that time was at a low, almost primitive level, and Shin-Bet had little trouble uncovering Arab spies and arresting them. Early in 1950, however, the Arabs opened a new front by engaging secret agents of other nationalities, principally from among the U.N. observers, many of whom were officers in their own country's army. Since they had diplomatic immunity they could move freely between Jerusalem and the capitals of the Arab world, and so could acquire valuable information.

The desirable hostesses of the Melody Bar in Haifa soon became informers for Shin-Bet, for after two or three drinks with them the U.N. observers would gossip indiscreetly. And when hidden microphones were found in the rooms of Tel Aviv's Hotel Kete Dan, where most of the observers stayed, all hell broke loose. The missionaries of peace put on their war paint and descended upon the Foreign Ministry with blood in their eyes. The Ministry's officials listened to their stories impassively and made formal apologies, but one was heard to remark: "The least we can do is listen to those whom we cannot arrest."

In 1950 Shin-Bet had to undertake an unwelcome campaign against the black market. Owing to Israel's perilous economic situation the Food Ministry had rationed supplies and inaugurated an austerity program. Very soon afterward the thriving black market that had come into existence made Ben-Gurion apprehensive for the national morale, and he decided that Iser Harel should undertake a crusade against the black marketers. The Shin-Bet agents, of course, raged at being sent to hunt down such piddling quarry as speculators in nylon stockings and beefsteak.

The crusade turned into a comic opera fiasco. The agents did apprehend a few terrified grandmothers who were trying to smuggle a dozen eggs, but the big operators slipped through their fingers. Even when they managed to snare one they reflected bitterly that all he would get was a fine of two hundred Israeli pounds, whereas he had made two hundred thousand.

Ben-Gurion, however, would not retreat, and when he learned that a company was dealing in bathtubs on the black market, he sent Iser Harel the following directive:

1. Find out how many bathtubs have been manufactured during the last six months.

2. Establish how many bathtubs have been delivered to wholesalers and at what price.
3. What is the price to retailers?
4. How many bathtubs did wholesalers buy from the factory during the last six months and what did they pay?
5. Compile a list of all retailers who bought bathtubs.
6. Check on each dealer as to how many bathtubs he bought and at what price, and to whom he sold them and at what price.
7. Trace every bathtub bought to the purchaser's home.
8. Have our men buy bathtubs in the stores.

(Signed) DAVID BEN-GURION

"Fortunately for us bathtub-hunters," reminisces one of the old-timers, "the crusade against the black market didn't last long, and we were soon able to devote our efforts to more important matters."

Far more important matters were indeed waiting for their attention.

10

Rebellion

At the end of World War II a thin, pale man wearing a British sergeant's uniform was liberated from the German prisoner-of-war camp where he had been confined for several years. He was a Lithuanian Jew named Boris Guriel who had emigrated to Palestine, where he had fought with the Palestine Brigade of the British army until he was captured by the Germans.

Returning to Jerusalem in 1945, this vigorous, keen-eyed man of extraordinary intelligence had not had time to change from his uniform into civvies before he was summoned to Shai headquarters. He did not even know what Shai was, for the years he had spent in the stalag had isolated him from the activities of Haganah, of which he had once been an active member.

Israel Amir immediately appointed Guriel head of Department M (for *medinit;* that is, "political"), whose business was to spy on the British army and authorities during the Mandate.

After the State of Israel came into existence Guriel was ordered to report to Foreign Minister Moshe Sharett, who told him: "My ministry is in the process of creating a secret division to be known as the Political Department. You are to be its director, reporting directly to Reuven Shiloach."

Shiloach, at that time the Ministry's adviser on special projects, held a long work session with Guriel, during which it was decided that Shiloach would effect a liaison between the Political Department and the Foreign Ministry, and coordinate the two. Guriel was given extremely wide powers with which to accomplish the objectives of his division, the principal one of which was gathering, in other countries, political and military intelligence vital for Israel. While Aman and Shin-Bet were limited to the territory of Israel, the Political Department became the Secret Service branch operating abroad.

Guriel assembled a staff of intelligent young Israelis whom he instructed in the technique of secret activities. Among them might be mentioned Dan Avni, an officer of the parachute corps and a future diplomat and professor of international relations, Moshe Gali, Gershon Peres, and Meir de Shalit, the future director of the Israeli Tourist Ministry. Soon the disciples of Guriel were scattered to the four corners of the earth, and confidential information began to flow into the department's headquarters in Tel Aviv.

After Iser Be'eri's fall Vivian Herzog was appointed head of Aman. This young Irishman with curly hair and a russet mustache, the son of the Grand Rabbi of Israel, had accomplished important missions for the British Military Intelligence during World War II, and afterward had directed a huge Intelligence bureau in Germany for the benefit of the Allies. He had returned to Israel just in time to undertake several missions for Shai, which he accomplished brilliantly, and he had subsequently conducted the first course of instruction for Shai agents.

After the state was established, Herzog became Be'eri's deputy. Because of his prodigious familiarity with military intelligence Herzog was entrusted by Ben-Gurion with planning the organizational structure of Aman, and the Prime Minister approved his blueprints on August 20, 1948. Appointed head of Aman in December of that year, Herzog proceeded to organize the Service into divisions corresponding to the several duties assigned to it and set up operational procedures that proved their worth during the years to come.

Not long after he took office Herzog proposed the establishment of a superstructural organization that would embrace all Israeli Secret Services — Aman, Shin-Bet, and the Political Department — which hitherto had been independent, reporting to different ministries. Thus their activities would be coordinated as they were in Great Britain. Reuven Shiloach was named president of this new commission, which included the director of the Political Department, the head of Aman, the head of Shin-Bet, and the chief of police.

Vivian Herzog remained head of Aman until April 1950, when Colonel Benjamin Gibli, who had been one of Be'eri's henchmen and one of Toubianski's judges, took over. Influential persons had demanded that Gibli be dismissed from the army, but finally he had been maintained at his functions. He managed his agency decisively and firmly.

Although its wings were clipped after the Be'eri scandal, Aman was still entrusted with numerous functions of vital importance, including gathering information on the Arab armies, which were being reorganized.

By the beginning of 1951 the Political Department came in for a good deal of criticism. The easy life that Guriel's agents allegedly led in foreign capitals offended several Israeli leaders. They were accused of being amateur actors who had gone abroad for the sake of parts in a spy melodrama, and they were blamed for holding secret conferences in lavish Geneva hotels. They defended themselves by saying: "If we meet on the shores of Lake Geneva, at least we aren't watched there. If we held our conferences on the Rue des Rosiers in Paris, we would be uncovered in no time." And to those who charged them with luxurious living they replied: "After all, in Europe do as the Europeans do. We can't wear shorts and sandals on the streets of

Paris or Rome or London as if we were in a kibbutz. We have to adapt our way of life to where we are."

Other criticisms were directed at Guriel's conception of information and the kind of information he wanted. The very name of his department indicated that its chief concern was with political developments, and it is true that he sometimes neglected military information for diplomatic, for very few of his agents were properly trained for gathering military information. Guriel also thought military intelligence less important than political.

"Perhaps I was somewhat to blame," Guriel told this writer some years later. "My theory was to teach my men how to gather information, not to collect such and such specific item. I wanted them to get a general view of a situation and of the problems confronting us. Information had to be of a political nature. The service had to discover what direction the politics of a country was taking in order to forecast a realistic chain of events. We had to know which way the wind was blowing so that we could prevent undesirable things from happening. Perhaps I was wrong, but . . ."

Apparently Moshe Sharett was none too enthusiastic about what he heard of Guriel's theories. During a conference with him and Shiloach he asked Guriel just what his conception of intelligence was.

"We need political intelligence."

"What does that mean?"

"Lithuania, my native country, is a small one," Guriel said. "Not long ago it was independent. I have always been convinced that it lost its freedom because it didn't gather political intelligence."

"What difference would that have made?"

"There was an unpublicized paragraph in the famous Ribbentrop-Molotov Pact of August 1939 that dealt with Russia's annexation of the Baltic countries — Lithuania, Latvia, Estonia.

If the Lithuanians had known this paragraph existed . . ."

"What if they had known?" Sharett interrupted.

"They could have done something, like set up a government in exile . . ."

Sharett made no answer. With the threat of a new war, and with enemies all around her, Israel had urgent need of military intelligence — details of Arab armies, their bases, their equipment, their capabilities. Political intelligence would not supply this need, and Guriel's theories were not relevant to the situation confronting Israel at that time.

After long high-level conferences Shiloach came to the inevitable conclusion that the Political Department should be replaced by a new service.

Shiloach's decision was received with bitter anger by the executives of the Political Department, who felt they were being unjustly treated. To them Shiloach was a turncoat who had listened only to the criticism leveled at the department. Guriel was summoned to Ben-Gurion's office, where he explained his theories at length. He left with the impression that he had convinced the Old Man of their value.

He was mistaken, however, as appeared when a select committee met with Ben-Gurion to decide the department's fate. Present were General Ygael Yadin, the Commander in Chief of the Army, Moshe Sharett, Reuven Shiloach, and the Director of the Foreign Ministry, Walter Eytan. Their final decision was that the Political Department must be abolished.

It was to continue officially to exist, however, within the Foreign Ministry, but was to deal only with such political matters as the Ministry would hand it. The gathering of intelligence abroad, as well as special operations outside of Israel, was assigned to a new service called the Central Institute for Intelligence and Special Missions — or *Mossad*, the Hebrew word for "institute." Reuven Shiloach was appointed its director.

On the night after the committee meeting Walter Eytan

came to Guriel's home. "The death sentence has been decreed," he said. The executives and agents, a homogeneous group, were furious. Their first reaction was astonishment. Then they rebelled, refusing to acknowledge or effect the decision. They held several secret meetings in Guriel's seaside apartment in Tel Aviv. Telephone messages camouflaged with allusions and double meanings summoned home all the agents who were in Europe. Some came on the run; those who stayed at their post organized secret meetings of their own.

"We're all resigning," they told Boris Guriel, who himself was the first to tender his resignation. Once his division chiefs and the agents had done likewise, they refused to collaborate further with Shiloach, even to handing over current operations to the new director and his assistants.

The consequences of this rebellion — unprecedented in Israel, and in any other secret service of the world for that matter — could have been disastrous, for it exposed the new State of Israel and left it paralyzed in its efforts to learn what was going on in the hostile Arab capitals.

Reuven Shiloach responded firmly to the challenge by appointing a commission to dissolve the Political Department, keep things moving, and organize the transferral of its powers to Mossad. But even after the service had been obliterated and Guriel's men had been officially forbidden to hold meetings or to leave their posts abroad, they continued to confer in secret and plan their next moves.

Boris Guriel and all his subordinates had resigned. Nevertheless the new Mossad and the Foreign Ministry held out their hand to the former head of the Political Department and were ready to reinstate him. Guriel, however, refused to accept their offers and left the Foreign Ministry forever after insulting Moshe Sharett to his face. Shiloach then ordered severe punishments for the rebels, demanding that those who had led the insurrection and ordered the mass resignations and refusals to cooperate be summarily dismissed from the Foreign Ministry and refused employment in any other branch of the government.

The episode still rankles. One of Shiloach's deputies minces no words in speaking of the Political Department. "They were all adventurers," he says, "trying to imitate James Bond in some amateur production. I have heard plenty about their sumptuous conferences in Europe, and also about the secret meetings they held after they had been officially ordered to stop all such concerted action."

On the other hand, one of the former members of the ousted department says: "That's not true. The rebellion was not intended to be taken so seriously. It was a mistake, I admit, but there was none of us who couldn't have been reasoned with."

Boris Guriel is not so absolute. "One or two years after our resignation," he told me, "we were called to police headquarters to sign a paper by which we swore to keep our former activities a secret. I refused to go. I said the police chief knew my address and could come to my house if he wanted my signature." As to the rebellion: "We were wrong. I wonder now how we could have dared rebel against the government."

In the fall of 1951 Reuven Shiloach assumed the direction of Mossad.

A great admirer of Shiloach says that this man of mystery par excellence represented the queen in Ben-Gurion's chess game. Some see him as a Cardinal Richelieu; others, as a wily manipulator with an uncanny ability to pull strings behind the scenes. There is no doubt that from 1948 to 1952 Shiloach was the greatest enigma in the Israeli government.

One other government official shared that quality with him — Shaul Avigur, the taciturn head of the Bureau of Immigration (Mossad le-Alia Bet). But after the proclamation of the state Shiloach alone had the full confidence of both Ben-Gurion and Sharett. He was the supreme authority in everything connected with Intelligence, espionage, state secrets, and special operations.

Although the truth is less romantic, no one can dispute the great influence Reuven Shiloach exerted on the structural organization, the procedures, and the theories of the Israeli Secret Service. All his life he had been engaged in secret missions, and he had made an endless study of such deep and dark matters in order to perfect his procedures and techniques.

Shiloach, the son of Rabbi Zaslanski, was born in the Old City of Jerusalem. He first attracted attention in the early 1930s, when the political division of the workers' federation appointed him one of the "Arab troika" — three young hopefuls who were sent to various Middle Eastern capitals to study the Arab question at first hand. Eliahu Eilat* went to Beirut; Eliahu Sasson† was sent to Damascus; Shiloach arrived in Baghdad under a double disguise — teacher, and foreign correspondent of the Palestine *Bulletin*. He stayed three years in Iraq, making a complete inspection of the country and plumbing the depths of the problems of Jews and Arabs in that country.

When Shiloach returned to Palestine he was employed as an expert on Arab affairs in the political division of the workers' federation. In 1936 he was transferred to the political department of the Jewish Agency as a liaison officer with the British authorities. In 1939 he was one of the counselors to Ben-Gurion and Chaim Weizmann, the leaders of the Jewish delegation at the Round Table Conference in St. James's Palace, London. But he did not truly achieve prominence until World War II, when he became Moshe Sharett's right-hand man responsible for special operations.

At Sharett's side he negotiated in Cairo the formation of the

---

* Future Israeli ambassador to London and president of the Hebrew University in Jerusalem.
† Future postmaster general and later police minister.

Jewish Commando Corps, which was to accomplish sabotage operations in Occupied Europe. He was partially responsible for sending twenty-three Jewish commandos into Syria, where they disappeared without a trace, and he was among the promoters of the Palestine Scheme, a top-secret program for a network of spies and guerrilla fighters in Palestine trained to make radio broadcasts and to offer armed resistance if the country fell into the hands of the Germans. He also took part in the formation of two special Palmach units: the Arab Battalion, whose members, disguised as Arabs and speaking flawless Arabic, were to accomplish special missions in Arab territory, and the German Battalion, which was equipped with German uniforms and arms and sent on suicide missions behind the enemy lines.

A few months later, along with Avigur, Shiloach wrenched out of the British their agreement to parachute Palestinian Jews into Occupied Europe in order to organize a Jewish Resistance. At Bari, Italy, he negotiated with the directors of the British Secret Service for sending into the Balkans Jewish self-defense units.

Immediately after the war Shiloach went with Ben-Gurion to the United States, where he helped the Old Man persuade a small group of Jewish millionaires to form a dummy company fur buying the latest machines for arms manufacture. Smuggled into Palestine, those became the nucleus of Israel's munitions industry.

During the War of Independence Shiloach was once again at Sharett's side as a special adviser in the Foreign Ministry. He was one of the Israeli delegation to Rhodes, which negotiated an armistice with Egypt on February 24 and Transjordan on April 3, 1949. Several times between 1948 and 1950 he met in the deepest secrecy with King Abdullah.

Ben-Gurion said of Shiloach: "He was one of our most talented experts in the area of foreign relations. He excelled in establishing and then in strengthening ties between us and other chiefs of state. He made a great contribution to Israel's international status, particularly among the nations of the East."

Somewhat bald, Shiloach had a triangular face with cold eyes of a light color — fish eyes, say his enemies. His few intimates are fond of telling anecdotes about his coolness, his extraordinary memory, his self-control, and his rigid self-discipline.

"When he is talking to me," said a young Israeli journalist, "I get the impression that I am seeing right into his skull, watching the little wheels go round."

Those who like to tease Shiloach for eternally wearing a cloak of secrecy say that once he hailed a taxi. "Where to?" asked the driver. Shiloach replied: "It's a state secret."

His keen analytical mind was matched by a rare quality of imagination. He could detect the most subtle nuances in the words of those he was talking to, and his reports were masterpieces of a comprehensive grasp of the subject matter on the one hand and of precise detail on the other.

David Ben-Gurion and Moshe Sharett thought they had found in Reuven Shiloach the ideal man to establish and maintain good relations between the government and the Secret Services of the new state. Iser Harel, however, had a different opinion of Shiloach.

To Iser many of the legendary talents that had created such a halo around Shiloach did not exist and never had existed. Little Iser was always cautious with Shiloach and invariably greeted him with the same question: "Did Ben-Gurion send you?" Much as he appreciated Shiloach's vast knowledge, fertile mind, and astonishingly brilliant ideas, Iser believed Shiloach lacked common sense and had small capacity for organizing and executing a program. Several of Shiloach's colleagues thought the same.

When Shiloach was named head of Mossad, Iser offered him full cooperation and put at his disposal all the resources of Shin-Bet, including its staff. In a way, he had to do so, for the rebellion in the Political Department left Mossad with practically no trained people either at home or abroad. Iser's own deputy became assistant director of Mossad.

Reuven Shiloach had hardly assumed his new duties when a disaster struck the Israeli Secret Service — the Baghdad affair.

11

The Gallows
of Baghdad

WHEN THE NAZI REGIME of Rashid Ali, an adventurer who had taken power in Iraq, toppled on June 1, 1941, there were violent riots, and the mobs that swarmed through the streets of Baghdad shouted for a sacrifice. A thousand-year-old tradition of pogroms dictated their choice of victim — the Jews.

Out of the warm, humid Oriental night swept a wave of bloodthirsty men with rifles, knives, and clubs. It broke on the Jewish quarter, and when it ebbed two days later the police tally of the wreckage came to 2731 stores and 6558 apartments looted and burned, hundreds of women raped, 2118 Jews wounded, and 179 Jews killed.

When the staggering news reached Palestine, the Haganah leaders sprang into action and decided to put a Jewish self-defense system into operation in Iraq at once.

A few months later two officers in well-tailored British army uniforms appeared at the home of the influential Skeik family in Baghdad's ghetto. "Gabriel sent us," they said.

The patriarch of the family burst into tears. "So you've come at last! Our house is yours." Then, turning to his two sons, he added: "They're from Israel, and for Israel we would suffer anything, even the gallows!"

The two officers were the first secret emissaries of Haganah. Others would follow, disguised as Arabs, soldiers, American tourists, Iranian traders, construction company representatives, army chauffeurs. They were the best type of young Palestinian, and all were agents of Shaul Avigur's Bureau of Clandestine Immigration, which operated all over the world arranging means for Jews to escape to Palestine in boats manned by captains and crews of various nationalities and sailing from harbors policed by accomplices or sympathizers with the plight of the persecuted.

Another emissary was Shmariahu Gutman, the amateur archeologist who had discovered Masada, the legendary fortress on the Dead Sea coast, where the last defenders of Jewish independence against the Roman Empire had perished.

There was also Enzo Sereni, an incorrigibly idealistic pacifist of almost insane recklessness, who would be parachuted into Occupied Italy two years later, captured by the Nazis, and put to death at Dachau. A girl, Malka Rofe, a radio operator, went to Baghdad too, disguised first as a soldier and then as a veiled Muslim woman.

There were plenty of others.

They quickly organized an underground branch of the Zionist Pioneer Movement, the purpose of which was to inspire young Iraqi Jews with determination to return to the Promised Land. Then they established a still more secret and selective body, The Order, which was to be the ears and eyes of Haganah in Baghdad and was also to get the Jewish self-defense system working. The two groups were mutually dependent, and many recruits belonged to both.

Haganah smuggled into Iraq supplies of revolvers, machine pistols, grenades, and explosives, which were hidden in sliks in

Baghdad's ghetto. Members of The Order were taught how to use these munitions and learned judo and the use of side arms. They also mapped out a detailed plan for the armed defense of the ghetto in the event of another pogrom.

Presently the young militant Zionists of Iraq undertook a third responsibility — undercover immigration. During the Second World War a secret exodus of Iraqi Jews began with small bands of young Zionists setting out for Palestine through Iran, Syria, and Transjordan, provided with forged papers and with transportation and escape routes arranged by the cell of Palestinian emissaries.

In 1948 Israel assigned them a new task — espionage.

October 1949 saw the unexpected arrival in Baghdad of one Nissim Moshe, a tall, lithe young fellow with an infectious smile. His real name was Ben-Porat, and he was an Israeli who had been promoted from the ranks to officer status during the War of Independence. When that war ended he resumed civilian dress and went to Baghdad as director of undercover immigration to Israel. It was a hazardous assignment, for since the War of Independence Iraq had become Israel's most implacable enemy, being the only Arab state that refused an armistice. An Israeli who entered this lion's den had little chance of coming out alive.

Perhaps that is why Ben-Porat was chosen. Iraq was quite familiar to him, for he had been born and brought up in Baghdad and had been a member of the Movement and The Order before emigrating to Palestine in 1944. He was about to marry a young Sabra when he was given the mission, but he yielded to the needs and wishes of the state.

Just before he left Israel he received a supplementary assignment, namely, to establish in Baghdad a spy system that would report on military and economic subjects. There was neither money nor time available for him to be trained for this duty; all he had got in that respect were a few documents from the Political Department and a pat on the back the night before he embarked on his career as a spy.

At Teheran Ben-Porat exchanged his Israeli passport for "Nissim Moshe's," thus becoming an Iraqi Jew living in Baghdad, where he presently arrived without incident. Soon he became the undisputed leader of all the underground activities that Israel had mounted in Iraq.

Back in Tel Aviv Shaul Avigur was fraught with anxiety because in underground warfare life insurance is spelled compartmentalization. Any contact whatever between the various spy systems operating in the same locality was strictly forbidden, and members of one network were never to know those of another, or even that they existed. Otherwise, the arrest of one could mean the ruin of all.

Ben-Porat's superiors were aware that this prohibition made his situation all the more precarious. He was to supervise everything—immigration, Zionist activities, self-defense, espionage. He also knew the directors of the other underground networks in Baghdad. If the Iraqis ever got their hands on him, the result would be catastrophic. All Israeli operations in Iraq would be annihilated, and for Ben-Porat there would be only one fate — the gallows.

The directors of the Bureau of Clandestine Immigration in Tel Aviv, therefore, began a campaign for the total separation of immigration from espionage. Their pressure increased in March 1950 because by then secret immigration had increased to an unprecedented degree, the Iraqi authorities having decided to let the Jews leave for "the country of their choice, with the exception of Israel."

On the heels of that decision one Richard Armstrong was admitted into Iraq on a British passport. His dark skin and his facial characteristics were hardly those of a pure-blooded Anglo-Saxon, but he explained that he was the by-blow of an Englishman's romance with a Hindu, a story that was accepted with sly winks. Armstrong negotiated directly with Prime Minister Tawfik El Sweidi for the airlift of tens of thousands of Iraqi Jews to Cyprus.

The Prime Minister might have been astonished to learn that the gentlemanly Mr. Armstrong who spoke such impeccable English was in reality the Israeli Shlomo Hillel,° who had been born in Baghdad and spoke perfect Arabic. At any rate, the airlift was promptly put into operation by a dummy company. Its planes at first flew straight to Nicosia, but after Iraqi surveillance relaxed, they landed at Israel's Lod Airport.

From his secret headquarters Ben-Porat prepared thousands of Jews for this massive migration, procuring transportation for them from remote districts to Baghdad's airport, instructing them in how to deal with Iraqi authorities, and scheduling the flights. In the daytime he appeared to be a minor employee of Shemtov, a Jewish community center, but at night he became "Zaki Haviv," a man of mystery whom only select initiates knew.

Israel finally yielded to Shaul Avigur's demands, and early in 1951 a young and dynamic Iranian landed at the Baghdad airport with a perfectly acceptable passport bearing the name of Zalihon. His true name, however, was Yehuda Taggar, and he was a Sabra from Jerusalem who had recently been released from the army, in which he had held the rank of captain. He had been sent to Iraq to relieve Ben-Porat of the espionage system.

Ben-Porat handed over to Taggar all its operations. Unfortunately the two networks remained closely connected, especially the link with headquarters in Israel. All communications from it to Taggar, as well as Taggar's dispatches and those of his associates, passed through Ben-Porat's hands.

The two men met frequently in order to coordinate their activities and to re-create a home atmosphere so that they might forget for a while the eternal peril in which they lived. For

° Later police minister of Israel.

conditions in the enemy land where they were compelled to exist sometimes drove them to the point of a nervous breakdown, particularly Taggar, who had no relatives or friends in Iraq. They would meet at some safe spot, then drive outside of Baghdad with the car windows closed, chatting in Hebrew or singing some familiar Israeli song.

Taggar was not the only one who knew about the other underground organizations. Several of his agents knew what the self-defense groups were doing. The principal slik for arms and ammunition was under the flagstones of the Shemtov synagogue, which also served as a departure center for the immigrants. There was little doubt that the place was infested with Iraqi spies.

Only one of the Israeli agents in Baghdad had never met Ben-Porat in person — a slender, tanned young man who carried a British passport identifying him as Rodney, a textile importer. Not that he hadn't tried to meet Zaki Haviv ever since his arrival in Baghdad, but Ben-Porat had refused to see him, and thus perhaps had saved his life.

Rodney's true name was Peter Yaniv, but in Israel he was better known by his nickname of "The Hindu." A former officer of the British Intelligence, he had accomplished several secret missions in India during World War II, had mastered Hindu dialects, and had married a native. Israel dispatched him to set up an autonomous spy system in Iraq, where his contact was no other than Yehuda Taggar.

Thus all of Israel's underground networks in Iraq wound up in a Kafkaesque tangle. Responsible for this situation were those who had not been able to dissolve the old-fashioned ties between The Order, the Movement, and Immigration as they existed before Israel became a state; those already engaged in setting up the spy system; and those who had kept in touch with the other organizations even after espionage had been separated from them.

*

On Rashid Street in the heart of Baghdad was a large department store named Ouruzdi Bek, whose necktie counter was near the entrance on the street floor. Its clerk at this time was a young Palestinian refugee named Assad, who had left his former home in Acre after the Israelis had captured that city. Shortly before Assad went to Iraq his cousin, a waiter in a café near the military governor's office, had fallen ill and asked him to take his place. For a week Assad served little cups of aromatic Turkish coffee to Israeli army officers, and he still vaguely remembered those young men in khaki uniforms.

One May morning in 1951, when Assad was minding his counter, he suddenly saw a familiar face among the customers — an Israeli officer whom he had waited on in Acre. He thought he must be dreaming, but it was indeed Yehuda Taggar, who had been stationed for three months in Acre. Assad ran after Taggar, but could not catch him, so he went to the nearest police station.

"I've seen an Israeli army officer right here in Baghdad!"

Since there had been rumors that Israeli spies were operating in Baghdad, the police took pains to instruct Assad as to what he should do in case he saw the officer again.

Yehuda Taggar wanted to buy a typewriter with Arabic characters and had tried the Ouruzdi Bek as the most likely place to find one. Not having seen one that pleased him, on May 25, 1951, he brought along his close friend Ben-Porat alias Nissim Moshe alias Zaki Haviv to help him locate one. Naturally they had to pass by Assad's necktie counter.

Assad did not waste a second.

Ben-Porat and Taggar had just started out of the store when suddenly three plainclothes men appeared. They were polite but firm. One whistled for a taxi. "If you please," he said, inviting the two Israelis to get into the taxi, which presently sped away.

Ben-Porat, on the rear seat between two of the detectives, tried to keep cool and think of a way to escape. He had been arrested twice while crossing the Iranian frontier, but both times he had got away at the last minute.

The first thing he had to do, he recognized, was to destroy any compromising papers he might have with him. He thrust his hands into his pockets one after the other and discovered in one trousers pocket a press clipping listing the Zionist fighters arrested in 1949. He had to get rid of it, for if it were found on his person it would be evidence of his interest in the underground Zionist movement. Taking out a handkerchief, he mopped the sweat that was streaming down his face, then tucked the damp cloth into his other pants pocket. In doing so he managed to extract the clipping, which he crumpled up and threw behind the seat. His guards appeared to have noticed nothing.

Ben-Porat had observed that the detectives considered him a person of no particular importance and were much more interested in their other prisoner, Taggar. Ben-Porat could not guess that the Iraqis already knew that Taggar was an Israeli, but he understood that they had nothing on him. The thing to do was pretend he himself was indeed an insignificant person and not too intelligent either.

"What you want with me?" he asked the detectives as they were shoving him into the interrogation room. "I'm only a petty civil servant in the Jewish community center. I met this tourist yesterday at a concert, and he asked me to show him around the stores." Taggar played along with this story, speaking English and pretending he knew no Arabic.

A moment before the two men were taken into separate rooms for questioning, Ben-Porat contrived to slip a note for his friends — and a tip — into the hand of the more gentle appearing of the detectives. It said simply "clean up and go home."

Ben-Porat was tortured for a week — strung up by the feet and then by the hands, beaten, and threatened with death. Four of his teeth were knocked out. But all he would say was: "What do you want with me? I don't know this tourist."

Taggar also kept silent.

The Iraqis, however, had more than one trick in their bag. They tied a black hood over Taggar's head, dragged him into the execution chamber, stood him on the trap door, and slipped a noose around his neck. "This is the end, Jew!"

He resigned himself to his fate, but he did not flinch, and finally he was returned to his cell.

After several days of this torture, Assad was brought in. Seeing him, Taggar realized that the game was up and he could no longer hide his nationality. He confessed that he was an Israeli officer. What was he doing in Baghdad? "I came to marry a Jewish girl," he said. His reply earned him only some mocking laughter, and more torture, but he told nothing.

The Special Branch of the Iraqi police profited not at all from Taggar's silence, but teams of experts went through his rooms in an Armenian boarding house in the Boustan El Khan section of Baghdad, and eventually, after smashing the furniture and drilling the walls, pried up the floor tiles and found in his private slik papers that revealed him as a spy. Among them were secret documents of a political and military nature that he had got through important personages in the National Assembly, and others dealing with economics that the Jewish banker Selim Mualem had tricked out of influential Iraqis.

Alerted by Ben-Porat's note, two Jewish underground workers went to Mualem at midnight and told him to get out of the country immediately.

"In the middle of the night?" Mualem said. "Don't panic. I'll take the first plane in the morning."

At two A.M. he was awakened again. This time it was the police.

Mualem's arrest triggered an avalanche of others, including the chiefs of the self-defense and espionage organizations. The interrogation rooms were never empty even for a minute. Rodney, The Hindu, at first indignantly protested that he was an English businessman, but torture dragged out of him that he was "an ambassador of peace" from Israel. Before they were through with him, he told all he knew.

Front-page headlines in the Beirut papers informed the world of the arrests.

Ben-Porat was dragged into The Hindu's cell. "Do you know this man?" Rodney was asked. "No." Ben-Porat heaved an inward sigh of relief. If The Hindu had known his true identity, he was sure everything would have come out.

After a week of torture Ben-Porat was released, thanks to the intervention of a well-known Kurdish lawyer. The Iraqi security officers had to admit there was no evidence against Nissim Moshe, for his story of having met Taggar at a concert conformed to Taggar's in every detail.

Ben-Porat's assistants worked out a plan for his escape, but he told them he had resolved to stay in Iraq. The exodus of Iraqi Jews was approaching its end as, day and night, planes jammed with Jews took off from Baghdad "for Cyprus." Ben-Porat believed he should stay at his post until all the Jews were out of Iraq. The police had dismissed the charges against him anyway and had not discovered his true function.

But the Iraqi secret agents were still on his trail, and their night raids and brutal questionings were beginning to bring them results. One name — Zaki Haviv — kept being mentioned in the interrogations as well as in the private papers and personal notebooks of the suspects. The Iraqis had not yet made the connection between the top man of the underground groups and the seedy Nissim Moshe, but it would not be long before they did, and meanwhile Ben-Porat's life hung by a thread.

Only two days after being released, Ben-Porat was awakened by the pounding of fists on his door.

"Who is it?"

"The police."

Caught like a rat in a trap, he feared the worst. There was no way he could get away, no chance of notifying his friends or of finding another hiding place. He resigned himself to his fate and opened the door.

The two policemen outside told him they had a warrant for his arrest.

"But what have I done?"

"Nothing serious." The policeman grinned. "Just an automobile accident. Come on, get dressed."

It took Ben-Porat a moment to recall that, strange as it seemed in the circumstances, he had indeed been in an automobile accident several months earlier and had received a summons. Now, while all the Baghdad police were searching high and low for Zaki Haviv, he was going to be tried for, of all things, careless driving.

The trial lasted barely an hour. "Two weeks in jail," pronounced the magistrate.

The penalty saved Ben-Porat's life, for shortly after his arrest the Iraqi secret agents finally established that Zaki Haviv and Nissim Moshe were the same person. It never occurred to them, however, that the dangerous Zaki Haviv was lodged in the Baghdad jail under the name of Nissim Moshe.

Ben-Porat's incarceration passed uneventfully. Then, a few hours before his release, a bribed guard thrust into his hand a slip of paper informing him that his identity had been discovered and that since he was being searched for everywhere he should get out of the country as soon as possible. His clothes and his personal possessions were returned to him, but he still had to have his fingerprints taken at the Special Branch headquarters where, Ben-Porat acknowledged, his name would be known. All he could do was hope.

The fingerprinting bureau was on the other side of Baghdad and some distance from the jail. Ben-Porat had to walk across the city to it between two policemen. As they entered the picturesque Shurja suq, its narrow twisting lanes crowded with colorfully dressed merchants, Ben-Porat found exactly the right moment to jostle his guards aside, dart down a side alley, and disappear into the throng of shoppers. The policemen figured that he was going to be free in a few minutes anyway, so why bother to chase after him?

When they reported the incident to headquarters, however, the storm broke. Nissim Moshe–Zaki Haviv–Ben-Porat had escaped again! Slipped right through the fingers of the police! A manhunt of unprecedented size and vigor began. The opposition press uncovered the details and doubled its attacks on the government. "Where is Haviv?" screamed the headlines — "In Tel Aviv!"

For a few days Haviv hid out with friends while the vise tightened on him. Meanwhile, in Tel Aviv, Shiloach's staff were working on ways to get him out of Iraq. And finally their escape plan was ready to its smallest detail.

On the night of June 12 Ben-Porat put on his best clothes. His friends drenched him with arrack, then helped the "drunk" downstairs and into a taxi with an Arab driver — a friend, though he did not know who his passenger was. Reeking with alcohol, Ben-Porat stretched out on the back seat and pretended to go to sleep. Fifteen minutes later the driver helped his fare out of the cab in a back street near the Baghdad airport.

The drunk stood erect. Then, clinging to the walls in order to keep in the dark as long as possible, he easily reached the airport fence. Having been instructed where the openings in the barbed wire were, he reached the main runway and squatted at its far end.

At the other end, outside the brightly illuminated terminal, the boarding stairs were removed from a giant plane, which presently turned and moved down the runway. The control tower gave it the signal to take off, and its engines began to roar. Suddenly the pilot turned on his headlights and aimed them at the searchlights on the control tower, momentarily blinding everyone facing the plane.

One of the plane's rear doors slid back, and through the narrow opening ten feet above the ground appeared a dangling rope. Ben-Porat darted out of the darkness, dashed to the rope, and hauled himself up into the plane, which increased its speed and slowly rose into the air. None of the ground crew had seen the escape, and the passengers were too busy fastening their seat belts to pay attention to the newcomer in the cabin.

As the plane passed over the city one of a small group on a rooftop said: "See if it blinks its lights." Just at that moment the plane lights flashed on and off three times.

"God be praised!" murmured the watchers of the skies.

Today Ben-Porat is a member of the Knesset, and assistant secretary general of the Israeli Labor party.

The nightmare of arrests, beatings, imprisonments, and torture continued in Baghdad, however. One of the espionage directors, a lawyer named Yoseph Bazri, was arrested in a friend's apartment after the police learned that a recent trip of his to Iran was not, as he had stated, to spend a vacation but to receive a new assignment.

Another important person in the Jewish underground was eighteen-year-old Shalom Salach, who was in charge of the arms caches. He had known for some time that the police were on his trail, but he had decided to postpone leaving Iraq for twenty-four hours in order to get a new suit of clothes from his tailor. It was a fatal mistake. On June 10 he was arrested opposite the Shemtov synagogue.

The boy broke under torture and revealed to the police where The Order's arms were hidden. Iraqi soldiers equipped with mine detectors searched the Shemtov synagogue and other houses of prayer, as well as private apartments and cultural centers. They found documents, maps, lists of names and addresses, and armaments amounting to 436 grenades, 33 machine pistols, 186 revolvers, 97 machine gun cassettes, 32 commando knives, and 25,000 cartridges.

It suddenly dawned on the Iraqis that their country might be at war with Israel but that the Israeli army was right in the middle of their capital city.

Shalom Salach and Yoseph Bazrí were brought to trial toward the end of 1951, accused of possessing explosives in order to effect assassinations of a "political nature." They were sentenced to death by hanging. Taggar, along with twenty-one other Jews, was tried for being a member of a subversive organization and sentenced to life imprisonment.

Taggar and Bazri were then tried together for espionage. Twenty Jews and Arabs were tried on the same charge, among them Peter Yaniv, The Hindu. For the second time Bazri was sentenced to death on the gallows and Taggar to life imprisonment, but thanks to his British passport as Mr. Rodney, Yaniv got only five years in jail. Dozens of other Jews drew long prison sentences.

Yehuda Taggar had been arrested in May 1951 during the interregnum in the Israeli Secret Service; the Political Department had just been dissolved, and the Mossad had not been created. Reuven Shiloach had only one assistant and one secretary.

When his assistant, Joseph Rotem, heard over the radio of Taggar's arrest, he immediately notified one of his friends, Yair. Both these men worked in secret day and night for a year to save the life of Taggar and his friends. It appeared that the Iraqis themselves were not too interested in executing Taggar, hoping they might in time worm precious information out of him. But no one succeeded in getting Bazri's and Salach's sentence of death commuted.

The black hood that the hangman in Baghdad's central

square placed over Yoseph Bazri's face could not smother his shout of "Long live Israel!"

The Iraqi authorities finally yielded to the strong pressure exerted by the British ambassador in Baghdad and freed "Her Majesty's subject" Peter Yaniv, alias Mr. Rodney. And in 1956 a final group of eleven Jews were released from prison. The only ones who remained incarcerated were Yehuda Taggar and two Iraqi Jews.

Life in prison was a horrible nightmare for Taggar, constantly subjected as he was to physical and mental torture, but he kept trusting in his friends' efforts on his behalf, and they did not forget about him.

Then Iser Harel became personally interested in Taggar's plight and would not give up hope that he could be freed. He saw to it that none of Taggar's relatives claimed his salary and had it paid regularly into an account under the name of Yehuda Taggar in a Tel Aviv bank. "Some day Yehuda will return," Iser kept saying. "The money must be waiting for him."

Nine years later Taggar did return to Israel as a result of a masterpiece of negotiation — according to Radio Cairo — between the Israeli Secret Service and Iraq's dictator, General Abdul Karim Kassem. Afterward Radio Cairo savagely attacked Kassem for being in the pay of Israel.

Before he left Baghdad Taggar was summoned to the old Royal Palace, where a guard of soldiers escorted him into a huge office. Behind an enormous desk sat a familiar figure — Kassem himself. Beside him were the commander in chief of the army and the military governor of Baghdad.

The Iraqi dictator studiously questioned the Israeli spy. "Tell me," he said, "if war were declared between Iraq and Israel, would you fight against us?"

"When I am back in my own country," Taggar replied, "I will do all I can to bring about understanding and peace between Israel and the Arab states. But if war should break out, I will fight for Israel, just as you have fought many times for your country."

Kassem seemed pleased with the answer. "Sit down," he said. The two men discussed the problems of the Middle East. Finally Kassem stood up. "When you get back home, tell your people that Iraq is an independent state now. We are not the lackeys of imperialism."

Taggar's friends who met him at the Tel Aviv airport had expected to greet a human wreck, but Yehuda was still the model of a vigorous, humorous, extroverted Sabra. His inner strength had surmounted the terrible experiences of his last ten years. Now married and a father, he holds an important post in Israel's Foreign Ministry.

On April 6, 1963, Iser Harel received a Passover greeting card, inscribed: "To Iser Harel, who set me free. With my deepest admiration. Yehuda Taggar."

With that entry Iser Harel marked the Baghdad file closed.

12

Iser Reaches the Top

AT THE END of Reuven Shiloach's first year as head of Mossad his lack of practicality, perseverance, and organizational ability became distressingly evident. In spite of some noteworthy achievements he had nevertheless failed to make Mossad dynamic or sufficiently well structured to handle its assignments — a fault that did not escape its employees.

Iser Harel and the brilliant Shiloach soon got into bitter private arguments. "You are incapable of directing Mossad," Iser finally told Shiloach. "You ought to resign." Shiloach's deputy, Joseph Rotem, was of the same opinion and told him so openly.

Shiloach himself felt that he was not cut out for the job. The record showed that he was indeed directing the agency's operations, but in reality it was the agents of other divisions of the Secret Service who were executing them.

Shiloach faced the facts. Although no complaint about him had reached Ben-Gurion, for Iser had not breathed a word about their violent quarrels, he submitted his resignation to the Old Man on September 19, 1952. At the same time he recommended to Ben-Gurion that Iser Harel be named his successor as head of Mossad and also made chairman of the committee of

Secret Service directors. Ben-Gurion agreed, and thereafter Iser Harel directed Mossad.

Shiloach, however, did not leave the Secret Service entirely. The Old Man offered him an important position as representative of the Prime Minister and the foreign minister to the Secret Service. The government charged him with supervising the work of the various branches of the Service and forming the policies by which all their activities of a political nature would be regulated: gathering intelligence abroad, foreign relations, special operations, and secret missions.

Iser had advanced a level, but Shiloach was still his superior and the boss of the other divisions as well, through his function of representing them to the government.

This new arrangement did not last long. Officially only Shiloach was the liaison with the authorities, but in practice things were quite different. The close association Iser had had with Ben-Gurion in the past now became closer. Gradually Shiloach noticed that he was being excluded from the Secret Service "community" and that he had neither power nor authority.

Once again he had the courage to face the facts. On February 8, 1953, he wrote to Ben-Gurion a second time, explaining that he had been unable to find a common language with Iser Harel and that their collaboration was therefore fruitless. Consequently — and for "personal reasons" — he wished to be relieved of his responsibilities. To his intimates Shiloach explained his decision by his serious automobile accident in the winter of 1952, which had appreciably diminished his physical ability.

His resignation was accepted. During their final meeting Shiloach recommended to Ben-Gurion that another high-level government official, Ehud Avriel, be appointed to the position he himself had held. Iser Harel, however, had had enough of these government representatives. He vigorously opposed the appointment and won his point. The post was abolished. Furthermore, the Old Man remarked to Iser: "Of course, you'll continue to direct Shin-Bet, even though you now have Mossad."

Since it was unprecedented for one man to be the head of two such big agencies, Iser put Joseph Rotem in charge of Shin-Bet. Rotem was to report only to Iser, who would represent both agencies to the government. Hence, Ben-Gurion created a new title for Iser Harel — chief executive of the Secret Services.

Iser's advancement marked the end of the long process of forming and organizing Israel's Secret Service. In 1952–1953 the community of secret services acquired its permanent form, and basic rules were established that defined the powers, the limits of authority, and the functions of the five bodies that composed the aggregate.

Of these Mossad was the most important. It was to gather intelligence abroad. The name of its director was kept a state secret. He was made personally responsible to the Prime Minister.

Aman reported to the commander in chief of the army and the defense minister. It researched and analyzed the military and strategical information furnished it by the various branches of the Secret Service, including Mossad and Shin-Bet, and issued definitive reports and appraisals. It also collected information on the deployment of enemy forces, their command posts, their headquarters, and their combat units; observed the movements of enemy troop formations; and collected works dealing with military subjects as they were published in the Arab countries.

Another of Aman's functions was to keep under constant observation the enemy's forces, their emplacements, their immediate purposes, their strength, and ways and means of transportation. To accomplish all these duties Aman had to have recourse to other sources of information than those supplied by Mossad. Additional top-secret responsibilities of Aman were security within the ranks of the army and censoring coverage of military matters by the press and the radio as well as what went through the mails.

The purpose of Shin-Bet (the Department of Internal Security) was to ferret out and destroy underground subversive movements, and to direct counterespionage while keeping watch on such possible sources of espionage against Israel as the Arab population, the communist party, the diplomatic colony, tourists, and certain Israelis. It ran the gamut of routine observation in order to prevent subversive activities and espionage within the country itself, but it was not authorized to assume the functions of the police.

The Special Branch of the Police Department, the fourth division of the Secret Service, supplemented Shin-Bet's activities by arresting suspects and interrogating them, expelling undesirable aliens, and keeping track of foreign visitors. It was under the authority of the police minister.

The fifth department, the Research Division of the Foreign Ministry, dealt with "legitimate espionage"; that is, analyzed information supplied by attachés in Israel's embassies, reports of talks with foreign diplomats, and articles in the periodicals and newspapers of other countries, particularly the Arab states.

These five branches were represented on the Committee of Department Heads by the directors of each and their deputies. The director of Mossad presided over this committee, whose function was to coordinate the departments and define their objectives.

Such was the theory behind the operational architecture of the community as constituted in the early 1950s. In practice matters soon took another course, for only three of the departments — Aman, Shin-Bet, and Mossad — were of prime importance; the others were poor relations.

The very nature of the Special Branch of the Police Department, for example, made it a subordinate body. On the other hand, it was by its own fault that the Research Division became actually a fifth wheel. Owing to Foreign Minister Moshe Sharett's indecisiveness and inability to see his objectives clearly, the Research Division was soon relegated to an insignificant status. It suffered from a lack of trained personnel, an inadequate budget, and poor research tools. Its director did not even participate in the routine meetings of department heads with the foreign minister. It quickly lapsed into idleness, making small use of its right to requisition from Mossad the secret information it needed.

Iser believed that to keep the branches in some sort of balance, the Research Division would have to be strengthened, and to that end he decided to add the director of the foreign ministry to the Committee of Department Heads. Even this step did no good, however, and the Research Division remained a negligible factor in the total scheme.

Although Iser was not responsible for analyzing and assessing information on the highest level (that was Aman's duty), his close relationship with Ben-Gurion provided him with a means of communicating his opinions to the Prime Minister whenever he thought it advisable to do so. Consequently he exercised considerable influence on final government decisions. His personal prerogatives also assured him an equally close relationship with the commander in chief of the army, and the high officials of the Defense Ministry greatly respected him.

By February of 1953, therefore, Iser Harel had reached the top of the ladder. One after another Be'eri, Guriel, and Shiloach had left the Secret Service, making it possible for Iser to assume the throne of a powerful bureaucracy. Except for Aman, which had a certain limited independence, Israel's Secret Service was under Iser Harel's control.

Less than five years after Ben-Gurion had discovered him, Iser had more power in Israel than anyone in the Intelligence community had held before him, or would acquire after him.

13

Rachel's Chauffeur

When Iser showed up to take possession of his new kingdom, he was hardly transported with joy. Mossad headquarters consisted of only three small rooms housing a secretary who was on the verge of a nervous breakdown due to not having been paid for several months and a handful of men who were directing the operations abroad. After Shin-Bet (which employed hundreds, was equipped with the latest devices, and had an adequate budget), it was hard for Iser to get used to his new situation.

The first established fact that confronted him was the empty treasury.

"Who is in charge of finances?" Iser inquired.

"Akivah."

"Where is he?"

It turned out that Akivah was in Paris with his wife, his children, and his mother-in-law. Iser wired him to come home at once.

Akivah appeared wreathed in smiles. "I've just arranged a loan of two million dollars for our Finance Minister, Levi Eshkol."

"Akivah," Iser interrupted, "instead of getting foreign loans for Eshkol, just find enough money to pay my secretary."

Iser lost no time in reorganizing Mossad. He brought over several of his most talented workers from Shin-Bet, including a tempestuous redhead named Rachel, a demon for administration. Together they set up a new procedural structure for Mossad.

Iser himself undertook to transform the branches of the Secret Service into communicating vessels, recruiting Shin-Bet agents, former employees of the Foreign Ministry, and veteran army officers. He thus gradually assembled a strong team that he personally supervised, trained, and assisted. Once his agents had proved their worth, however, he left them to their own devices. At work he seemed far more a friend of his people than their boss.

Although Iser had small use for protocol, his agents feared and respected him. No one dared chew gum or crack sunflower seeds in his presence. Yet when the doorman greeted him one morning as "Mister Iser," his response was: "No 'Misters' here, thank you. 'Iser' will do nicely."

Iser trained his staff to keep conferences brief, for he did not have the patience to sit through lengthy discussions, preferring to reach decisions promptly. Even in his conferences with Ben-Gurion he was like that. Sometimes he went so far as to say: "Look, Ben-Gurion, I'm dreadfully busy and I'm already late for a meeting. Please, let's get on with it.'

The higher echelons in Mossad admired Iser's astonishing flair for his work. "He was just as remarkable in operations as he was in organization," said the influential daily newspaper *Ha'aretz* of him later. "He had become master at getting information, coordinating techniques, and directing his department's activities. The secret of his success was his dedication, his perseverance, his personal involvement, and especially his foresight, in which last respect he was like a hunting dog."

More than once Iser let his fabulous intuition guide him in

uncovering the machinations of Israel's enemies, piercing the supposedly foolproof disguises of foreign spies, and finding the shortest ways to his ends. He knew how to put himself in the place of an adversary, guess his intentions, and foresee his reactions. He could effect plans so surprising that they thwarted enemy tactics before they were conceived. A joke among the Israeli secret agents was: "If you showed Iser Harel one side of a match folder, he could tell you without looking what's printed on the other side."

Iser, however, could be intolerant of subordinates whose points of view differed from his. He would listen to them, but he never altered his own approach to a problem. Sometimes he would say to his opponents: "You may think as you please, but you shall do as I say." He was always sure of being right, and from the moment that he thought he was, he would convince himself that he could not act otherwise. Sometimes he overestimated the enemy's strength and would take more precautions than necessary in order to avoid the slightest rebuff, but those who reproached him for this had to admit that what he undertook would undoubtedly succeed.

Nevertheless, agents going abroad on an assignment were none too pleased to have Iser along, for he made their life hard. If disagreements arose as to what methods should be adopted, he never left his subordinates, especially his deputies, in peace, deluging them with arguments and last-minute instructions until they were exhausted. Still, he never let his men down, and if any made a mistake, Iser took the blame for it. But if he caught one in a lie, he fired him at once.

Iser treated his men as his equals. Whenever a chauffeur or any other kind of messenger came to his house at night with an urgent telegram, Iser would make him come in, pour him a cup of coffee, cut him a slice of watermelon, or hand him a glass of brandy. He was not above sending on a mission an agent whose wife was about to give birth, but he also saw to her accouchement. He disliked giving orders; occasionally he would go to an agent's house at three o'clock in the morning and say: "An emergency. Could you possibly catch the five A.M. plane for Europe?" The agent would still be rubbing the sleep out of his eyes when Iser was at the door, saying: "Thanks a lot. Shalom."

Rachel tells a story about two friends who came to see her when she was not at home. While they were outside her door a small man appeared and invited them to wait for her in his apartment. He gave them cakes and coffee, and when Rachel still did not come home, drove them to their own house in his car.

"Are you Rachel's chauffeur?" they asked.

"That's right."

Rachel did not know anything about it until her friends said: "What an extraordinary chauffeur you have! He's quite a fellow."

Yossi, Iser Harel's own chauffeur, was also his confidant, keeping a key to Iser's apartment and making himself at home in it. A handsome, blue-eyed fellow, he was Rivka's secret source of information on what her husband was up to.

Iser would introduce Yossi as his "friend," and when he was going to one of his beloved football games with Joseph Nahmias, the Chief of Police, he always invited Yossi along, saying: "Today I'm going to be your chauffeur." When business took them outside Tel Aviv they always ate together, and after Iser resigned, people would ask: "What's become of his deputy we used to see having lunch with him?"

Sometimes Yossi would look into Iser's office and see him walking up and down the room. "It s conspiracy day," Iser would say with a wink. He would get up early to prepare a coup by making notes on scraps of paper for projects that would develop into Mossad's celebrated exploits.

Iser never hesitated to invest as much money, means, and personnel as were necessary to insure the success of one of his coups, but his own way of life was modest. Even after prosper-

ity had come to Israel, and ministers and high officials patro-
nized luxury restaurants, Iser continued going to a simple place
in midtown Tel Aviv for his usual lunch of vegetable salad, yo-
gurt, and custard.

When Iser took up his new post he found that he needed to
know English. After a strenuous three months' course he was
able to read English and to carry on a conversation, though not
to perfection.

His favorite books now dealt with politics. He read Winston
Churchill's memoirs three times, and he loved autobiographies
of statesmen and political leaders. He methodically read all the
works of former secret service chiefs. He also liked Voltaire.
For relaxation he read Agatha Christie, but spy novels irritated
him because they approached problems of espionage in what
seemed to him a ridiculously puerile way. "My men solve problems much more complicated than the ones in those books," he
would say, and the only spy novel he really liked was *The Spy
Who Came in from the Cold,* by John Le Carré. "Things are
better handled in that book," he once said, but hastened to add:
"Still it's a crime to manipulate people like that as if they were
pawns. A man who undertakes a mission ought to know what
he is doing and why he's doing it." He also enjoyed Graham
Greene's satire on espionage, *Our Man in Havana.*

Spy movies also exasperated him. After some astounded Shin-
Bet agents saw him leaving a James Bond movie, they asked his
opinion of it. "I had been hearing so much about it," Iser said
with a groan, "that I wanted to see what it was all about."
Then he added: "Nonsense!" and disappeared into the crowd.
He much preferred the dated humor of English farces like
Laughter in Paradise, The Ladykillers, and *Kind Hearts and
Coronets,* and French movies, especially those with Jean Gabin.

When he traveled abroad he went to the opera or to a concert
in the evening, and he also liked musical comedies, but at home
in summer he would put on a bathing suit and keep a transistor
radio to his ear. "When I'm listening to a good concert," he told

Yossi, "I can relax and at the same time plot my little coups. I never get bored."

"He lacks only one thing," some of his friends said, "a sense of humor. His jokes are hoary, but if anyone told him so, he would be the most astonished man in the world."

His new post required Iser to take more pains with his personal appearance. Previously he cared hardly at all about clothes and was perfectly at ease in shorts and a sweater. Until he took his first trip abroad he did not know how to knot a necktie. One of his friends tied it for him, but Iser couldn't learn to do it himself, and so all during the trip he would take his tie off and put it on again as if it were a noose. Since his new duties required better grooming, he began to take some pains to give his neighborhood dry cleaner a great deal of business. He would get up early in the morning just to iron a shirt himself, telling Rivka: "It gives me a nice feeling."

After living for one year in Jaffa, and for two years in central Tel Aviv, the Harels moved to the tree-shaded suburb of Zahal. The austerity program and rationing were then still in effect, but for the high priests of the Secret Service it was the era of Rivka's "economy cakes," which she served at her Thursday evening parties for the elite of the "world of shadows." Reuven Shiloach, Benjamin Gibli, and others from the high echelons of the Service would come to these parties, which became as regular an institution as the meetings of the Committee of Department Heads.

Iser would give another kind of party at the end of every difficult and dangerous operation, inviting all who had taken part in it as well as the commander in chief of the army, the foreign minister, and high-ranking army officers. For men who lived and worked in secrecy and anonymity these parties were a great source of pleasure, for they could see at them that the most important men in the government were familiar with their activities and appreciated their contribution to Israel's preservation.

One of the reasons Little Iser got his job was his close relationship with Ben-Gurion, about which *Ha'aretz* wrote later:

The resemblance between Iser Harel and David Ben-Gurion, his superior for many years, is striking. They have the same small, piercing eyes, the same forceful chin, the same quick and vigorous gestures, the same short stature. Those who know the two say they have the same nature also. Perhaps this resemblance explains their mutual affection and the entire confidence they have had in each other for over fifteen years . . . Ben-Gurion discovered Iser, and entrusted him with great responsibilities. In return, Iser has demonstrated his loyalty by creating a Secret Service respected all over the world.

There was always a reason for their conferences; Iser never went to see Ben-Gurion just to chat or gossip. "I have never brought him Greek texts, or bought presents for his wife," Iser once said in allusion to some members of the Old Man's court who spared no pains to get into his good graces.

The understanding between Iser and Ben-Gurion could not help arousing jealousy among the Prime Minister's close associates, who envied the direct line between them and the almost unlimited powers the Old Man had conferred upon the head of the Secret Service. Iser was the only man in Israel who had the exceptional privilege of a private interview with Ben-Gurion; not even Colonel Argov, who knew all Ben-Gurion's secrets, was admitted to their conferences — something that considerably vexed Argov, who did not conceal his annoyance. As a matter of fact, there was friction between Iser and Ben-Gurion's associates that lasted until the day he left the Service.

One October night in 1953, two men, Naftali and David, Shin-Bet department heads, were driving from Jerusalem to Tel

Aviv. Suddenly Naftali jammed on the brakes. He had just
caught sight of a strange rectangular object in the road. David
jumped out and came running back with a black leather briefcase without initials or other identification. When they opened
it they were dumfounded, for inside was the kind of treasure
every spy or secret agent dreams of discovering.

The briefcase contained inestimably valuable papers: the
private diary of Foreign Minister Moshe Sharett, a bundle of
telegrams from the various foreign embassies, several notebooks in which Sharett had jotted his strictly private thoughts
about who should be the next Prime Minister, how the members of the next cabinet would relate to one another, what his
personal opinion of Ben-Gurion and other leaders was. It could
not be other than Moshe Sharett's briefcase, which must have
fallen out of a car, perhaps the minister's own.

As soon as they reached Tel Aviv Naftali telephoned the
chief of Shin-Bet. "I must see you at once. I have just found
something extraordinary." After listening to Naftali's brief account of what had happened, the chief said: "Go straight to
Iser."

Naftali sped out to Zahal, informed Iser of what had happened, and offered him the briefcase. He thought that surely
Iser would be delighted to have the private papers of Moshe
Sharett, for he was involved in politics and could doubtless
profit from an examination of the documents. Iser never
touched the briefcase, but merely looked at Naftali with astonishment. "Why did you bring this here?" he asked. "Take it to
Sharett."

Naftali reacted as if he had been slapped in the face. He
drove off to Sharett's house in Tel Benjamin. The foreign minister, who had been informed by Shin-Bet that the briefcase
had been found, received him in a dressing gown on the steps of
his country house. His expression was surly, and his voice,
angry.

"You sure get around, don't you?"

Naftali went away without saying anything. Some hours later the mystery was solved. Returning from Jerusalem, Sharett had stopped to pick up a hitchhiking soldier and in opening the door of the car had dropped the briefcase.

Naftali did not bother to give Sharett these facts. He knew that the minister would never believe that Shin-Bet had found the briefcase on the road, much less that the head of the Secret Service, who enjoyed Ben-Gurion's complete confidence, would not have read and photostated his private papers.

14

Dangerous Games

IN THE DARK, silent little synagogue of the fanatical orthodox religionists in Jerusalem three young men with beards and side curls and wearing the traditional black caftan and soft hat of the sect were moving among the prayer benches one April night in 1950. The only light came from a flickering candle on the table that held the Torah scroll, behind which several absolutely motionless men could be dimly perceived.

"Who is the candidate?" came a voice from the gloom.

One of the three young men stepped forward. "I am."

"Have you made up your mind to join us?"

"Yes."

The voice chanted an ancient prayer, then intoned: "Our road is long and hard and strewn with hazards. Sacrifice without end will be required of all who take that road to our supreme and sacred goal.

"On this day you become one of a body whose purpose is to enforce the laws of our holy religion on the country and on the nation by whatever means are necessary, even violence.

"Repeat after me: 'Lord, I shall hate those that hate thee. I shall fight against those who fight against thee. I shall hate them with all my heart, and they shall be my enemies. Search me and know my heart; try me and know my thoughts; and lead me in the way everlasting.'

"In the name of the Creator of the world, in the name of the great, the terrible, the omnipotent — blessed be His name — God of Israel, God of the faithful, may our thoughts, our wills, and our deeds find grace with Him. May He bless and guide our steps, receive our acts, watch over our way, which is the spirit of His laws. May the pillar of fire which is His law, may the light of His spirit, illumine our faithful in the fulfillment of their sacred duty. Amen."

The candidate took the oath. Then after a silence the voice resumed: "Henceforth from this moment thou art a soldier in an army fighting that the Law of the Lord be honored and that it may reign and spread its glory."

The ceremony ended. A new member had been admitted into the Union of Fanatics.

That Union had been founded on the feast of Passover in the year 5710 (1950) by five young orthodox Jews who had met in Jerusalem and vowed to create a secret organization devoted to enforcing on the state the principles of the Jewish religion by all possible means. Its leaders — Rider, Rephuel, and Eliahu — had previously been members of the Stern Gang's extremist religious faction. Disgusted by secular ways of life, which they thought imperiled the Jewish character of the State of Israel, they resorted to a method of the past — an underground campaign. Within a few months they had managed to recruit a sizable membership, largely from students in Talmudic schools and from religious youth movements. They divided their converts into cells of five members, each with a commander. Then the members took pseudonyms and closely adhered to all the rules of conspiracy. There was also a cell called Judith for girls that gathered information.

The whole of 1950 was devoted to getting ready for action. The conspirators managed to procure explosives, steal weapons from a military camp in Jerusalem, and manufacture incendiary bombs. They trained in some woods beside their headquarters — a youth hostel near St. John's Hospital.

The clandestine organization got moral and material support from well-known leaders of the religious community, such as Rabbi Frank, the future Grand Rabbi of Jerusalem, who had the final approval of all its operations. A municipal councilor, as well as one of the leaders of an ultra-orthodox political party, was also among the invisible directors of the Union's activities.

On the night of January 18, 1951, the Fanatics went into action by setting fire to eight automobiles owned by persons in the northern section of Jerusalem who had broken the Sabbath laws. To hide their trail they scattered tracts signed by Neture-Karta, an ultra-orthodox religious sect that opposed Zionism and the State of Israel. During the following weeks they set fire to twelve other cars and also to a butcher shop in the center of the city that was selling nonkosher meat. Shortly afterward a bomb was thrown into the Expresso Restaurant on King David Street.

In the spring of 1951 the Fanatics decided to attack by daylight. Their plan was to throw Molotov cocktails into nonkosher butcher shops and burn the records of the Army Recruiting Station in Jerusalem in order to stop the mobilization of women. Their final action was to be a spectacular assault on the Knesset on May 14.

On that day the Knesset agenda carried a proposed law for inducting orthodox Jewish women into the army. The law had already produced such a storm of protests and threats from the orthodox community and kindled such a flame of wrath in religious circles that on the eve of the debate there was considerable tension in Jerusalem.

The next afternoon the gallery of the Knesset was so full of spectators, among whom were many orthodox Jews with beards and wide-brimmed hats, that no one noticed the few youths who had mingled with the crowd to execute the plan they had prepared with great care. Outside, a bearded young man named Wormser was casually strolling in front of the building that housed the generator which furnished the Knesset with electricity. He was pretending to look at the sky, but actually he was watching the windows of the Knesset gallery. As soon as he got the signal from Rephuel inside, he intended to break down the door to the generator with a crowbar and cut off the current. His fellow conspirators, already at their posts as liaisons and as actors, would carry on from there. Several had got into the Knesset individually and found seats in the gallery. In the center of the front row sat a man whose thick cloak concealed a bomb made of a tobacco can filled with explosives.

The man never took his eyes off Rephuel calmly waiting by the window with a flashlight with which he would signal Wormser as soon as the voting on the law commenced. Wormser would cut the current, and in the resulting darkness the man in the front row would toss his bomb into the semicircle of desks below.

At seven P.M. Joseph Shprinzak, the President of the Knesset, took his place on the tribune and raised his gavel. The man in the cloak had his hand on the tobacco can. Rephuel was fingering the flashlight in his pocket. Wormser's eyes were glued on the window through which he could see the outline of his accomplice. All three held their breath.

Shprinzak banged his gavel.

That morning Shprinzak had received an unexpected call from Iser Harel.

There was no love lost between the two men. Shprinzak had been one of Ben-Gurion's most active opponents before the creation of the State of Israel, and afterward he had refused to submit to the Old Man's authority, insisting on the independence of the Knesset, which he considered his private domain. The first time Iser came before the Knesset to explain the security measures he planned for it, Shprinzak said to his face: "I suppose Ben-Gurion sent you even here." Nor did he make any attempt to conceal his distrust of Iser's motives and spiked his guns on every possible occasion. Iser finally installed some security apparatus after great difficulty and then thanks only to the cooperation of the Knesset guards.

On this occasion, however, Shprinzak did not argue with Iser, but gave him close attention, for the head of the Secret Service had a very serious matter to communicate:

"Our office has discovered a clandestine organization of religious extremists who are sworn to stop at nothing to prevent the passage of the law for mobilizing orthodox girls. Shin-Bet has managed to slip some agents into the organization, and we know all its plans. Today some of its leaders will be inside the Knesset, and as soon as the voting begins they are going to cut the current and throw a bomb into the chamber."

"What do you plan to do?"

"Arrest the man before he can throw the bomb," Iser said. "I am taking complete responsibility for that, because it is extremely important that I catch him in the act. It's the only way of dealing the organization a death blow."

"And how do you intend to go about it?"

"I'll tell you exactly how. As soon as he enters, I will have my men surround him without his noticing. At the right moment, we'll grab him. He must be arrested within the Knesset and with the bomb on him."

Anxiously Shprinzak asked whether it wouldn't be better to cancel the session. Iser replied that doing so would endanger it more, for the Union of Fanatics would try again, and the next time Shin-Bet might not be able to discover the date. Shprinzak had to accept that answer. It was agreed between them that Shprinzak would preside over the session as if nothing were to happen and that he would give the guards instructions to admit the Shin-Bet agents into the gallery to lay the trap.

All went as planned. The agents acted discreetly and efficiently. As the zero hour approached they were all at their posts, some watching Wormser, others sitting beside the man with the bomb, or standing beside Rephuel at the window. No detail had been overlooked.

Shprinzak banged his gavel.

The session was declared open. The voting would begin in a few minutes, but for the time being the President of the Knesset held the floor. All eyes were on him.

Nervously Joseph Shprinzak began to speak. Shouts of protest and insults came from the gallery, where had gathered the religious groups who knew nothing of the plot but had come to oppose the "infamous" law. That was enough for Shprinzak to bang his gavel again and declare the session adjourned.

Iser was beside himself. His men had encircled the bomber, and in a few seconds Iser would have had the secret organization in his clutches and been able to crush it. Shprinzak had obviously panicked. His adjournment of the session spoiled the entire plan, and thereafter it would be impossible to catch the subversives inside the Knesset.

Grimly Iser watched the leaders of the conspiracy mingle with the spectators and leave for their homes in safety. Now that he could no longer catch them in the act, he had no choice but to resort to more conventional methods of apprehending them. He ordered a net thrown over the city.

That night, in accordance with instructions from Shin-Bet, the police searched dozens of apartments and religious institutions in Jerusalem. By morning they had arrested over fifty suspects and had seized the papers, the arms, and the explosives hidden in their apartments. The bomb that should have exploded in the Knesset was found at Wormser's, and sliks of arms and explosives were uncovered in St. John's Hospital and in a nearby machine shop. The captured documents removed all mystery about the nature and the extent of the Union of Fanatics, and by May 15 all its members were behind bars.

Only the four leaders were brought to trial. They received from six months to a year in prison. Shin-Bet, as usual, had recommended a light penalty, wishing not to wreck any man's life, but merely to cause him to lose his appetite for subversive activity, and to crush the organization.

The trial of the Fanatics heralded a wave of subversive sabotage throughout the country. Now, three years after the assassination of Bernadotte and the *Altalena* affair had halted the activities of underground organizations, their survivors were coming to life again. Among the reasons for this revival of subversive activity were force of habit, bitterness over the government's "betrayal of the cause," and a natural impulse to settle affairs by the terrorism used during the British Mandate.

Faith in the new nation had reached a critical point. Many Israelis, worthy men among them, had failed to comprehend what independence and national sovereignty really meant. It would be ten years more before Shin-Bet could relax its efforts against underground movements. Meanwhile its campaign continued as old secret organizations came to the surface, were suppressed, returned to hibernation, and emerged once more. Their final extinction had to wait until the "desert generation" grew weak with age and a later generation brought up under independence took its place.

Shortly after the Fanatics' plot Iser encountered a dangerous resurgence of terrorism due to the fiery opinions aroused by the subject of German reparations.

David Ben-Gurion had proposed to the Knesset that the reparations payments offered by the Federal Republic of West Germany be accepted in order that Israel might absorb the survivors of Nazi persecution and effect a wide program of construction and development. Various circles, especially those known as "nationalist" — former members of the Stern Gang and Irgun — rebelled against such "shame." "German money cannot wash away the blood of six million martyrs," proclaimed their slogans.

On January 9, 1952, when Ben-Gurion laid the matter before the Knesset, he encountered open defiance. At the same time that the session opened, Menachem Begin, the leader of the Herut party and the former chief of Irgun, began a violent harangue in Zion Square in the heart of Jerusalem. He exhorted his enthusiastic audience to oppose the government by every method and let it be understood that his party would lead the way in resuming the old Resistance. "It will be a fight to the death," he shouted. "Today I shall give the command — Blood!"

The hysterical crowd rushed toward the Knesset, broke through the police lines, and bombarded the parliament with stones, some of which broke windows in the gallery and injured several deputies. The police and the army had a hard time repulsing the attack. Menachem Begin was expelled from the chamber for three months. A new wave of terrorism loomed.

Menachem Begin, however, did not resume his underground warfare, preferring to fight within the law. Several attempts at sabotage were foiled. In the corridors of the Foreign Ministry a Herut member named Dov Shilanski was arrested in the act of setting a time bomb. Others attempted to do the same for different motives, such as the youths who protested against Religious Minister Pinkas' restrictions on Sabbath traffic by leaving a time bomb in the vestibule of his house. The damage was considerable, but no one was hurt, and the incident was unimportant, merely a sign of the times.

In November 1952 a fresh wave of terrorism broke. At Shin-Bet headquarters the evidence was clear that a new secret organization had gone into action. The question was which one.

In Czechoslovakia the judges of the scandalous Prague trials had just rendered their verdict: Rudolf Slanski and eleven other defendants, mostly Jews, were sentenced to be executed for spying and treason. Two Israelis, Oren and Orenstein, who were visiting Czechoslovakia, were given long prison sentences. On the following day a bomb exploded outside the Czech legation in Tel Aviv.

The Slanski trial was part of an anti-Zionist and anti-Semitic campaign behind the Iron Curtain. On January 13, 1953, the Kremlin announced the discovery of a "doctor conspiracy," alleging that nine Jewish doctors, members of a Jewish "nationalist organization," had plotted the assassination of some top-ranking Soviet leaders.

Late in the evening of February 6 a violent explosion shook the Soviet Embassy on Rothschild Boulevard in Tel Aviv. Four persons were injured, including the ambassador's wife, and the damage was extensive. Two days later the U.S.S.R. severed diplomatic relations with Israel.

The Secret Service was far from happy. In the middle of the night Ben-Gurion notified Iser Harel and asked him to spare no effort to find the perpetrators of the crime. But all the efforts of Shin-Bet came to nothing.

In April 1953 violinist Jascha Heifetz gave a series of recitals in Israel. One program included some works by the German composer Richard Strauss, a well-known Nazi sympathizer. On the day before this concert Heifetz received an anonymous letter:

> You know as well as we that it is our memorial day for the martyrs of the ghettoes, and yet you have the effrontery to play a work by one of those who took part in the extermination of our people. Why don't you end your concert with *Deutschland Über Alles?* A curse upon you! See that you do not repeat your crime. In the name of all the most revered and sacred principles of the nation, be accursed! We warn you!
>
>   (signed) The Defenders of the Nation's Honor

On the following day Heifetz was the victim of a typical act of aggression as he entered the King David Hotel in Jerusalem. A youth flung himself upon the violinist, struck his arm with an iron bar, and fled. Apparently he had hoped to break Heifetz's wrist and thus prevent him from performing.

Ha'aretz wrote:

The wave of violence, whose most serious manifestation was the bombing of the Soviet Embassy, made its appearance during the last six months of last year. At first there were two reasons for it: religious fanaticism and the reticence of certain groups — especially those once part of the Resistance movement active before the State was established — to face realities. With the exception of the religious fanatics there seems to be no definite ideology behind the slogans of the "Empire of Israel" or "The Black Boot" or "The White Boot." Nevertheless, in the course of the last months butcher shops selling non-kosher meat, bookstores carrying Russian books, and other establishments have received an increasing number of threatening letters. The attack on Jascha Heifetz has aroused general censure.

On May 26, 1953, two students in a Talmudic school were caught in the act of depositing explosives in the Ministry of National Education in Jerusalem as a protest against the law providing for secular education, which they thought threatened religious education. Following their arrest, the police and Shin-Bet unearthed a secret religious organization, some of whose members had formerly belonged to the religious faction of the Stern Gang.

During their investigation Shin-Bet agents observed that several suspects kept talking about enterprises and operations that had nothing to do with their own organization. What came to light as the investigation proceeded was that some members of religious groups fought for wildly nationalistic ideals in other underground movements more secret and efficient than their own.

Hence the discovery of the Empire of Israel.

Sixteen former terrorists who had belonged to the Stern Gang were dreaming of creating a Hebrew empire that would stretch from the Nile to the Euphrates like the ancient kingdoms of Israel and Judah. At their first meeting in Tel Aviv's Hadassah Park they swore to sacrifice their life for that empire. "The State of Israel is but one step on the road that leads to our goal — the Empire of Israel," wrote Heruti, the visionary of the organization.

The members were divided into cells of eight. Nocturnal initiation ceremonies involved an oath on the Bible, the national flag, and a revolver. They took pseudonyms, practiced the manual of arms, and committed a series of holdups in order to fill their treasury.

Old hands at terrorism and conspiracy, they were nevertheless amateurs on an ideological level. They had a definite goal, but it was a dim and distant one, and their immediate objectives were even less clear. They blindly attacked everything opposed to their nationalistic theories, whether institutions that cast a slur on religion, communist groups, or pro-Nazis.

After apprehending the religious terrorists Shin-Bet went after the empire builders. In one drive the police managed to snare all the Stern Gang's members and to capture a good supply of machine pistols, revolvers, explosives, and ammunition that had been hidden in apartments, in a grotto in the Valley of Kidron, and in barrels buried in Tel Aviv.

In July 1953 the sixteen suspects were tried before a military tribunal near Tel Aviv. They were accused of burning butcher shops, bombing the Czech Legation and the Soviet Embassy, burning communist clubs, bombing the weekly magazine *Haolam Haze*, spying on army bases and munitions factories, stealing military documents, possessing weapons illegally, and planning acts of terrorism.

The public prosecutor was unable to prove all the charges, but he easily convinced the court that the most dangerous secret organization yet created within the State of Israel was before it. When sympathetic groups left over from the Stern Gang tried to exploit the trial for political ends, the presiding judge, Benjamin Halevy, felt constrained to say: "We are not trying the political opinions of the accused. They have been brought to justice because they belong to a terrorist organization that has broken the laws of Israel and committed acts of violence. The State of Israel cannot tolerate, only five years after it came into being, the existence of any organization which breaks the law, perpetrates bombings, and employs methods used by certain of its members before Independence."

The verdict was harsh. Thirteen defendants were sentenced to long prison terms. The lengthiest were given to one Bachar (twelve years) and to Heruti (ten years).

Once more the condemned paid only part of their penalty. The last of them was freed less than two years after the trial, on April 25, 1955, the eve of Independence Day. Iser Harel had recommended to Ben-Gurion a suspension of the sentences "in order that the prisoners may take part in the celebration of our Independence as free citizens."

15

Iser Harel's Mikes

AT MIDNIGHT on January 28, 1953, a torrential thunderstorm deluged Tel Aviv, but even the suspension of electricity it caused did not stop two shadowy figures from reaching a dilapidated house at 20 Halevy Street, in the southern part of the city, the headquarters of the extreme left-wing Mapam (United Workers Party), which was opposed to the government. Muffled in raincoats, they stealthily climbed to the fourth floor, where with a flashlight they located the door they wanted.

A shout of "There they are!" echoed in the dark building, as several young men leaped on the intruders and pinned them to the floor.

"Who are you?"

The two prisoners hesitated before giving their names: Abraham Barad, thirty-two years old, from Jaffa; Shlomo Zahavi, twenty-four years old, from Tel Aviv. They said they came from Eastern Europe.

"Who sent you?"

There was no answer. Nothing could get the men to talk.

The Mapam workers searched them thoroughly, found bunches of keys and lock-picking tools, and in Zahavi's pocket a typewritten sheet headed: "Course Outline, January 19, 1953," followed by sections entitled: "Tapping," "Monitoring," "Electric Current," and "Telephone Tapping."

"Who sent you?"

No answer.

On the following day one of the Mapam leaders, Natan Peled, held a press conference at 20 Halevy Street, during which he showed the reporters a tiny transmitter with a very sensitive microphone inside. The whole thing, of American manufacture, was smaller than a package of cigarettes and, once it was concealed in a piece of furniture, could receive and transmit everything said in a room.

Peled, a short-legged man of medium height, told the reporters in his heavy Russian accent: "For some time we have noticed that our most secret meetings have been unaccountably leaked to the press. Our men searched the room of Meir Ya'ari, the Secretary General of the party, and found this apparatus on the underside of his desk. We laid a trap, and last night we caught two men whom we turned over to the police after having questioned them."

"Who are they?" asked a reporter.

"Mapai spies for Ben-Gurion."

The next day banner headlines carried the story on the front page of the newspapers, and public opinion was outraged. The opposition parties, led by Mapam, were crusading against the government, and Mapam was accusing Mapai (Israel Labor Party) of spying on the leaders of the other parties and making use of secret tactics. According to Mapam the leaders of the opposition parties were being trailed; their telephone conversations monitored and recorded; microphones hidden in their offices; spies planted in the directorial circles of rival parties and reporting to Ben-Gurion, who everyone knew had engaged them. Embarrassed, Mapai had flatly denied these accusations.

One month later the two men who had planted the mike under Ya'ari's desk were brought before a magistrate, who imposed token fines of fifty pounds apiece. But the opposition gave Mapai no peace. Ben-Gurion's party continued its categorical denial of having had any connection whatever with the mikes.

That was only partly true. Now it can be confidently stated that David Ben-Gurion and several other Mapai officials who at that time occupied key positions in the government were aware of the situation. They were of the opinion that Mapam ought to be kept under surveillance by the Israeli Secret Service. Iser Harel frankly states that it was he personally who ordered the mike hidden in Ya'ari's office. "I was right, too," he adds.

In the early 1950s it came to Shin-Bet's attention that a secret Mapam committee was making a great effort to obtain information on political, diplomatic, and military topics. This news boded no good for Iser, who for some time had been following the activities of Mapam, which was drifting more and more to the Left and showing pro-communist tendencies.

Mapam was indeed a Zionist party whose members had fought valiantly for the creation of the state. Its kibbutzim, located in the middle of the barren desert, struggled under constant enemy shellfire to become established, and its young people had furnished Palmach with superb fighters. Mapam, nevertheless, was now on a dangerous ideological course, owing to its slavish admiration for the Kremlin, whose directives it followed almost to the letter.

When the Korean War broke out, Mapam howled with rage against the "aggressors of South Korea." Its periodicals sang hymns to Stalin, "the sun of the nations," severely criticized Tito as a "lackey of American imperialism," and termed Eisenhower's election to the presidency of the United States "a threat to world peace." When an American loan rescued Israel from her serious economic crisis, Mapam proclaimed that "step by step we are being enslaved by the infernal machine of American capitalism."

On the anniversary of the October Revolution, November 7,

1952, Mapam's central committee said in a greeting address to the Israeli soldiers: "Let us remember the Red Army of liberation and fight for the transformation of our own forces into a People's Red Army in the noble tradition of Palmach." Neither the Prague trials, nor the wave of anti-Semitism that followed them in November 1952, nor the trial of the doctors in Moscow in January 1953 could shatter the mystical faith of Mapam. On the day Stalin died, one of Mapam's leaders delivered a public oration in Tel Aviv, in which he said: "If there is one grave in the world to which the Jewish people ought to make a grateful pilgrimage, it is Joseph Stalin's."

As the party continued its drift to the Left, the country's leaders grew more and more worried, fearing that some of Mapam's factions, which were close to the Soviet Embassy in Tel Aviv, might unconsciously become tools of the communists.

In 1952 Iser Harel's agents uncovered evidence that the Israeli communist party had undertaken to create communist cells within Mapam. The leaders of the communist party were trailed and watched, and Shin-Bet found that they were plotting to get control of Mapam by infiltrating it.

"A group of extreme Leftists had been set up in the heart of Mapam," Iser says, "and were fighting to annex it to the communist party. The Mapam leaders did not know of this group, whose leader was Moshe Sneh, the former chief of Haganah. Apparently the Soviet Embassy was directing by remote control a subversive plan which the leaders of the communist party and of communist groups inside Mapam were putting into execution, all unbeknownst to the Mapam leaders. To me, Mapam was first and foremost a Zionist party, and I made up my mind to stop its drift toward communism. Through a friend I informed Meir Ya'ari about the conspiracy that was going on behind his back."

Meir Ya'ari, however, violently objected to Iser Harel's interference. Shin-Bet, therefore, decided to keep a close watch on the activities of the communist faction inside Mapam, and that was why the mike had been installed in Ya'ari's office.

It was no use for Mapam to be angry about Mapai's "spying"; it was soon to be proved that Iser's information was well-founded. Right in the middle of the mike crisis Mapam split. Sneh's communistic group separated and shortly afterward joined the communist party.

Only then did the Mapam leaders wake up. Too late they found that the communist subversion in their ranks was no figment of Iser Harel's imagination. After the schism a special committee of Mapam made a secret purge of its groups and removed every element suspected of having contacts with the communists.

The mike business came to the surface again in 1955, when Mapam finally joined the coalition government on condition that an interministerial commission be appointed to audit the activities of the Secret Service.

"What's your opinion of that?" Ben-Gurion asked Iser.

"It's a good thing. I'm for it."

At the first meeting of the commission Iser sketched the various activities of his bureaus. "We keep under surveillance only subversive or underground activities," he said. "No one else."

"Just a minute," interrupted Justice Minister Pinhas Rosen, a member of the Liberal Party. "If you're telling the truth, then why did you place a microphone under Ya'ari's desk? Who was responsible for that?"

"I was," Iser replied. "I ordered it done."

"I don't understand," Rosen said. "That's just the opposite of what you said a moment ago."

"Not at all," Iser said, staring at a Mapam minister with a glint of amusement in his blue-gray eyes. "I can easily give you all the details of why I acted as I did."

The Mapam minister rose. "No," he said. "This commission

was created to deal with current matters, not delve into the past."

The curtain fell on the mike affair, but unfortunately it did not end the Mapam affair.

Late in the morning of May 11, 1955, Israel Neubauer, who owned a small café on Elath Street in Tel Aviv, found a sealed envelope under a chair. Clearly one of his patrons had forgotten it. Since it had no address, Neubauer decided to open it. What he found inside amazed him — a bundle of papers marked "top-secret." Neubauer hastily resealed the envelope and locked it in a desk drawer.

Hardly had he finished when a seventeen-year-old boy rushed in. "Did you find an envelope?" he panted.

"Who are you? How do I know it's yours?"

"I can get people to prove it is."

"No," said Neubauer thoughtfully. "I would rather give the envelope to the police and let them decide what to do with it."

"So call the police."

Having no telephone of his own, Neubauer asked the boy to go with him to a nearby store to make the call. He was talking to the police station operator when the boy said: "I'll be back in a second."

He ran out of the store and never came back.

A few minutes later Neubauer was describing him to the police officers who had just arrived. "A good-looking, tall, well-built boy in khaki shorts and sandals. He had the Mapam youth emblem on his shirt."

The officers opened the envelope and found in it confidential reports of the Foreign Affairs Ministry and various departments of the Defense Ministry, names of members of three Mapam kibbutzim, and details on important persons connected with them.

That evening the envelope was laid on Iser's desk. From its contents he deduced that "Mapam had set up an underground network which was operating out of the very bosom of the Defense Ministry, the army, and the Foreign Ministry." He ordered an investigation. Various leads brought the Shin-Bet agents to a Mapam youth club near Neubauer's café. The boy who had come after the envelope, however, did not belong to it and had disappeared without a trace.

For a year the investigation marked time, and it was not until 1956 that the Shin-Bet agents uncovered the man who had assembled the papers. His name was David, and he was a high official in the Foreign Ministry, an active member of Mapam, and a former member of a Mapam kibbutz. In 1952 he had been recruited by a secret committee within Mapam that systematically gathered information on diplomatic and military subjects.

Iser knew that such a committee existed, for it had aroused his suspicions as early as 1950. At that time, he had no evidence, but now things were clearer. When questioned, David admitted that he was a spy for Mapam between 1952 and 1955, during which period he had regularly supplied that party with classified papers, for which he had been paid thirty pounds a month at first, later one hundred and one hundred and fifty pounds, and after April 1954, four hundred pounds.

Iser had to think a long time about what to do with this fellow, who was hardly a confirmed spy, for the documents had not been handed over to foreign agents but to a legitimate Israeli political party. Neither had that party given information to foreign agents or foreign embassies. Furthermore, Mapam had recently got rid of its communist elements, had become part of the government, and was cooperating with the Secret Service.

Iser suspected that Mapam itself might want to get rid of its former spy, David, and followed his hunch. David was fired from the Foreign Ministry, but his file was closed, and he was not brought to trial. A convenient exit had been provided for Mapam, as in the past for the Stern Gang, Irgun, and other opposition groups.

To put an end to the affair, Iser went to one of his close friends, an influential member of Mapam. A third man joined them — Reuven, one of Mapam's leaders and an expert on security matters. Iser informed them about David. "For the good of public and national interests," Iser said, "this business should be kept secret. David has been put out of the Ministry. Let me suggest that you break all connections with him."

Reuven looked at Iser in astonishment. "I have never heard about this person and this whole business until now."

Iser did not doubt his sincerity. "This is what I recommend," he said. "Check this story out with your people on the security committee. If they confirm that David worked for them, then forget about me. But if they say they had nothing to do with David, then telephone me at once, and I will reopen the investigation."

The other two men agreed.

They did as they promised, and his friends never got back to Iser about the David affair.

16

Three-Act Tragedy

CAPTAIN HASSAN EL MANADI, of the Special Branch of the Alexandria Police Force, was on duty on July 23, 1954, at the Rio Movie Theater, for in the Cairo and Alexandria movie theaters during the past several weeks homemade bombs had caused damage and panic. Fortunately no one had been killed.

The perpetrators of these disturbances were unknown. The new revolutionary regime of Colonel Nasser was still popular a year after he had seized power, but it had its opponents in conservative middle-class circles, and especially in the powerful secret society known as the Muslim Brethren, an organization of religious fanatics who were experts in sabotage and subversive activities and who had started a wave of disturbances on the eve of the anniversary of the revolution.

Hassan El Manadi did not notice a young man dressed in the European style of light trousers and summer jacket who was in the crowd waiting for admission to the theater until he attracted the captain's attention by falling to the ground and writhing and shrieking in agony. A flame shot out of his pocket.

El Manadi rushed to his assistance, tore off the young man's jacket, and extinguished the flames. Out of the burning pocket he extracted a charred spectacles case, from which a wisp of smoke was still curling. Inside it were cinders of explosives.

The immediate arrest of the young man, Philip Nathanson, a nineteen-year-old Jew, produced the most serious disaster that Israel's Secret Service was ever to encounter.

The case had begun three years earlier in mid-1951, when a traveling salesman for a British electrical apparatus firm landed at Cairo airport. His British passport gave his name as John Darling, but his real name was Avraham Dar, an Israeli army officer and one of Aman's best agents.

On the following day he presented himself to Dr. Victor Sa'adi, a fervent Zionist Jew, who headed a small underground organization called Together, which had two major objectives — espionage and the undercover immigration of Egyptian Jews into Israel.

John Darling explained to Sa'adi that the purpose of his mission was to set up a secret network designed to accomplish special operations on strategic positions behind the enemy lines. Sa'adi put himself at Darling's disposal. During the following month he recruited several young Jews of good family who were active members of Zionist youth movements. Darling divided them into two cells, one in Cairo and the other in Alexandria.

The directors of the cells were Samuel Azar, a teacher in Alexandria, and Dr. Moshe Marzuk, of the Jewish Hospital in Cairo. Darling and Sa'adi made a magnificent girl named Victorine Ninio the liaison between these cells after they had questioned her at length on the terrace of a big café near Cairo's Al Nasser Movie Theater. The charming Victorine was the athletic champion of Cairo's Helio-Lido Club and held many records in swimming and gymnastics. She was given the alias of Marcelle.

In 1952–1953, following instructions from Tel Aviv, several

young members of the network went to France "on vacation." There they boarded an Israeli ship that was to sail for Haifa, even though they had no visas. As soon as they disembarked they were sent to the Israeli army's Intelligence School.

In a seemingly vacant building in Jaffa the young Zionists were trained in the use of explosives and invisible inks, learned to code and decode and to operate walkie-talkies, and were introduced to photography and surveying. A young army officer named Rachel taught them how to manufacture explosives from chemicals easily obtainable in any drugstore. They also learned how to sabotage.

They returned to Egypt at the end of 1953, via France again, and received their first assignment on postcards from Europe to Marcelle, who would dip the cards in a chemical solution that made words written in sympathetic ink appear between the lines. The network directors were instructed to purchase in drugstores chemicals for making explosives, set up a secret laboratory for their manufacture, and compile a list of places to be sabotaged in due time.

Soon the network members were equipped with the latest devices for communication. John Darling received a transceiver and commenced regular exchanges with Tel Aviv headquarters.

Still in its infancy, the network was poorly organized and was incapable of undertaking operational assignments. The youthful enthusiasm of its members caused them to ignore the rigid rules for conspirators, and they would leave in their rooms compromising documents and photographs. The fact that they had been badly trained made no difference, for the network was not designed for immediate action; in fact, it was to be kept on ice for later work in case of war between Israel and Egypt. There was plenty of time for it to improve its techniques.

Then, in 1954, a situation arose that completely upset those plans.

*

In the beginning of that year Israel's security began waning as bloody incidents kept occurring on her frontiers. The Western powers refused to supply her with arms, and the new American Secretary of State, John Foster Dulles, exchanged the sympathetic policy of his predecessors for one of "American neutrality" in the Middle East.

The corrupt regime of King Farouk had been overthrown in 1952 by a military junta headed by General Mohammed Naguib, and a year and a half later Naguib had been ousted by the strong man of the revolution, young Colonel Gamal Abdel Nasser.

These changes did not disturb Israel too much, although she was certainly aware that Nasser's Egypt had been in the past her principal enemy in the Middle East. But Jerusalem had confidence that the presence of the British army in Egypt would have a restraining influence on the Egyptian government. Furthermore, so long as the British kept their bases in the Suez Canal Zone, they would be scapegoats for the hatred of the populace.

In the late spring of 1954, however, coded telegrams from London brought the alarming news that Churchill had decided, in view of pressure from the Egyptian government and a wave of bloody terrorism, to abandon the canal and evacuate Egypt, all with the blessing of the United States. He would do so in accordance with an agreement under negotiation to guarantee the future of the bases and the protection of British investments in Egypt.

The news caused consternation in Israel, for without the presence of the British in Egypt, the precarious situation in the Middle East could collapse and produce a new outbreak of hostilities between Israel and Egypt. The great question was how to avoid this eventuality.

The Israeli government was ill-equipped to deal with the problem. At the age of sixty-eight Ben-Gurion had resigned as Prime Minister at the close of 1953, had retired for two or three years, as he said, and had taken up residence in the Sde Boker kibbutz in the Negev, where he hoped to encourage young people to overcome the hazards of life in the desert. Moshe Sharett had become Prime Minister, and Pinhas Lavon, defense minister.

Lavon was a strange, brilliant man of strong character. He had all the qualities needed for being great, but his arrogance, his cynicism, and his sarcastic tongue created a barrier between him and his associates. The Mapai leaders considered him a dangerous and aggressive intriguer. Golda Meir, Levi Eshkol, and Shaul Avigur had all warned Ben-Gurion of the risks he ran in making Lavon defense minister.

They were right. Lavon quickly incurred the antipathy of the army by getting involved in intrigues against the young director of the Defense Ministry, Shimon Peres, and against the Commander in Chief of the Army, General Moshe Dayan. In June 1954 Dayan had even gone so far as to tender his resignation, and only a long talk with Ben-Gurion kept him in his post. Isolated from his party and from the army, Lavon proceeded to alienate Sharett also by ridiculing him and being so insubordinate that Sharett almost resigned.

Iser Harel was on Sharett's side, for his relations with Lavon were very cool. Furthermore, for the first time there was an unbearable tension between Iser and the head of Aman, Colonel Benjamin Gibli. Lavon had established a close and confidential tie with Gibli by short-circuiting Moshe Dayan, whom they excluded, along with Iser, from their secret conferences.

According to the information from London, Churchill was on the point of signing the agreement for the evacuation of the Canal Zone, but there were violent objections to this treaty from the young conservatives within Churchill's own party. Some circles in Israel let themselves be fooled into thinking that hope was not lost and that perhaps Great Britain could be forced to remain in Egypt.

Ben Dan wrote of this situation:

That is when the new Defense Minister, Pinhas Lavon, already fifty years old, stepped on the stage. The drama that followed was played out in an Egyptian setting. Dreamed up in Tel Aviv and directed by the head of the Bureau of Military Intelligence, Col. Benjamin Gibli, the scenario provided for sabotage in Egypt. As a reaction to the eventuality of a withdrawal of British troops from Suez to Cyprus, the plan devised in Israel's Defense Ministry was terroristic and amoral — in fact, a Machiavellian scheme providing for the destruction of American and British buildings in Egypt, especially in Cairo, thus endangering British and American lives. If such machinations could be laid at the Egyptians' door, public indignation in Great Britain and the United States might effect a change of policy. Having been shown the irresponsibility of the Egyptian government, the West would be obliged to keep its troops in Egypt to protect the vital artery of the Suez Canal. This project was prepared in the Israeli Defense Ministry without being communicated to the Prime Minister, or even to the Commander in Chief of the army. Worse yet, the plan was put into effect without the government or its Prime Minister knowing anything about it.*

"Operation Egypt" matured. As soon as they got the order to go into action, the Alexandria and Cairo networks were to light a flame of terrorism in the two cities by attacking institutions belonging to Great Britain — libraries, cultural centers, embassies, consulates, etc. These acts would be attributed to the government itself or to the Muslim Brethren and would demonstrate the weakness of the administration and the lack of confidence the British could have in its promises. Thus the British would be compelled to re-examine their determinations and might decide to cancel the evacuation of the canal.

Machiavellian though the plan undoubtedly was, it was also criminally stupid. The men who conceived it must have been naive to believe that such an enterprise would ever induce Great Britain to alter her plans. A few of those who were in on the plan raised objections, but they were not heeded.

* *The Spy from Israel* (Prayer Book Press, 1969), pp. 29–31.

For some weeks the networks in Cairo and Alexandria, to whom the execution of the plan had been entrusted had had a new director named Robert, a handsome young Israeli with blond hair and blue eyes. He had been furnished with a German passport bearing the name of Paul Frank and was supposedly representing a large German electrical equipment firm. Shortly before he arrived in Egypt another Israeli, Max Bennett, had been admitted into Egypt as the representative of a German firm that specialized in prosthetic devices for veterans. Bennett had nothing to do with the networks of Paul Frank and John Darling, but was on a mission of pure espionage, in the course of which he established close relationships with the high-ranking officers, including Naguib himself.

Early in May 1954 Paul Frank was urgently summoned to Europe. On May 26 he met in France a special Israeli envoy, Avner, who ordered him to return to Egypt and to launch his men on Egyptian, British, and American targets in Cairo and Alexandria. On June 25, Paul Frank returned to Egypt, and a week later his men showed up. On July 2 their homemade explosives — boxes of VIM soap powder and eyeglass cases saturated with a chemical solution — exploded in a post office and a public checkroom in the El Ramal section of Alexandria. The damage was inconsequential — a slight fire and a little smoke. On July 14 similar explosions occurred at American information centers in Cairo and Alexandria as well as at the American consulates in those cities. Once again, the damage was slight, and the tiny blazes kindled by the eyeglass cases were easily quenched by the fire department.

On July 15, 1954, the Arab News Service circulated for the first time a dispatch that mentioned the wave of sabotage in Egypt, and on July 16, 1954, *Ha'aretz* reprinted it. On the same day and following days instructions were sent from Israel to Paul Frank to attack Egyptian and British objectives.

Finally, on July 23, the anniversary of the revolution, Paul Frank launched his operations on five targets at once: two movie theaters in Cairo, two in Alexandria, and the checkroom of Cairo's central railway station. This time the fuses of the time bombs did not work, and four never went off.

The fifth exploded too soon, outside the Rio Movie Theater, in the pocket of Philip Nathanson.

The whole network exploded along with Nathanson's bomb. The police raided his living quarters and found papers, explosives, and, in a darkroom, pictures of Philip's friends, among them one of Victor Levi, a student. When he was apprehended Levi confessed to having helped make the bombs and place them. In the pages of one of his books, the Egyptian detectives found a tiny transmitter.

In Cairo another transmitter was fished out of an oil can in the trunk of Dr. Moshe Marzuk's car. The police found that Marzuk had four apartments in the capital.

As one after another of the network was arrested, documents were discovered in their lodgings, as well as maps, a printing press, and several transceivers. Marcelle was arrested at the seashore, where she was taking a vacation. A check on her previous contacts led the Egyptian detectives to the only Israeli agent who had had nothing to do with the networks and who had been a lone wolf — Max Bennett. Avraham Dar (John Darling) had left Egypt some time before. Strangely enough, Paul Frank was not even bothered, although all trails led to him. He calmly settled his business, sold his car, and went to Europe.

One of the underground apartments in Cairo had been rented by a young Egyptian Jew, but although the police arrested and questioned him, he managed to convince them of his innocence and was released from custody. His name was Eli Cohen. Eleven years later, after having become the most celebrated of all Israeli secret agents, he was hanged in Damascus as a spy.

On July 26 the Egyptian police had eleven prisoners. The newspaper headlines called them a Zionist Gang that had tried to set movie theaters afire and were suspected of the bombings of the American and British institutions.

In Tel Aviv the directors of Operation Egypt learned from the newspapers that their enterprise had been a fiasco.

The curtain fell on the first act.

Prime Minister Moshe Sharett was in distress. As soon as he heard the news he labeled the Egyptian charges "despicable slanders designed to harass the Jews in Egypt." Then he was discreetly told that the "slanders" were actually the truth. In his humiliation he demanded an accounting.

Iser Harel was white as a sheet. The men who had conceived the project, Defense Minister Lavon and the chief of Aman, Colonel Benjamin Gibli, blamed one another. Throughout the country everyone feared the worst for the young Jews who had been arrested in Cairo.

On December 11, 1954, their trial began before a military tribunal. The night before, an Egyptian Jew named Carmona, who had apparently been connected with the network, hanged himself. On December 21 Max Bennett also committed suicide after being accused of having been an Israeli Intelligence officer; he took a rusty nail from his cell door and slit his veins. Marcelle was tortured. Twice she tried to throw herself out the windows of police headquarters, but was rescued, and now she, too, sat in the defendants' box.

On January 27, 1955, sentence was pronounced. Two of the accused were released for want of evidence against them. Six others were given seven years to life at hard labor. The two directors of the networks were condemned to death.

Demands for clemency flooded in from all over the world, and such prominent statesmen as French Foreign Minister Edgar Faure wrote personal appeals to Nasser. All to no avail.

On January 31, 1955, Dr. Marzuk and Samuel Azar were hanged at dawn in the courtyard of Cairo's central prison.

The irresponsible project had resulted in disaster for Israel's moral and political reputation. The disclosure of Israel's attack on British and American buildings greatly weakened the new state's ties with those countries. Worst of all, the perpetrators of the fiasco tried to take refuge in lies, mutual accusations, and slander.

Some days after the executions in Cairo, Israel recognized her need for a strong leader who would be resolute in matters involving her defense. On February 17, 1955, Ben-Gurion came home from Sde Boker and became defense minister.

End of Act Two.

According to Ben Dan the lamentable Cairo episode had a third act, whose principal was Paul Frank. Ben Dan relates what happened to Frank after he managed to escape from Egypt:

He had a right to advancement in the Israeli Secret Service, and he continued to work for it in Germany and Austria, thanks to his pretended career in the SS. His superiors ordered him to have no contact with Egyptians in Europe, but he still kept meeting Egyptians, among whom was Adm. Suleiman, whom he had known in Cairo and who now held a diplomatic post in Bonn. (In Cairo Frank had also established contact with high administration officials, notably with Zakariah Mohieddin, the future Prime Minister, and with Col. Osman Nuri, the head of military intelligence at that time.) Frank was suspected by his Israeli superiors of working for the Egyptians as well as for them.

Frank was commanded to return to Israel, where he was brought before a military tribunal in Jerusalem in 1959, and sentenced to ten years in prison. During his trial the Cairo episode came up again. The Secret Service reached the appalling conclusion that Paul Frank had been collaborating with the Egyptians even then, had confessed that purpose of his mission, had disclosed the project of political sabotage, and had been paid for his revelations the sum of 40,000 German marks. This treachery explained how he had been able to get out of Egypt after July 23, 1954.[*]

[*] Ben Dan, *ibid.*, pp. 34–36.

17

Nasser's Secret Ally

AFTER FINAL AGREEMENTS for Great Britain's evacuation of the Suez Canal were signed in October 1954, the departure from Egypt of convoys packed with British soldiers boded no good for Israel.

Israel was justifiably anxious, but she did not know everything. She was ignorant, for example, of the fact that the enemy she feared most — Gamal Abdel Nasser — was being supported by a secret ally, the American CIA, whose influence was wide and whose power was great. Only now, almost twenty years later, when the heads of the CIA are writing their memoirs, has any light been shed on the CIA's biggest blunder in the Middle East — its association with Nasser.

In 1947, when the CIA was still in its infancy, its ingenuous policy-makers contrived a magic formula for extending American influence in the Middle East. All they needed to do, they thought, was to replace corrupt Arab governments with truly democratic administrations headed by incorruptible leaders. Syria was the guinea pig chosen for testing this theory, and presently men, money, and "experts in democratic government" were flowing into Damascus to set the stage for the first free elections. Such was the CIA's enthusiasm for its idealistic program that it even installed American voting machines. The Syrian elections, however, turned out to be just as corrupt as ever, the voters having been bribed and the tabulation of the ballots falsified.

The CIA, however, was not discouraged. For free elections it substituted a diametrically opposed solution of the problem — a coup d'état that would bring into power a strong man who would clean up all the corruption in the government. By March 1949 the CIA had laid the groundwork for a military coup in which General Husni Zayim, the Commander in Chief of the Syrian army, would follow the guidance of U.S. Colonel Steve Mead and seize power.

The jubilant CIA agents paid no attention to Dick Hinton, the American political attaché in Damascus, who said it was the most stupid and irresponsible enterprise ever to embarrass an embassy. "We have forged the first link of an endless chain," he said.

Soon it was apparent that the Americans had indeed started a series of bloody revolutions that were to make Syria's the most unstable government in the Middle East. They became disenchanted with the unspeakable Husni Zayim, who soon lost all influence with his own people and with his allies. On August 14, 1949, his army mutinied and massacred him without the slightest effort on the part of the Americans to rescue him.

Thwarted a second time, the CIA experts in democracy, nevertheless, lost none of their enthusiasm. The years from 1949 to 1952 they spent in combing the Arab world for a leader with enough charisma to gain and keep the loyalty of his people and inaugurate a new era in his country's history. The search led the CIA agents to Egypt, and there, in 1952, they found the Bonaparte of the East they had dreamed of. This custom-made hero of theirs was a young colonel, still a long

way from the power he would grasp, named Gamal Abdel
Nasser.

In March 1952 Kermit (Kim) Roosevelt, the grandson of
former U.S. President Theodore Roosevelt and an active CIA
agent, landed in Egypt, and shortly thereafter on three separate
occasions met with several army officers who belonged to the
Free Officers, a secret club headed by Nasser, who was in the
process of organizing a revolt against King Farouk. These absolutely secret conferences led to an agreement between them
that the army would seize power in Egypt and that democratic
government would be postponed for several years. When it did
emerge, the United States would recognize it and meanwhile
aid and support the new regime. In Washington Roosevelt informed Secretary of State Dean Acheson that the United States
would have to accept the fall of Farouk.

On July 22, 1952, General Mohammed Naguib forced King
Farouk out of Egypt. A junta of Free Officers took over, and for
some time Naguib appeared the new head of revolutionary
Egypt, though he was only a straw man for Nasser, who soon
became absolute dictator.

On the heels of the revolution there descended upon Egypt a
swarm of CIA agents, State Department experts, and public relations men. To organize propaganda against the opposition,
Paul Leinberger, formerly of the OSS, was loaned to the Egyptian government. James Eichelberger prepared a manual on
modern government intended for the new masters of Cairo,
which was later published under the name of Zakariah Mohieddin, Egypt's future vice president. Kim Roosevelt and Miles
Copeland, another CIA agent, established direct and efficient
contact with Nasser and his cabinet.

One result of this entente was the request of the Egyptians in
1953 for United States aid in organizing their army and secret
service. Preferring to furnish this help indirectly, the CIA men
blithely recommended the assistance of German specialists and

summoned to Cairo several former Wehrmacht officers under the direction of former Nazi General Wilhelm Farnbacher.

Nasser ordered his secret service patterned after the American in that it was to be headed by a General Intelligence Agency — in Arabic, *Mukhabarat El Aam* — an exact copy of the CIA. This new branch of the government was supplied with the latest equipment from America — electrical apparatus, tiny mikes, special cameras, tape recorders, and listening tables for wiretapping.

Thanks to the willing cooperation of the Americans it recruited several former officials of the Wehrmacht's Intelligence, who trained the Egyptians to use this equipment and taught them their own methods. The best known of these technical assistants, as they were called, was one of Hitler's right-hand men, Colonel Otto Skorzeni, who had rendered distinguished service in World War II and now, once he had met Nasser in person, proceeded to be lavish with his expert advice.

At the end of November 1953 a man carrying two large suitcases arrived from Beirut at Cairo Airport, where he was escorted to Miles Copeland's car. An hour later he was being received by Hassan Tuhami, Nasser's confidant, and two Egyptian secret service agents.

"Let's start the counting," said Copeland.

Inside the suitcases were bundles of small-denomination bills that totaled three million dollars of American secret funds, a gift from the CIA to Nasser, who mockingly used it for the construction of the absolutely useless Cairo Tower opposite the Nile-Hilton Hotel. The CIA agents were presenting this money to Nasser over and above the forty million dollars they had extracted from the State Department for their pet.

The close relations between the CIA agents and Nasser reached their peak in 1954 and 1955. Quite often Copeland and Roosevelt would dine informally with Nasser and his henchmen, calling one another by their first names and exchanging dirty stories. Under the spell of Nasser's charm Copeland and Roosevelt became his best advocates in Washington, where they managed to explain away even his most undemocratic measures and justify his undermining of other Arab states by calling it "union action against strikebreakers." Confident that these guardian angels from the CIA would report him favorably in Washington, Nasser proceeded to do everything he wanted.

In 1955 the CIA began campaigning in Washington for supplying Egypt with armaments. When they encountered resistance — for the American government had no wish to arm Israel's enemy — they defined "armaments" as mere parade equipment, such as helmets, shiny boots, and holsters to the value of twenty million dollars. Nasser, they said, needed this kind of show to impress the common people of Egypt, that's all.

While his friends were intervening for him in Washington, however, Nasser concluded a secret treaty with the U.S.S.R. for the delivery of an enormous supply of the latest real armaments.

On February 28, 1955, after Pinhas Lavon had resigned as Israel's defense minister, his successor, David Ben-Gurion, ordered a raid on Gaza in reprisal for a series of murders committed by Egyptian commandos in the Negev. Forty Egyptians were killed, and the Egyptian army sadly humiliated. As a result, Nasser began to search everywhere for armaments.

At the World Neutralist Conference in Bandung, Nasser met Chou En-lai, Premier of the People's Republic of China, whom he told of his urgent need for arms in order to resist Israeli aggression. Chou forwarded this information to Moscow, where it was immediately perceived that the chance of a lifetime had arrived for Russia to get into the private hunt club of the West, called the Middle East.

Telegrams from the Kremlin deluged the Soviet ambassador in Cairo, and on September 27, 1955, Nasser informed an astonished world that an agreement for the delivery of a fabulous quantity of arms had just been concluded between Egypt and Czechoslovakia. Egypt was to receive two hundred MIG 15s and 17s, twenty-five Ilyushin bombers, one hundred Stalin tanks, six submarines, and hundreds of half-tracks, cannons, and light arms.

The delicate balance of forces in the Middle East was now broken, and the Israeli Secret Service was caught short, having gathered no information about the secret conferences between the Russians and the Egyptians. The Israeli leaders minced no words in blaming Mossad for this serious failure.

The Israeli Secret Service, however, was not the only one to be taken by surprise. The CIA knew no more than the Israelis did. The United States had got wind of the Moscow-Cairo negotiations only a few days before the conclusion of the agreement was announced.

In mid-September 1955, Kim Roosevelt had received in Washington a personal letter from Nasser. "I intend to sign an agreement with the Russians," wrote the Egyptian colonel. "If you do not want me to, come to Cairo." When Roosevelt reported this letter to the CIA, he was told that Nasser had already signed. Baffled as they were by their "dear Gamal," the CIA's Egyptian experts could not grasp the significance of that piece of news, namely, that the Russians were now firmly entrenched in Egypt. Instead of acting to prevent further disaster, they resorted to their custom of "understanding" Nasser and justifying him. The agreement with the Russians, they said, would only strengthen Egypt's independence.

Roosevelt and Copeland took the next plane for Cairo, where they personally advised Nasser to forestall adverse world opinion by announcing that the agreement had been concluded with Czechoslovakia, not with the U.S.S.R. In 1948 Czechoslovakia had furnished arms to Israel during her War of Independence, and so a similar agreement between Egypt and the same country would soften the West's reactions. Nasser followed their advice, even though the Czechs had had nothing to do with the agreement.

Then Kim Roosevelt learned that Undersecretary of State George Allen was making an emergency flight to Cairo with a letter from John Foster Dulles, described by the press as an ultimatum from the United States to Egypt. He dashed to Koubba Palace and persuaded Nasser not to take Dulles' letter seriously, for it could have no practical consequences. Roosevelt also contrived to see George Allen before Nasser could receive him and persuaded him to speak softly and read Nasser only the least extreme sentences in Dulles' letter.

At this time, when, contrary to America's best interests, the CIA was doing everything possible to smooth over Nasser's relations with the outraged United States, Iser Harel was sent to Washington.

Unaware of the bond between Nasser and the CIA, Iser saw in the arms treaty the Soviets' first attempt to become involved in the Middle Eastern situation. The U.S.S.R., moreover, seemed to him to be acting cautiously, spying out the land and waiting to see what the United States would do. On this premise he based his policy.

"The behavior of the United States at that time," Iser says, "was very strange. One word from them would have been enough to make the communists back down, but it was never spoken. On the contrary, it appeared that the United States was looking with favor on Soviet intervention. The only way I can explain that attitude is by the Americans' 'Arab complex.' My reasoning was that once the arms treaty became public knowledge, it could easily be deduced that Nasser would ally himself with the Devil in order to get arms to fight Israel. It would also be clear that the U.S.S.R. was moving into the Mediterranean. But instead of seeing the danger as we did, the Americans supported Nasser, explaining that he had no intention of letting the Soviets into Egypt and stressing that the Russians had signed merely a commercial agreement. Yet all that went on during a Republican administration in the U.S., and during McCarthy's witch hunt, when the Americans were hysterical about the threat of communism and were determined to halt its spread everywhere. Everywhere, that is, but in the Middle East. Israel had the distinct impression that the West was leaving her helpless against a Russo-Egyptian coalition."

Iser decided first to explain that the Soviets wanted to upset the balance between the free world and the communist bloc by gaining a foothold in the Middle East and Africa, and that if the United States did not agree with him, Israel would not wait until the Arabs had become so militarily superior that they could crush the Jewish state.

"If you give us arms," Iser told the Americans, "there will be no war. Nasser won't dare attack us, and Israel will be preserved. But if Israel gets no arms, there will be war!"

Nasser's advocates in the American government and with the American oil interests, however, argued that Nasser had only peaceful motives and was a friend of America. He needed the Czech arms in order to deal with Israel on an equal footing.

"If Nasser truly wants peace," Iser counterattacked, "then he has no need of the Czech arms."

"Well, are you Israelis sincerely interested in peace?" said Iser's opponents.

"Yes."

Hence, Robert Anderson's secret mission.

Robert Anderson, a dynamic businessman, was Eisenhower's assistant secretary of defense and would be secretary of the treasury. He had considerable influence with the oil companies, was thoroughly familiar with the Middle East and knew several of its leaders, and enjoyed Eisenhower's personal esteem. In fact, it was due to Eisenhower's own recommendation that Anderson set out for the Middle East on a secret mission.

Anderson landed at Cairo in November 1955 and went directly to Koubba Palace, where Nasser greeted him with smiles and promises. Yes, he sincerely wanted peace. Yes, he would be disposed to hold talks with Israel if Anderson would arrange them. Anderson did not understand that Nasser's sole aim was to allay America's fears about the Soviets and forestall any attempt of the United States to abrogate his agreement with the Russians.

After his private interview with Nasser, Anderson went to Athens to change planes, then flew to Tel Aviv, where he was driven to Jerusalem on a mission of such absolute secrecy that he was lodged in the villa of a leading citizen who had put it at the disposal of the government on the personal request of Paula Ben-Gurion. The house was surrounded by secret agents, and the Secret Service let it be known that the mysterious visitor was none other than a special envoy from Chancellor Konrad Adenauer. Not even the American ambassador knew that Anderson was in Jerusalem. To avoid the press, Anderson did not appear at government headquarters, but met with Ben-Gurion at the President Hotel.

"Tell Nasser," Ben-Gurion said, "that I am ready to meet with him at any time in any place, even in Cairo, in order to discuss peaceful relations between Israel and Egypt."

Anderson returned to Tel Aviv, where he received a team of experts' reports on the diplomatic and military situation in the Middle East, as well as on the Arab-Israeli conflict.

Fortified with all this knowledge, Anderson went back to Cairo, where a different Nasser received him. The Egyptian President saw that he had been caught in his own trap and had gone too far with his smokescreen. The Israelis and the Americans had taken him too seriously. The truth was that he had not the slightest intention, now that his strength was about to be increased, of coming to terms with Israel. He was, therefore, content with giving Anderson an answer that he would repeat many times in the future: "I would have been ready to meet with Ben-Gurion as you suggested, but now, if I did, I would be assassinated within the hour. It is too risky. In fact, it is impossible."

Anderson had to tell Ben-Gurion that his mission had failed.

Once again the American statesmen failed to draw the inevitable conclusion. More special envoys had been sent from Israel to Washington. They laid their cards on the table: "Through Nasser's duplicity, and thanks to the armament treaty, the Russians are going to establish themselves in Egypt and never leave it. If you want to stop the Russians, your only way to do it is to overthrow Nasser at once. That's perfectly feasible."

The Americans smiled at them. "You see communists under every bed and in every dark corner. Nasser is o.k. He is anticommunist. We can count on him. The Czech agreement is nothing but a commercial treaty."

When Ben-Gurion learned of the Americans' final statement, he recognized that in the circumstances war with Egypt was almost inevitable. In April 1956 he convened his closest associates to discuss preventive war. After listening to the reports of the military he concluded: "If we could get a certain number of tanks and fighter planes, the forces of the Middle East would be in balance again, and we could avoid war. War is no solution. Even if we win, the Arabs will start hostilities all over again. But if we can create an army that commands their respect, war will be avoided."

Immediately Ben-Gurion sent envoys abroad. Shimon Peres went to Paris to confer with Premier Guy Mollet. Another flew to Washington, where he met with the foreign policy experts.

"I will tell you a state secret," he said, handing them a sheaf of papers. "Here are Ben-Gurion's proposals, the results of a secret conference of the highest echelons in the Israeli government. His ideas and his policies are clearly expressed in them.

Ben-Gurion does not want war, but if we cannot obtain arms
for our defense, there will be war."

The Americans could not be persuaded. They were interested only in learning that Ben-Gurion did not want war. That
information relieved their anxiety, but they still firmly refused
to give Israel arms.

Once more Iser Harel flew to America.

"I was convinced," he says, "that if the balance of military
strength was upset, war was inevitable. The Arab states were
only looking for a weak spot in Israel's armor, and if they found
it, they would make war."

Still the Americans would not budge from their position.

A few months later a secret alliance between Israel and
France and Great Britain was solemnized by the Protocol of
Sèvres. Israel commenced her preparations for the Sinai War.

On October 29, 1956, Israeli troops attacked Egypt and in a
flash got control of the Sinai Peninsula and reached the Suez
Canal. President Eisenhower was furious that Israel, France,
and Great Britain had been scheming behind his back. The
CIA, which had categorically stated that Israel would not go to
war, had been wrong all the way down the line.

The United States and Israel exchanged violent notes. The
Americans accused Israel of having deliberately deceived them
by repeating over and over again that she did not want war.
Washington demanded that Israel recall her army and end all
military operations. The Israeli leaders replied that indeed
they had not wanted war and recalled their warnings to the
Americans' mind.

After the Sinai War the United States' attitude toward Israel
was distinctly wary for several years. Not until the summer of
1958 did it change. For in July 1958 the Middle East burst into
flames. A bloody rebellion in Iraq brought a military junta into
power. U.S. Marines had to intervene in a civil war in Leba-
non. King Hussein of Jordan's life was saved in a military

putsch only by the British parachutists he requested who were sent by airlift from Cyprus to fight the insurgents from the roof of the royal palace in Amman.

The common denominator of most of these incidents was the systematic efforts of Nasser and the U.S.S.R. to overturn the pro-Western governments of the Middle East. At last the American statesmen, including John Foster Dulles, had to admit that the Israelis had been right back in 1955 and that they themselves had been deceived. America tried to pull her chestnuts out of the fire and keep her influence in the Middle East, but it was too late. The Soviet Union had established strong positions in the Arab world and was determined not to abandon them.

It cannot be denied that the Central Intelligence Agency, through its naive trust in Nasser and its stubborn defense of him, had made a great contribution to opening the doors of the Middle East to communist expansion.

18

In Vino Veritas

AMONG ISER HAREL'S DUTIES was constant travel. In September 1955 he made a secret visit to Argentina at the time of Peron's fall; in October 1955, and again in May 1956, he was on a diplomatic mission to Washington; later he went to Germany. Frequently these trips involved a certain amount of danger, for some of the countries were not on very friendly terms with Israel. Also he often went abroad to direct his agents in some particularly complicated operation.

When he had to pass through or remain in unfriendly countries, Iser traveled with false papers, and sometimes in disguise. He was a man whom no one noticed or remembered anyway. He knew how to appear insignificant, and in hotels, planes, and airports he was never inquisitive and shrouded himself in a veil of silence. No one stopped him to look more closely at his papers or ask him questions, and never in his life were his suitcases opened by a customs inspector.

Before he returned to Israel from Europe he always took pains to buy something for Rivka, for he kept her measurements in his notebook. Nor did he forget his colleagues, or Yossi, his chauffeur, or any of his relatives. All got a little gift.

The Mossad comptroller used to say: "He is the only one of our people who pays back at least some of his travel allowance."

In Israel, too, he cultivated anonymity, which was not always easy to achieve. Often he would have to confer with the new Foreign Minister Golda Meir, but every time the police guards at her house would question him thoroughly before letting him in. Once Yossi tried to spare him this examination by winking at the policeman and whispering: "The gentleman is director general of the United National Dairies."

The next time Iser had to see Golda Meir, the policeman saluted, opened the door, and loudly announced: "The director of dairies to see the foreign minister."

When the story got back to Mossad headquarters, everyone made haste to congratulate the boss on his recent promotion.

In 1957 Prime Minister David Ben-Gurion, for the first time in the history of Israel, divulged to the Knesset the existence of Shin-Bet. "The Department of Internal Security," he said, "is one of the most efficient in the entire government of Israel, and no matter what the political opinions of any Israel government may be, it can be proud of its achievements. Its principal duty is to see that no fifth column exists in Israel, to uncover terrorist organizations, and to foil foreign espionage."

As a matter of fact, foreign espionage in Israel had, during the last few years, become more and more aggressive. In 1957, a file containing a fantastic story of espionage was laid on Iser's desk.

It had all begun one night in January 1954 in a cosy little restaurant in Tel Aviv. At one of the tables sat a rather pretty girl and a blond young man with a well-trimmed mustache and a shirt open at the collar in the Israeli style. He was in high spirits, and after dinner he kept drinking one bottle of beer after another until he was glassy-eyed.

"You call this beer?" he said to the girl. "In my country we have real beer!"

"What country are you talking about?" It was the first time she had had a date with Gabriel Zussmann.

"Germany, of course. Don't you believe me? Look." Gabriel Zussmann fished out his wallet and extracted an old snapshot that he held before the girl's eyes.

The girl froze. There was a somewhat younger Gabriel Zussmann in an SS uniform. She could hardly get control of herself.

A few days later there was a knock at Zussmann's door in Haifa. He opened it to find some policemen and Shin-Bet agents, who politely asked him to go with them to the neighborhood police station and answer a few questions.

"Your name?"

"Gabriel Zussmann."

"Is that your real name?"

Zussmann hesitated before replying. "No. My name is Ulrich Schnefft."

Then he told the astonished policemen the incredible story of his life.

Ulrich Schnefft had been born in 1923 in Königsberg, Germany, of Protestant parents. After their death he was adopted by a German family named Muller, who had also adopted a Jewish boy named Edward Klein.

In 1941 Ulrich was called to the colors and volunteered for the SS. Promoted to corporal, he fought on the eastern front, and after being wounded in Russia was sent back to Germany and then transferred to Italy, where he was taken prisoner by the Americans in the Po valley. He feared for his life, for the SS was not very popular. Fortunately the shell that had wounded Schnefft in Russia had left a scar on the underside of his left arm that obliterated his SS tattoo. He had taken the precaution of destroying all his papers and further to conceal his identity

had the happy idea of turning himself into a Jew, thinking that
no one would suspect a poor refugee from the gas ovens.

A German military doctor circumcised him. Shortly afterward Schnefft was released, and he returned to Germany. He
was sent to Munich, where, in a displaced persons' internment,
he noticed that his Jewish impersonation was serving him well.
The Jews were benefiting from the clothing and food that efficient organizations procured for them, and Ulrich saw no reason why he should not profit from the same source too.

In 1947 Ulrich Schnefft reached Cologne, where he went to
the Hebrew Sheltering and Immigrant Society (HIAS) office
and announced himself as Gabriel Zuss, a Jew, born in a village
near Königsberg. His father, Julius Zuss, as well as his mother,
had been massacred by the Nazis, and he had been sent to
forced labor in a small factory near Berlin. Since no one
doubted the truth of this story, Gabriel Zuss conceived a still
bolder plan. In order to escape eventual detection, and also to
get away from the severe unemployment crisis in Germany, he
entered his name at the Jewish Agency for transportation to
Israel.

Thereafter everything moved on greased wheels. He received the necessary papers and left on a special immigrant
train for Marseille. In December 1947 he embarked on the *Haganah* for the Promised Land.

Things on the voyage, however, did not go so smoothly. The
ship was stopped by the British navy, and Zussmann-Schnefft
found himself interned again, this time in Cyprus. With the aid
of the local branch of Haganah he made two escape attempts,
but finally reached Israel only in February 1949. He enlisted in
the Israeli army, and after attending officers' training school
was promoted to the rank of lieutenant in the artillery, where
he proved to be so good a soldier and instructor that his superiors could hardly believe that he had not been in an army before. After being demobilized, he stayed for a while in the
Kiryat Anavim kibbutz, then bought a farm of his own in the

village of Migdal Ashkelon, where he made friends and a life
for himself. Aside from his fondness for drink, no one could
find any fault in his character.

An unhappy love affair led him to leave the village and set
himself up in Haifa. It was when he was spending a weekend
in Tel Aviv that the girl he picked up there found out he was
the former SS Corporal Ulrich Schnefft under the almost perfect disguise of the Jew Gabriel Zussmann.

The Secret Service suspected that Schnefft had been involved
in a massacre of Russian Jews. One of the witnesses said he had
seen in Schnefft's possession a snapshot of him laughing at a
burning synagogue, but it was never found again, and the police had no evidence of the alleged war crimes of Ulrich
Schnefft. Since he could not be brought to justice, the Secret
Service decided to expel him from the country. On February 4,
1954, he boarded the *Negba* as a vacationer and a week later
landed at Genoa. Gabriel Zussmann, Israeli army officer and
farmer, was no more. In his place stood the adventurer and spy
Ulrich Schnefft.

On the day of his arrival he went to the German Consulate in
Genoa, told the consul of his military past, and asked to join the
German secret service, which had just been formed. The consul immediately detected whom he was dealing with and
showed Schnefft the door. He did not despair, however, but
managed to get in touch with East German agents in Italy,
whom he persuaded that he could set himself up in Paris as an
Israeli Jew and make contact with NATO employees through
whom he could get valuable information for the communist
bloc. The East Germans gave him a small amount of money
and sent him to Paris.

But the extroverted Schnefft was more interested in cabarets
and nightclubs than in his mission. Soon he was broke, and the
secret service of East Germany ended all relations with him.
Then he decided to approach the Egyptians.

The military attaché of the Egyptian Embassy in Paris was quite interested in the young man and his story. Schnefft was given a test in which he was quizzed on the composition and extent of the Israeli armed forces. The Egyptians, satisfied with his answers, took him on.

A few days later Schnefft went to Rome, where he received a passport bearing the name of Robert Hayat, and then flew to Cairo, where he told the Egyptian Intelligence officers all he knew about Israel. They made him a proposition — go back to Israel, enlist in the army, get stationed in a Negev base, and set up a spy network.

Schnefft refused. He wanted only to be sent back to Germany. Finally, with the 170,000 lire the Egyptian secret service paid him, and with his forged passport, Robert Hayat left for Germany. In Frankfurt he found his foster brother, Edward Klein, who gave him a job in the drugstore he managed. He met Inga. It seemed as if the espionage chapter in his life was about to close. But Schnefft kept running after women, frequenting bars, and spending money like a drunken sailor. Soon he was broke again. The Egyptians, who were waiting for that to happen, made him another proposition. Early in 1956 Schnefft was back in Cairo, and this time as an employee of the Egyptian secret service.

Schnefft was given several responsibilities in the General Intelligence Agency in Cairo, such as assembling files complete with blueprints and maps on all the Israeli military installations he knew: training camps, airplane bases, artillery bases, fortifications, electric plants, factories, minefields near the Egyptian border. He lectured before the experts in the Israel Section of the Agency and conducted a course for high-ranking Egyptian officers. Frequently he went to the Gaza Strip and gave lessons in Hebrew to the suicide-commandos — the Fedayeen — who were about to raid Israel. He also made many trips to Marseille as a special messenger for the Egyptian secret service.

By 1957 the Egyptians found that they had insufficient information on Israel. A new State of Israel had emerged from the Suez War. The files and the information that Schnefft had assembled on the Israeli armed forces were now out of date and useless. The Agency had no further use for Ulrich Schnefft. With no job and no money, Schnefft knocked about Cairo until he was desperate.

That was when the Egyptians made him one last offer. They would reinstate him if he would undertake the assignment of entering Israel as an Egyptian spy. Since he had no alternative, he accepted, perilous though he knew the mission would be.

At the end of 1957 a foreign tourist of Jewish extraction landed at Haifa with a passport made out to David Weizberg. Dark glasses partially concealed his features. In his pocket was a tiny pistol in the form of a fountain pen.

Schnefft had come back fearing the worst, but he was pleasantly surprised to find that he encountered no difficulty with the immigration or customs officials. He registered at a big hotel on Mount Carmel, loaded his camera, and began photographing the harbor and the hills above it, the fortifications, the gun emplacements, the battleships, and the radar stations. No one seemed to be following him.

The only precaution he failed to take was to stay out of bars near the harbor, where he would have a drink or two — or three. One night he came out drunkenly brandishing his tiny pistol in front of Israeli sailors and shouting in German: "I can kill you just like I killed Jews for the Führer."

Arrested by the Israeli police and Shin-Bet, Ulrich Schnefft was tried in a closed court. The pistol, the notebooks, and the films that were found in his hotel room were enough to convict him. The defense pleaded mental illness caused by the wound he had received on the Russian front. Schnefft himself pleaded his unhappy love affair. Because an Israeli girl had rejected him, he said, he wanted revenge on the whole State of Israel.

Sentenced to seven years in prison, Schnefft was expelled from Israel after having served two thirds of his term. No one knows what became of the soldier who had fought under the swastika, the star of David, and the Egyptian crescent.

19

Traitors

THE SCHNEFFT STORY never reached the press, but another trial for espionage made front-page headlines in all Israeli newspapers, not that it was important in itself, but because it seemed to be right out of a Hollywood farce.

They nicknamed him "Politruk" because in Russian that signifies the political instruction work he did for the Palmach unit in which he served, but his real name was Alexander Yulin, and he was known for his cheerful, colorful, amusing personality. After the War of Independence he lived quietly in the ancient city of Beersheba, the capital of the Negev District, until the day he decided to take his chances in Europe.

His attempts in Zurich to get a visa for Moscow having failed, he applied for assistance to the Jewish community, posing as a refugee from Russia, but they would have none of him. He then went to Munich and offered his services as a former Palmach officer to United States Intelligence. Thrown out again, he went to Vienna and repeated his offer to an Intelligence officer in the Soviet Embassy.

"I am an Israeli officer," he said, "and I can furnish you with information about my country."

The Russians bit. Yulin got his instructions and an advance on his salary, but not enough to satisfy him. Consequently he boarded a plane for Paris and sang the same tune to the military attaché of the Egyptian Embassy.

The Egyptian secret service welcomed him and put him on the next plane to Athens, where the Egyptian secret agents gave him a German passport made out in the name of Peter Fritz. Then he went to Cairo, where for three weeks he lived the life of Riley. He told his new bosses all he knew about the Israeli army, gave them much practical advice on the psychological warfare programs that Radio Cairo was broadcasting in Hebrew, and learned the Egyptian codes and the use of invisible ink. Then he took his salary of $1500 and a bottle of invisible ink with him to Tel Aviv, via Athens.

At Lod Airport he got through customs easily and went back to Beersheba, where he resumed his former way of life. It was there that he conceived the extraordinary plan of adding Shin-Bet to his roster of clients and ingenuously presented himself at the Central Police Station.

"I have a proposition for you," he whispered to the desk sergeant. "I can set up a spy network against Egypt."

The sergeant smiled. "What do you know about Egypt?"

"What do I know about Egypt? I've just come from there."

That's how "Politruk" got five years in prison.

He was, of course, just the opposite of a genuine spy, but his arrest caused a reaction. Here was the exceptional case of an Israeli who knew what went on in the army and had been photographed with Ben-Gurion, Ygal Allon, Israel Galili, and other celebrities, being connected with an act of espionage. Furthermore, the enthusiasm with which the Egyptians had hired this ingratiating clown demonstrated the extreme importance they attached to agents of Israeli nationality.

The case of Alexander Yulin, unimportant intrinsically, was nonetheless a bad omen for the Israeli Secret Service, for it introduced a new type of spy — the traitor. Yulin was no local

Arab or foreign tourist in the pay of the enemy's talent scouts, but an Israeli — "one of us" — who, unsuspected by his neighbors, could find out about all works in progress. Such a rare species was extremely dangerous to the security of the country.

Arab spies and foreigners, nevertheless, were and still are the favorite villains of sensational articles and "documentaries" on espionage in Israel. Anyone who reads merely the first paragraph of such a work is immediately immersed in a sea of Arab names and melodramatic descriptions of "cells" and "networks" operating in the Negev, in Galilee, or in Tel Aviv. The authors spare no pains to convince their readers that so-called Arab spies are the most insidious since the time of Genesis and that their capture has saved Israel from a dreadful fate.

The reader can also find intriguing chapters about foreign spies of diabolical ingenuity insinuating themselves into the Holy Land with orders from the secret services of Egypt, Jordan, Syria, and Iraq. Over and over again appears the story of the American journalist Mary Frances Hagen; of the German Helgard Otto, "the spy with the golden hair"; of the roguish Greek Alcibiades Kokas; of the "Turkish fox," Shahap Tan; of the Coptic priest El Anthony; and of the Egyptian "journalist" Ahmed Outhman, who came to report but intended to escape with all the military secrets of Israel in his notebook.

Doubtless all those spies came to Israel with high and earnest ambitions, but they never constituted much of a threat to Israel's safety. Their fantastic operations have acquired a greater reputation for deception than they actually deserved. The vast majority of Arab spies in Israel did little more than buy maps and periodicals at newsstands and seldom got further than revealing the location of such and such a military base, or following briefly the movement of a tank column or of an infantry division, or "discovering" the existence of certain types of weapon — generally obsolete — in the arsenals of Israel.

To do them justice, it was not their lack of experience that caused their failure, but the unique character of the Israelis.

Israelis know a lot of military secrets, but no outsider can worm his way into their intimate groups. A good example is the nature of a kibbutz. A sizable majority of the young people in kibbutzim serve in the special units of the army as commandos, frogmen, or parachutists. They talk freely about their experiences, especially at the Friday evening parties in the refectories. The same is true elsewhere. Hundreds of reporters, thousands of professional soldiers, employees of the Defense Ministry, politicians, Palmach veterans, high officials, soldiers' families — all know plenty of military secrets. Frequently during an evening among friends the principal topic of conversation is these secrets, the very mention of which would send an enemy spy into ecstasies.

A curious instinct, however, restrains an Israeli's gossip. He becomes dumb as a mackerel whenever he encounters someone who is not "in," whether he be another Israeli or a foreigner. Consequently, very important secrets may be known to thousands of Israelis, but are impenetrable for an outsider. Hence the reason that the secret services of other countries, having tried out Arabs and tourists, have finally resolved that the only source of information of any value to them is a well-informed Israeli willing to betray his country. The Arab secret services especially have been foiled in this respect, for it would be extremely difficult to find a single Jewish spy who has ever given the Arabs any information of value. Other foreign secret services, however, have tried to overcome this handicap with imagination.

Late in the fall of 1960 an American observation plane — the same type as the U-2 shot down over Russia that year — appeared in the skies of Israel, flying at an altitude of seventy thousand feet, far beyond the reach of Israeli fighter planes. It traversed the Negev and vanished over Dimona. On December

19, 1960, the world press published a picture taken during that flight — of a plant the Israeli authorities claimed was a textile factory but which was actually a powerful atomic reactor.

Two years later Israeli jets intercepted three other American planes above the Negev and forced them to land at Lod Airport. These, however, were slow and heavy planes that allegedly belonged to NASA. The pilots insisted that they were merely gathering meteorological data and had lost their bearings, but the rumor spread in Israel that their instruments had little to do with weather observation. Nevertheless, there was small danger to Israel involved.

One other Intelligence agency, however, became interested in Israel. Its headquarters were in Moscow.

From the very beginning of Israel's independence, the Russians had a rich source of information in the communists and communist sympathizers in the country. They also had the requisite tools in their own embassy and the legations of their satellite countries. Well before the end of the British Mandate, however, Shai had created Department C (for communist), which kept both active and sympathetic communists under surveillance throughout the country. After the State of Israel was proclaimed, this surveillance was enlarged to include trailing communist party leaders and tapping their telephones.

In 1950 Shin-Bet found that the source of the Israeli communist party's money was Moscow, though it was distributed through Soviet-controlled business and industrial firms in Israel. In January 1950 the first communist spy network was destroyed quite by accident.

During a street demonstration in Jerusalem, the police arrested a young party member named Uri Winter and found in his briefcase confidential military papers. Then they arrested a friend of his, Gustave Gulovner, and finally a third spy, Sergeant Major Reicher, a communist who was furnishing the secret documents.

The Russians learned their lesson from this first — and also last — arrest of their communist spies in Israel and thereafter were careful not to let them be in jeopardy from the close watch the Israelis were keeping on communists. The surest way to get the party annihilated, they saw, was to have it engage in espionage.

Actually Shin-Bet was well informed about everything that went on within the party. It learned, for example, of the top-secret project the communist leaders were trying to mount by introducing into Israeli territory guerrillas like those of Algeria who would fight for "the liberation of Palestine." Iser Harel took no measures simply because the party itself decided to abandon the project as impractical.

In January 1958 Shin-Bet uncovered a conspiracy within the party itself. Aroused by the creation of the United Arab Republic, Arab communists were organizing cells inside the party, making contact with Nasser's agents across the frontier, plotting the destruction of Israel with the connivance of Nasser, and at the same time getting rid of the Jewish communist leaders.

Iser Harel rose to the occasion by informing the Jewish communist leaders of the plot against them. They reacted immediately, and the party was shaken by stormy confrontations that almost dissolved the pretense of a union between Jewish and Arab communists. The quarrel eventually split the party into the Maki, with a Jewish majority and nationalist ideology, and the Rakah, with a preponderance of Arabs and a violently anti-Israel policy.

This schism also persuaded the Russians that they would have to recruit their spies somewhere else, and immediately after the Czech-Egyptian agreement of September 1955 the Soviet KGB launched a colossal underground offensive in Israel.

Confronted with this expansion of secret activity on the part of the Soviets, Shin-Bet developed a new division to study Russian theories and methods of espionage. Experts thoroughly analyzed the confessions of unmasked spies, the testimony of double agents, books and articles dealing with Russian espionage, and a body of classified material from other sources. Their earliest investigations revealed that the Russians' efforts in Israel were as massive as if Israel were the U.S.S.R.'s deadliest enemy. They also learned that the Russians did not believe a single word in the Israeli press.

"The outstanding characteristic of Soviet espionage," Iser Harel says, "is never to believe anything that issues from an official source, probably because their own press seldom publishes the truth. They spare no effort to check on official releases. If, for example, they learn that a new road has just been built, they arrive on the scene with as many precautions as if they were involved in a master plot. They go to heroic extremes to find out about anything at all, no matter how commonplace it may be or how fully the newspapers have reported it. The instructions they get from Moscow are as detailed as those sent from the Arab capitals to the Arab spies in Israel. They study every strategic point that could possibly be of interest to a world power.

"They are also deeply concerned with economic, scientific, social, and political matters — from the manufacture of nails to the construction of a major highway. They just have to know everything, and they don't stop until they do."

Russian methods of espionage are savagely cruel. An Israeli diplomat posted to Moscow was drugged during a formal dinner party, and when he woke up found himself in an unfamiliar room surrounded by Russian policemen.

"Your wife is in our hands," they told him. "Her life is in danger. We will release her on the one condition that you agree to work for us."

In Israel Russian agents almost always resort to blackmailing Israelis whose parents are still in the Soviet Union or elsewhere behind the Iron Curtain. Either their victims spy for them, or their parents will meet a sad end. Dozens of persons who yielded to this kind of blackmail have been uncovered as spies in Israel. In some cases the Russians have got them into their clutches before they left for Israel and compelled them to take courses in espionage. Then, long after their arrival in Israel, they contact the immigrants and give them secret missions.

Sometimes Soviet methods are more subtle. One fine summer day Avraham, a metallurgical engineer from Russia, was walking along a sunny street in the heart of Jerusalem when someone bumped into him.

"I'm sorry," said the jostler in Russian.

"Oh, you speak Russian?"

"Yes, I am a Soviet citizen."

Avraham was happy to meet another Russian. The two men chatted for a while on the sidewalk, then went for a drink together. Avraham learned that his new acquaintance was the head of the Soviet scientific delegation in Israel. His name was Ivan Zaitzev, and he enjoyed diplomatic status. The delighted Avraham told him that he had a mother and a sister in Russia and asked whether Zaitzev could help them get an exit visa.

The Russian promised to do all he could. The two met frequently thereafter, and Zaitzev willingly agreed to send Avraham's letters to his relatives in the diplomatic pouch.

Then Zaitzev began asking questions, harmless at first, which Avraham answered innocently. Even after Avraham had moved from Jerusalem to Acre they continued to meet in an old Russian monastery in Haifa.

Zaitzev's questions were now becoming more precise. What was going to be manufactured in the electric hearth that had just been ordered for the steel mill in Acre? What are the relations among the political parties in Israel? What is the capacity of the oil refineries in Haifa?

One day he showed up with a friend, whom he introduced as Comrade Vissagonov, Secretary of the Soviet Embassy in Tel

Aviv. The newcomer also asked all kinds of questions about the Weizmann Institute, the Institute of Technology in Haifa, scientific research centers belonging to the army, military preparations, secret immigration of Russian Jews.

At last Avraham recognized that he was in the power of the Russians and that the freedom and even the very lives of his family depended upon him. Fearing the worst, he refrained from contacting the police or Shin-Bet, but that was a serious mistake. He was finally arrested and sentenced to nine years in prison.

During his trial it was discovered that Zaitzev had not bumped into him accidentally. The Russians had known about Avraham for a long time — his origins, his profession, his address, his ties to his family in the U.S.S.R. When they had everything ready for action, Zaitzev had "just happened" to jostle Avraham in the middle of a crowded pedestrian crossing.

Blackmail is only one of the Russians' methods of recruiting spies. Another, still more dangerous to Israel, is to "cultivate" assiduously spies among the admirers of Russian communism and those who practically worship the U.S.S.R. as the one true country of the People. They stay away from the communist party of Israel, but they make approaches to its first cousin, Mapam, whose members, patriotic though they might be, also often are dedicated to a second "fatherland."

20

Nocturnal Visitors

ON THE EVENING of April 15, 1958, Police Sergeant Aloni was patrolling the Tiv'on Road north of Haifa, when he noticed a car with its lights out parked at the entrance of the Sha'ar-Ha'amakim kibbutz. Leaving his radio cruiser beside the road, he approached and deduced from its license plate, CD 19872, that the strange car must belong to the diplomatic corps. The hood was up, and a man was peering into the engine, while another sat inside.

"Can I help?"

The man inside the car answered in Hebrew with a strong Russian accent: "We don't need anything."

Aloni wrote the license number on the back of his hand and left. On the following day he was again passing the kibbutz, and there was the same situation. Aloni wisely noted the number of the second car and then suddenly recalled that one night exactly a month earlier he had seen a diplomatic car parked at the same place. He decided to report these incidents to his superiors.

By April 25 his report was in the hands of the director of Shin-Bet's Department of Counterespionage — European Division. A check of the license numbers revealed that the cars belonged to the Soviet Embassy. One was registered under the name of Vissagonov, who was known to be involved with espionage in Israel, and the other belonged to his associate Sokolov, also known to Shin-Bet as a controller of spies.

The discovery of Vissagonov's car solved a puzzle that had stumped Shin-Bet for some months. On several occasions its own cars had trailed Vissagonov's automobile as it roared away from the Soviet Embassy in Tel Aviv and headed north. The Shin-Bet officials were convinced that a spy in the pay of the Russians was operating in the northern part of the country, but they had been unable to catch him. The expert chauffeur of Vissagonov's car had always managed to elude their pursuit.

Now here was the car at the entrance of the Sha'ar-Ha'amakim kibbutz. Could the Russian spy be a member of it? The Shin-Bet agents did not want to jump to conclusions, but they knew Soviet espionage operated on a rigid schedule, and since the Russians had met someone at Sha'ar-Ha'amakim on March 15 and April 15, it was probable that the next meeting would be on May 15.

On the morning of that day a team of secret agents occupied a hill two hundred yards from Sha'ar-Ha'amakim and trained their binoculars on the kibbutz. When night fell, they moved nearer to it and hid in the bushes along the road and behind the concrete shelter at the bus stop.

A little after nine o'clock a diplomatic car pulled up and turned off its headlights. Two persons got out and stepped into the beams of the headlights of a car that "luckily" happened to be coming from the opposite direction. The Shin-Bet watchers thus could see that one of the unknown persons was wearing khaki, the other a blue business suit. The two men disappeared into the kibbutz, but their car turned around and sped off toward Haifa.

An hour and a half later the diplomatic car came back, stopped, picked up the two visitors, and vanished into the night

— all in a matter of seconds. It did not succed, however, in shaking off its pursuers, who, less than an hour later, found it parked in front of the railway station restaurant on Haifa's Independence Avenue. Again the Shin-Bet agents saw the nocturnal visitors to Sha'ar-Ha'amakim, and this time they could definitely identify the man in the blue suit as Comrade Vitali Pavlovski, the Deputy Director of the Mission of the Russo-Palestinian Society of the Soviet Academy of Sciences in Jerusalem and a secret agent of the KGB.

When that institution had opened its doors on January 16, 1956, the influential evening newspaper *Ma'ariv* remarked that it seemed strange that none of the members had a university degree.

That fact did not seem so strange to Shin-Bet, whose experts knew from the start that all the members were regular agents of the Soviet secret service. The head of the Mission was Ivan Zaitzev, who passed sometimes as an engineer, sometimes as a journalist or as an archeologist. Before coming to Israel he had "worked" in China and Armenia. In Jerusalem he got in touch with scholars, paid them surprise visits, and asked them questions. He liked to ask them to meet him at the Armenian's Garage, where he could chat at length with his informers without fear of being overheard.

This was the same Zaitzev who had made contact with Avraham and, along with Vissagonov, got plenty of information out of him. He was a brutal man, fond of drink, who did not even try to act like a spy but relied entirely on his diplomatic immunity. Often during a conversation with an Israeli scholar he would forget himself and exclaim: "What the hell do you want out of me? I don't know a damned thing about your scientific research. I'm only a representative of our Academy of Sciences."

Ivan Zaitzev left Israel in 1957 and was replaced as head of the Mission and also of the local KGB branch by Nikolai Gulin, a man with a supercilious manner, blond hair, and a bushy mustache, who pretended to be a surgeon. His deputy, Vitali Pavlovski, passed as a historian, but he had only to open his mouth to betray that he had never been enrolled in a university.

Shin-Bet was quickly able to establish that the Mission was a cover for an extremely active den of spies. It discreetly warned the scholars and diplomats who met regularly with Comrades Gulin, Zaitzev, and Pavlovski about the true character of these "scientists," but in most cases the warnings were unnecessary; the Israeli scholars had known at once whom they were dealing with.

On May 15, 1958, the picture became very clear to Shin-Bet headquarters. Pavlovski, one of the chiefs of Russian espionage in Israel, was secretly meeting a member of the Sha'ar-Ha'amakim kibbutz once a month. The next question was the identity of the kibbutz member. To answer it, Shin-Bet laid another ambush for June 15 at the same time and place.

The man who appeared on the roadside that evening was rather short of stature, wide-shouldered, bald, and wore thick-lensed spectacles. He paid no attention to the boy and the girl sitting in the bus stop shelter, but they kept their eyes glued on him. At nine o'clock the diplomatic car stopped as usual, and Pavlovski got out. The bald man greeted him, and together they went into the kibbutz. The Shin-Bet agents followed them quietly.

On the same night a report was telephoned to Shin-Bet headquarters that Pavlovski's friend had been identified as Aaron Cohen, a well-known member of the Mapam central committee who had acquired a reputation as an Arabic scholar and was well-versed in Middle Eastern matters. The Shin-Bet directors were deeply disturbed.

In spite of his small size, the near-sighted Cohen was a hardy individual who possessed a pleasant manner, had a keen sense of humor, and was a good speaker. A native of Bessarabia, he had come to Palestine in 1937 and had been active in the extreme Left wing of his party. During World War II he had worked in League V, an association that gave material aid to besieged Russia. He was passionately devoted to the Peace Movement, and he believed with all his heart in the World of Tomorrow as defined by communist philosophy. He had flirted for some time with the Mapam pro-communist faction, but he had refrained from quitting the party during the schism of 1953. Nevertheless, his unyielding Stalinism brought him into some disgrace, and he was banished from the party's directorial circles.

That political exile was almost welcome to Cohen, a man who liked to be alone and undisturbed so that he might devote his time to his studies of Arab problems. In the past he had worked for the League for Jewish-Arab Reconciliation, and before Israel became a state he had frequently met with Arab leaders, never failing to criticize severely the Zionist leaders, especially Ben-Gurion, who he thought had wrecked all chances of a permanent settlement with the Arabs. In 1955 and 1958 he had published two works on the Arab world that lacked objectivity because of his unqualified admiration for the Arab national movement and because he confused his Marxist opinions with ethnic theories.

Could it be that Cohen was a Russian spy? The only way to prove this suspicion was to catch him red-handed. If the regular series of meetings between Cohen and Pavlovski was still continuing, then it was likely that they would meet on August 15.

At nightfall that day a team of detectives and Shin-Bet

agents surrounded the kibbutz. Their chiefs, equipped with duly signed search and arrest warrants, intended to arrest Cohen just at the moment he was delivering material to the Soviet diplomat. But Pavlovski did not show up, and the team left without attracting any attention from the kibbutz.

Iser Harel did not want to wait, but he also did not want to act hastily. Over the years he had succeeded in establishing close contacts with Mapam, which was making earnest efforts to purge its ranks of communist and subversive elements. But the arrest of so prominent a member of the party as Cohen would cause a national scandal. If Cohen were to be arrested, it would have to be done in the least embarrassing way for the party.

Iser decided that since he had no positive proof that Cohen was a spy, he would give him a loyalty test. If Cohen managed to convince him of his innocence, Iser would not bother him, but if the opposite proved true, Cohen would be arrested and charged according to law.

On October 17, 1958, Aaron Cohen came to the Liaison Office of the Foreign Ministry in Tel Aviv on the telephoned invitation of Samuel Divon, the Director of the Middle East Division, who, the previous evening, had asked him "to confer on some matters of mutual interest." Cohen had met Divon frequently and so found the invitation perfectly natural. When he arrived, he was calm, self-confident, and good-humored.

Joel Morag, the new head of Shin-Bet, Iser Harel, and some of their men had stationed themselves in the next room. The conversation between Divon and Cohen was brief. "I asked you here at someone else's request," Divon said, and left the room. Then Iser entered, to be greeted calmly by Cohen.

"You know," said Iser, using the informal mode of address, "that my business is national security. Recently some things have happened that have cast suspicion on you. We are investigating them. We could have turned this whole business over to the police, but you are a well-known man, and I myself am on excellent terms with Mapam. So I have a proposition to offer you. I shall ask you several questions, and if you answer them to my satisfaction, you will be free to go and will not be bothered further — providing, of course, that you tell the truth. I want to assure you that I didn't bring you here to cause you trouble or to embarrass you with your kibbutz, but I warn you that if you do not answer my questions, I shall have to turn you over to the police and Shin-Bet. You will not be able to go back to your home, but will be arrested right here."

Cohen kept his composure. "Go ahead and ask me your questions. I'm ready to answer them."

"You don't know what we know," Iser said. "Don't forget to tell the truth, for if you do not, then my suspicions will be confirmed."

"I understand," said Cohen. "Go ahead. I'm ready to answer."

"Have you had any contacts with the Russians?"

"Yes. I go to the Soviet Academy of Sciences from time to time, and I sometimes telephone it."

That, Iser thought to himself, is what the Russians must have told him to say, for they ought to know we tap their wires. To Cohen he said: "You have had no other contacts or meetings with them?"

"No!"

"Absolutely no other contact of any kind?"

"No!"

Iser got to his feet. "You are lying to me. My suspicions are confirmed. I am turning you over to Shin-Bet for further questioning."

Iser summoned the men from the next room, and instructed them to take charge of Cohen. He was convinced Cohen was a spy. If not, why would Cohen have lied? Why would he have concealed his meetings with Pavlovski?

Iser went to Ben-Gurion. "I'm about to arrest Aaron Cohen," he said.

"You're sure he's suspect?" the Old Man asked calmly.

"Yes. We have checked all the details."

"In that event, you must do your duty." Ben-Gurion understood that such things are inevitable and must be accepted.

While being questioned, Cohen got deeper and deeper into the mire. First he denied having met Pavlovski; later he admitted it but pretended that they had kept their meetings secret so as not to be disturbed. At another time he asserted that some of the Mapam leaders who knew that Cohen and Pavlovski had been in contact in the past had forbidden him to see the Russian again, but Cohen had disobeyed.

Cohen's pocket notebook revealed other staggering evidence. He had entered the dates of his meetings with the Russians in a childish kind of code that was easily deciphered. Sometimes he had written, "Nine P.M. — Mr. Gates," meaning that he would meet Pavlovski at the kibbutz entrance at that time. Sometimes he entered Pavlovski's name in its Arabic form and used the Arabic word for entrance. While Zaitzev was still in Israel, Cohen had written: "Nine P.M. — Mr. Hare." (The word for "hare" in Russian is *zaitzev.*) Or he would spell the Russian names backward. Iser Harel's name also appeared in Cohen's notebook and after it the letters "P.K.M.," the initials of Shin-Bet's divisions.

Flipping through the pages of the engagement book, Cohen's inquisitors found a cryptic entry for the date of October 28, 1956, the eve of the day when the Sinai War broke out as a result of a secret treaty with France:

Uri S. Visitors. French come for fuel. No idle watching while they're getting together. Wait. France will attack Nasser in Suez, we in Jordan and Syria. There will be peace for twenty years. USSR too busy with its own affairs to help.

This was translated as: "French airplanes have arrived and are filling their tanks with fuel. Israel will act in concert with them and will attack Jordan and Syria while France attacks Egypt. That will assure peace on Israel's frontiers for the next twenty years. The U.S.S.R. is too occupied with the revolution in Hungary to intervene."

October 28, the date on which the entry had been made; Israel's alliance with France; the presence of French planes in Israel — all were state secrets. Had Aaron Cohen revealed them to the Russians?

Cohen's well-kept calendar disclosed other secrets. On the page for March 18, 1958, appeared the names of Moshe Gat, Gideon Shimron, Haim Ya'ari — two diplomats and an Israeli journalist who had gone on a mission to Moscow and Warsaw. Shin-Bet had learned from other sources that the KGB had investigated these diplomats. Cohen had entered the names after a meeting with Pavlovski, who had asked him to collect information about all three. In addition, a notation was discovered which clearly proved that on the orders of the Russians Cohen had done research on the Semitic Action movement directed by Uri Avneri and had given the Russians the data obtained.

An unobtrusive search of Cohen's lodgings in the kibbutz brought Shin-Bet, among other things, a political document that Cohen had doubtless prepared for the Russians. It contained no military information, only analyses of the government's general intentions, currents of opinion in Mapam, and the government's position on matters of security and foreign policy.

The Russians themselves furnished further proof of Cohen's suspicious activities. Barely two days after Cohen's arrest was known to the public, Comrade Vitali Pavlovski went to the Foreign Ministry and asked to be given an exit visa immediately. Then he and his wife jumped on the first plane out of Israel and disappeared forever.

Aaron Cohen was treated well. At first his arrest was kept a secret. His kibbutz was told merely that he had been unavoidably detained in Tel Aviv and was unable to return. At his request he was permitted to meet one of the Mapam leaders, Ya'akov Hazan, in the privacy of Hazan's automobile.

Early in November the first rumors of Cohen's detention began to circulate, and on November 9, 1958, three weeks after the arrest, the newspapers got hold of the whole story.

What followed was a frenzied war dance throughout the country. Cohen's capture furnished the sworn enemies of Mapam with the excuse they had longed dreamed of for an attack on that party that would drag it in the mud, slander its leaders and its politics, and increase suspicion of its loyalty to the state.

David Ben-Gurion tried to stop this movement by a release that he signed himself: "I sincerely deplore the efforts of certain newspapers to fling mud at an entire community, well known for its pioneer efforts and for its loyalty to the nation, simply because one of its members is suspected of a crime for which he is yet to be tried."

Mapam also took the offensive, labeling the Cohen affair "provocation," accusing Shin-Bet of a low and cynical conspiracy, and trying to prove that the whole thing was only a plot to discredit Mapam on the eve of the 1959 elections. The Mapam leaders, who had not changed much over the years, were determined to view Shin-Bet as a sinister organization that spent its time weaving diabolical schemes with which to entrap the sainted men of their party — all under orders from Mapai and its unspeakable leader David Ben-Gurion. They found respectable allies in the persons of several distinguished professors of the Hebrew University, among whom was Martin Buber, who unhesitatingly declared that in their opinion Cohen was beyond doubt innocent.

Cohen's trial was postponed until 1960 so as not to influence the general elections of November 1959. It was a closed trial — the name of the "foreign power" concerned was not revealed —

and lasted almost a year. Finally the Haifa court pronounced Cohen guilty of collecting information intended for the use of Israel's enemies and of giving information to the agent of a foreign power. He was sentenced to five years' imprisonment.

Cohen appealed the verdict to the Supreme Court, which overruled one of the charges and reduced the penalty by one half. The Supreme Court decision, however, made it clear that "Aaron Cohen did deliver to an agent of foreign espionage information on what was going on all over Israel, except for questions of security in the technical sense of that word. In doing so, Cohen acted from motives designed to injure Israel's safety."

Cohen was pardoned by the President of Israel and released from prison on June 15, 1963.

Aaron Cohen's was the first major trial for espionage in Israel. It outraged public opinion, not simply because of the secrets the traitor had revealed to the Soviets, for those were actually unimportant, but because it was the first capture of a spy who belonged to the highest stratum of Israeli society. Cohen was a celebrated man who had devoted his best years to Israel's development and belonged to the exclusive group known as the "Founding Fathers" of the nation. Until he was apprehended, most captured spies had been Arabs, foreigners, or marginal Israelis who were not a part of Israeli life or had been rejected by it. The Cohen affair was a grievous blow to the country's leadership, which suddenly discovered that espionage was not limited to outcasts, the downtrodden, or the maladjusted, but was a contagious disease capable of afflicting those of the best circles and the most secure.

Aaron Cohen may have been the first of these aristocratic spies, but he was not to be the last.

On July 14, 1960, a squad of police officers knocked at the door of a house on Haifa's Horizon Street. It was opened by a well-dressed, distinguished-looking man in his fifties who spoke Hebrew with difficulty.

"Professor Sitta? We have a warrant for your arrest."

The arrest utterly astonished the scientific world, for Kurt Sitta enjoyed international fame as a scholar and had one of the most brilliant minds in Israel. He held several chairs at Haifa's Institute of Technology, where he was pursuing his researches into outer space.

Sitta was not a Jew but a Czech from the Sudetenland. Since his youth he had been politically progressive, and after Hitler's occupation of Czechoslovakia he had been sent to Buchenwald. After the war he returned to his native country, but not for long. In 1948 he crossed the Iron Curtain and joined a team of scientists at the University of Edinburgh. Then he worked for a while at the University of Manchester before accepting an invitation to join the faculty of the University of Syracuse. In 1953 he was similarly honored by the University of São Paulo, Brazil, and the following year he agreed to come to Israel.

His advancement in Haifa was electrifying. Within two years he had become head of the Physics Department. He attended many scientific conferences in both Western and Eastern Europe and had recently been put in charge of a research project on cosmic rays for the U.S. Army.

The Institute's administrators were quietly told on the day after Sitta's arrest that he had been accused of espionage for the benefit of a foreign power and would soon be brought to justice. The news shocked the learned men on the faculty and made them suspicious and sullen, for many feared the trial would reflect on the Institute's reputation. Through a high-placed intermediary they brought pressure to bear on the government to have the matter hushed up and Sitta surreptitiously expelled from the country.

Some professors simply refused to believe in Sitta's guilt. Professor Ari Jabotinski headed a drive in all scientific circles throughout Israel to save poor Professor Sitta from martyrdom at the hands of insensitive men. This drive gathered strength after the news of Sitta's arrest was made public. On September 1, 1960, Jabotinski published a manifesto signed by Institute professors against "the infamous slanders on the character, life, and work of Professor Sitta that have appeared in the press." The scholars cried scandal, accused Shin-Bet of witch-hunting, and got away with it because of the position they enjoyed in Israeli society.

Consequently, when the trial opened in Haifa on November 5, 1960, a privileged group was allowed into the closed sessions. It was composed of scholars from Haifa's Institute of Technology, the Hebrew University in Jerusalem, and the Weizmann Institute, whose colleagues had sent envoys to check on the witnesses, the lawyers, and the court itself so that there would be no departure from the principles of law and justice.

They had to bow before the truth. Kurt Sitta was indeed a spy, planted in Israel by the Czech secret service acting on Moscow's orders. He had been sent to Israel with instructions to establish himself there and get an important position in the field of scientific research — and wait for further orders.

That, however, was not the most sensational disclosure of the trial. Shin-Bet succeeded in proving that Israel was not the first country in which Sitta had been a spy, but that for years he had been guided by the remote control of his secret masters wherever he happened to be.

The authentic biography of Kurt Sitta was revealed in the courtroom. While a prisoner in Buchenwald he had formed friendships with other prisoners who, after their liberation, had been given key positions in the Czech secret service. During the years 1945 to 1948 Sitta held a position in a special division of that service and, brilliant scientist though he was, rarely visited its research laboratcries, being engaged in purging Sudetenland Germans of all Nazi elements. In 1948 Sitta said he "chose freedom" and went to England, but he had actually been sent abroad by the Czech secret service, which had made him an attractive proposition, namely, that he could pursue his research in all the great universities of the world and under the best conditions, providing he would furnish the Czechoslovak Socialist Republic with classified information.

That is what he did everywhere, but not always with complete success. While he was in the United States, he was duly contacted by Czech agents and told to get information on the American scientific potential. The FBI suspected his activities and even tried to make him a double agent, but they got nowhere. In 1953, however, the American immigration authorities refused to renew Sitta's visa. It was in Brazil that he received the invitation from the Technological Institute in Haifa, but he did not accept until he had got the green light from Prague.

In the summer of 1955, just a few days after the conclusion of the Czech-Egyptian arms agreement, Sitta was getting down to work one fine morning when he was stopped on the Institute's main staircase by a pleasant blond youth who smilingly introduced himself as an employee of the Czech Consulate in Tel Aviv and offered as references the employees of the Czech Consulate in the United States who had directed Sitta's secret activities. Then he introduced one of his colleagues, and the three men got down to business — means of communication, schedules of meetings at different times and places, strict prohibition of telephone conversations, means of transferring information.

Over a period of five years Sitta and his controllers met many times, mostly in Haifa's cafés, especially the Krips and the Sternheim, and sometimes on benches in Benjamin Park. During that period Sitta made several trips to Czechoslovakia to "see his sister," but in reality to report at length and viva voce to the secret service. Then his masters ordered him to extend his sphere of action by attending a scientific congress in West Germany, where he was to get information on United

States aid to German scientific institutions and also on the activities of the Max Planck Institute in Göttingen.

In Israel this charming, brilliant, highly respected man regularly delivered information on scientific research for the military and on the Israeli Atomic Commission. Quite often he had to stoop to giving the Czechs names of students of his from communist countries whom they might recruit as spies.

After his arrest Sitta came to be known as "the Israeli Klaus Fuchs." Perhaps he deserved that title when, under cover of darkness, he was handing his masters reports on scientific and military research in Israel, but when he met them on a bench in Benjamin Park and slipped them the names of students to be seduced into espionage — then this "Klaus Fuchs" was transformed into a desperate spy performing an infamous deed.

Kurt Sitta was found guilty and sentenced to five years in prison. In 1963, pardoned by the President of Israel, he left the country for good.

Then came the Beer scandal.

21

Room at the Top

DURING THE EARLY 1960s there kept turning up in the private conversations of politicians and army officers the name of a man who was thought to be Ben-Gurion's private military adviser. Some called him the Liddell Hart of Israel. He was a talented journalist, a brilliant military expert, an enthralling speaker, and a theorist of international reputation — Dr. Israel Beer.

Beer had a brilliant mind, but his manner was biting and arrogant. Thin as a skeleton, he had a bald head like a skull that had been covered with a sheet of parchment in a futile effort to disguise its shape. A graying mustache drooped over protruding yellow horse teeth from which always dangled a damp cigarette. His condescending attitude offended most people, but all his faults were compensated for by his unusual facility of expression, his profound knowledge of political and military matters, and his extraordinary analytical capacity. Always self-confident, Israel Beer had used his natural talents to rise to heights of power, sometimes by ruthlessly trampling on the intervening ranks.

Beer had landed in Palestine from Vienna in November 1938, his only baggage the story of his adventurous life, which made young Sabras gape at him in wonder. They thrilled to his descriptions of his youth in Vienna, the atmosphere of the Stubenbastei high school, and his brilliant university career in which he had won a doctorate. Their admiration grew when he recounted his military deeds on Vienna's barricades in the ranks of the Republikanischer Schützbund (League for the Defense of the Republic) during the 1934 workers' uprising against Dollfuss' dictatorship. Then as a brave student-officer at the Military Academy of Wiener Neustadt, he had taken part in the resistance to the Nazis in Austria, and, in 1936, had joined the International Brigade in Spain.

The Spanish episode was doubtless the most stirring of all Israel Beer's adventures. Under the names of Jose Gregorio and Miguel Diaz, he had fought at Madrid, Guadalajara, Brunete, and Teruel and had emerged from that bloody struggle for liberty and human dignity as a lieutenant colonel. In 1938 he left Spain in despair that was relieved only by memories of his gallant comrades-in-arms: the Englishmen Wilfrid MacCartney and Tom Wintrigham, the Russian Ivan Koniev, Lazlo Rajk, General Julius Deutsch, and the writer Ludwig Renn.

Back home, he wandered through the gay city of Vienna like a soul in torment until the memorable night when his whole existence changed by his picking up Alex Bein's biography of Theodor Herzl. He read it through at one sitting. Thereafter a new flame burned in his mind — Zionism. Three days after he landed in Haifa he enlisted in Haganah.

Lieutenant Colonel Israel Beer was of inestimable help to that secret army fighting for the State of Israel, for in addition to his other qualifications, he had an extensive knowledge of history, diplomacy, and military strategy. At both Palmach and Haganah headquarters he was in great demand. He was appointed head of Haganah's operations in the Galilee District, later assigned to the Planning Section, and during the War of Independence, when the Israeli army was created, became one of the principal adjutants of General Ygal Yadin.

At the end of the war Beer was promoted to chief of planning and operations, but from that moment on, his military enthusiasm began to wane. Some say that he had been gravely disappointed by the dissolution of Palmach; others think his pride was hurt because he was not made adjutant to the new commander in chief, his old friend Yadin. Whatever the reason, Israel Beer resigned from the army in 1950 and went into journalism and politics.

In 1944 Beer had joined the extreme Left wing of Mapam and thereafter followed Moshe Sneh even further to the left. He became military reporter for Mapam's organ, *Al Hamishmar* and expounded his leftist politics in highly praised articles in which he never missed a chance to show his admiration for communism, especially during the Korean War.

Ben-Gurion was one of Beer's favorite targets, and he attacked him with all the force of his vitriolic style. In a chapter he wrote in 1953 for the *History of Palmach* he lit into the Old Man with such force that its editors, Israel Galili and Yigal Allon, decided not to include it.

The same year 1953 was a turning point in Beer's political career. Shortly after the split in Mapam he abruptly reversed his politics and went over to Mapai. "I was on the wrong road," he told his friends. "When I took a long hard look at the subject I found I was wrong and Ben-Gurion was right."

Beer also left *Al Hamishmar* and joined *Davar*, the official organ of Mapai, and also began writing for various magazines and army publications as well as for foreign papers. Gradually he carved out a niche for himself in military circles and regained the confidence of the government leaders. In 1955, on Shaul Avigur's recommendation, he was engaged by the Defense Ministry to write the official history of the War of Independence. That work completely conformed to the "Ben-Gurionism" he had now adopted, even to his account of the extremely controversial battle of Latrun in 1948. Soon he had

become "one of us," and the Defense Ministry provided him
with a secretary and an office close to Ben-Gurion's.

"Israel is a marvelous country," Beer remarked rather cyni-
cally to a friend. "All you have to do is give a cheer for Ben-
Gurion and you can do whatever you like."

And that is just exactly what Beer did. Sporting his lieutenant colonel's uniform, he regularly attended the closed meetings of the high command, and even though he did not have
access to classified papers, everyone spoke freely in front of
him. He spent a large part of his time hanging around in the
apartments of high command and Defense Ministry officials,
getting from their own lips plenty of exact and detailed information on all subjects.

Beer's exceptional position in the Defense Ministry was the
subject of an article by Alain Guiney, *France Soir*'s Tel Aviv
correspondent, who wrote:

I met Israel Beer for the first time in the office of Shimon Peres,
then still the general director of the Defense Ministry, toward the
end of the Sinai War. The forces of Israel, France, and Great Britain
had just ended their campaign, and I wanted to learn from Peres
what Israel's future plans were . . .

"Let me introduce Dr. Israel Beer," Peres said . . . I was so
startled by his bizarre appearance that I could hardly listen to
Peres' explanation of Israel's diplomatic strategy. Shortly afterward
France's Ambassador Pierre Gilbert came in and started chatting
with Beer, to whom he expounded France's points of view, at the
same time criticizing Great Britain, the U.S.S.R., and the United
States. Beer listened closely and indicated his approval, and from
time to time interrupted the ambassador with some opinions of his
own . . . Ever since, I have not had the slightest doubt that Beer is
one of the *éminences grises* of the Defense Ministry.

One of the few persons who distrusted Dr. Israel Beer was
Commander in Chief Moshe Dayan, who could not stand the
doctor and even tried to get the editors of *Davar* to fire him.

"He has read a great deal about military matters," Dayan said, "but he has learned nothing." On several occasions Dayan told Beer not to wear his uniform, and when he found Beer present at a secret conference at army headquarters just before the Sinai War, he ordered him to leave. After that, Beer kept out of the general's way.

At the end of 1956 the influential and politically independent *Ha'aretz* hired Beer as its military editor, and his reputation both in Israel and abroad soared. In 1959 the University of Tel Aviv followed his recommendation and established for him a chair of military history, the inauguration of which was attended by David Ben-Gurion, General Haim Laskov, the new commander in chief, and several other directors of national defense. The Old Man congratulated Beer effusively on his address on this occasion. The chair raised Beer's prestige as a military expert to new heights, and many officers took courses with him in order to broaden their points of view and increase their knowledge. The courses included practical exercises and analyses of battles in the War of Independence, the Spanish Civil War, and World War II. Military developments between the two world wars were stressed.

More and more frequently now, Beer went abroad, for this was the time at which secret and mutually profitable bonds were being forged between Israel's Defense Ministry and that of West Germany under the direction of Shimon Peres for Israel and Franz Joseph Strauss for the Federal Republic of West Germany. According to Peres, Germany was a good rainy day friend.

The perspicacious Israel Beer knew how to make the most of this combination. He was much appreciated in Germany because of his thorough knowledge of the language, his international reputation, and his deep knowledge of various nations' attitudes toward events in the Middle East. Learned German societies invited him to speak at their conferences, and in 1958 he was guest speaker at the annual meeting of the German Association for Military Science. In 1959 a Munich publisher issued his book, *The Middle East — Crucial Battleground of East and West,* which was very well received.

On several occasions Beer was invited to lecture before the Bundeswehr officers and attend maneuvers of the West German army. He was a guest speaker at the Protestant Academy of Tübingen and other distinguished groups. He made friends with General Heusinger, Commander in Chief of the German army, General Partsch, Admiral Rieke, General Budersohn, and many other high-ranking officers.

Some of Beer's trips were paid for by the Israeli Trade Mission in Bonn, which highly approved of his visits to Germany. The Defense Ministry also looked with favor on Beer's treks, and Commander in Chief Laskov had no objection to Beer's lectures on strategy, for his theories derived from the Israeli high command's.

Beer's German career reached its apogee with his participation in a symposium for military officers on "Moral Principles in the Art of War," in which Defense Minister Strauss and an eminent professor of Heidelberg University also participated. When Beer returned from one of these journeys, he boasted of having been given the floor — "in spite of the objections of the Israeli Consulate in Stockholm" — at a conference of the high command of the Swedish army, of having visited the Norwegian defense ministry, and of having been invited by the European headquarters of NATO to inspect its bases in Germany.

In spite of having been officially forbidden to do so, Beer made several excursions into East Berlin. He reported enthusiastically to Gershom Shoken, the publisher of *Ha'aretz,* that in East Berlin he met the Polish ambassador and asked to be put in touch with Polish Defense Minister Kummer, who had been his comrade-in-arms in Spain, and that as soon as Kummer learned his dear old friend was in Berlin, he sent a special plane to bring him to Warsaw for a two-day reunion.

Between 1959 and 1960 Dr. Beer's private life underwent some changes. After the war he married Rivka Zinder, a hospital laboratory assistant. They had no children, but they did have a magnificent German shepherd dog named Azza, whose sudden death in mid-1959 seriously upset the couple's tranquil and simple home life. Beer began to go to bars and nightclubs, to chase women — preferably young ones — and to get drunk more and more often. In the old days in his native Vienna he would have been called *débauché*.

He could now be found quite regularly among the girls at the Adria or the Atom Bar, and at midnight he would invite many journalists and artists for several rounds of drinks in the Jaffa cabarets. Beer always picked up the check. Even abroad he spent freely. Once in Cologne he invited most of the employees of the Trade Mission to a cabaret and paid the outrageous bill without flinching.

His married life began to go downhill, for he took a young divorcée as his mistress and spent a good deal of money on installing her in a fine apartment. He even tried to get her a job at Radio Israel.

Early in 1961 Beer was rushed to a hospital with several fractured ribs and other physical damage. When he returned to work — minus a few teeth — he pretended to have been in an automobile accident, but he got so entangled in the web of lies with which he answered his colleagues' questions that he finally had to admit there had been no accident but that his mistress' ex-husband had beaten him up in the street. None of that, however, hurt his career.

On March 31, 1961, Iser Harel for once found himself with a free evening. He left his office earlier than usual and hurried home to get a bath and change his clothes, for Yossi had got him tickets for the theater. Iser and his Rivka had a snack for dinner. Before leaving for the theater Iser gave the switchboard operator at headquarters the number of his seat so that he could be reached in an emergency. He had picked up the car keys and was on the threshhold of his house when the telephone rang.

"Good evening, Iser. Avraham Michaeli speaking."

Avraham Michaeli was the chief of counterespionage at Shin-Bet.

"What's the trouble?"

"I phoned you because I can't reach Joel Morag. He's not home this evening. It all has to do with . . ."

Avraham resorted to allusions and unfinished sentences, but Iser quickly understood that a decision had to be made at once — and certainly not over the telephone.

"Where are you, Avraham?"

Michaeli gave Iser the name of a café in Tel Aviv.

"Where are you parked? Right. Wait for me in your car. I'm on my way."

Iser hung up the phone. "I'm terribly sorry, Rivka, but you'll have to get someone else to take you to the theater. This is an emergency."

Fifteen minutes later Iser was in Avraham's car in a quiet back street in the center of Tel Aviv. Avraham was very excited. He said that his agents had happened on a meeting between a Soviet diplomat and an unknown person in a dark street, and a black briefcase had been handed by one to the other. The Shin-Bet men had followed the unknown man to his house, which they were completely astonished to discover was 67 Brandeis Street, Israel Beer's address.

"It certainly points the finger at Israel Beer," said Avraham. "But what is to be done?" His voice betrayed his anxiety and embarrassment, for he knew how close Beer was to Ben-Gurion.

"Make one final check," Iser said. "If your suspicions are confirmed, go to Beer and arrest him. Call the police Special Branch right away and get the arrest and the search warrants you must have."

Avraham turned white. "What if we're wrong? What will Ben-Gurion say?"

Iser knew that if he asked him, the Old Man would tell him at once to arrest the suspect. So he snapped: "Just do as I say."

Iser went home and sat down at the desk in his study, skimming through files to kill time. Late that evening Avraham Michaeli telephoned him again.

"I finally got hold of Joel, and he thinks it would be better not to make the arrest tonight."

"Do what I told you," Iser said. "Make the arrest tonight. Also search the place. Get the police there at once." He hung up abruptly.

At half-past two in the morning there was a loud knocking on the door of Beer's apartment. When Beer opened it, he stared for a long time at the police and the agents on the landing. Without a flicker of expression he watched them unfold the warrant and read its official language.

"So," he said at last. "Do your duty."

On the following day, when Ben-Gurion was on a tour of inspection in the Negev, his aide, Colonel Ben-David ("Habad") got a telephone call from one of his associates, who spoke very guardedly, using only the customary allusions. "Tell the Old Man that the Little One has caught the Skull red-handed."

Israel Beer was no new "client" for Iser. For six years now Iser had had him under suspicion, had urged that he be fired from the Defense Ministry, and had warned everyone in it about Beer. He had also tried to have Beer's many trips abroad curtailed. There had been several violent quarrels between them, and Iser had seriously warned Beer again and again.

Their first important conversation was on December 30, 1955, shortly after Beer had joined the Defense Ministry, at which time Iser had grave doubts about him. Beer might not have been the only officer to resign after the dissolution of Palmach, but he was different from the rest in continuing to drift to the Left and take a stand with pro-communist groups. Iser also knew that Beer had been a member of Mapam's Security Committee, which at one time devoted its efforts to collecting military and political secret information.

Then just at the time that Sneh's faction left Mapam to join the communist party, Beer ran out on his friends. A prominent Mapam leader whispered to one of Iser's agents: "Don't trust Beer. I wouldn't be surprised if within a year or so he became an active member of Mapai. That would be good evidence that he's following a long-term plan according to instructions from afar." As it turned out, Beer did join Mapai less than two years later, after repenting before Shaul Avigur and confessing to Ben-Gurion at Sde Boker.

In his analysis of the case Iser deduced two possible reasons for Beer's behavior. One, Beer was a born opportunist; hence, his leaving the communists when their cause was in decline and going over to Ben-Gurion's winning side. The second of Iser's explanations had much more serious implications. Having made a thorough study of Soviet espionage, Iser knew how their agents operated. Frequently they would contact one of the most talented and loyal members of the communist party and tell him to get out of the party and penetrate government circles. Thus they create potential spies who dig themselves into government bureaus after having apparently dissolved their ties with communism. After a few years these men are ripe for spy missions.

The question in Iser's mind was whether Beer was in the process of becoming a communist spy, and to clear this up Iser got hold of Beer in December 1955 and asked him the reason for the sudden change in his political opinions.

"I shall give you the same explanation I gave Shaul Avigur and Ben-Gurion," Beer said with complete frankness. "When I was an officer in the International Brigade in Spain, it was not Jerusalem I was dreaming of, but Moscow. After my return to Vienna, however, I became a Zionist overnight as a result of reading Bein's life of Herzl." Then, as if to excuse himself, he added: "I know that if you were to read that story in a book, you would think it absurd, but it's the truth nonetheless."

Consequently Beer had chosen Jerusalem over Moscow. Afterward, so he said, when he had joined Mapam he had for several years believed a synthesis could be made of communism and Zionism, but the split in Mapam convinced him otherwise. Given the extremes of communism and Zionism, he had chosen the latter.

Iser was obliged to admit that Beer's explanation seemed both logical and sincere. But he was not satisfied all that easily. He began asking Beer about the military and political information that Mapam's Security Committee used to gather. He wanted to hear from the doctor's own lips what the aims of that underground activity were.

Beer answered that the committee paid persons who worked in the various ministries for the information they furnished it, but he absolutely denied knowing anything about military intelligence, and he emphasized that he had never been connected with that kind of information.

From then on, Iser was even more on guard, for he himself knew, and had evidence to boot, that Beer had got hold of classified documents of a military nature. He continued questioning the doctor, but Beer gave him only evasive answers. At the end of that long interview Iser's suspicions were by no means gone, but he knew that as a result of his questioning Beer would be very careful about undertaking any dangerous enterprise. Meanwhile Iser labeled him a potential danger to Israel's security.

Less than a year later, on September 28, 1956, Iser summoned Beer again. This time he gave the doctor a severe and definite warning.

The preparations for the Sinai War were coming to an end, and it was generally believed that hostilities would begin some time during the following month. About September 20 Ben-

Gurion cabled Shimon Peres in Paris to inform him of his consent to an alliance with France against Egypt for the end of October. Iser, who was in on the secret, knew that the slightest leakage on that subject might utterly defeat the whole project and result in much bloodshed. But many other Israelis knew at least part of the deal, and they had to be kept silent about it. Iser particularly distrusted certain Leftist persons who were close to high-ranking officers and also to officials of the Defense Ministry, because such persons also had regular conferences with the Soviets.

Iser drew up a list of ten names, most of which belonged to Mapam members well known for their pro-Soviet opinions, got them to meet with him under one pretext or another, and said to every one of them: "As you know, the Russians are nowadays very hostile to Israel. They have decided to bet the limit on the Arabs. I am certain that there have been communist cells in Mapam, and it is likely that some of Sneh's faction have stayed in the party to spy. Do you know anyone who is collaborating with the Russians?"

Several mentioned one or another person whose presence in Mapam after the split seemed strange. Others just said no. But it was not the communist agents in Mapam that interested Iser; he wanted to give his guests a subtle warning. He knew that whatever their political leanings were, they would be extremely careful after their session with him, and if one or two did have acquaintances among the Soviets, they would not be in contact with them during the next few weeks. And that was precisely what Iser wanted.

Israel Beer's name was close to the top of Iser's guest list.

Iser called to Beer's attention the military tension in the Middle East, put him on guard against the communist agents still in Mapam, and asked him to keep his eyes open. Then in guarded terms he began talking about the relations some persons had with various Soviets.

Suddenly Beer cut him off and told him that he had happened to meet one of the secretaries of the Soviet Embassy in Tel Aviv, who had asked for a series of regular interviews in order that he might make an objective study of Israel's problems. Beer agreed, but he had thought it wise to inform Colonel Argov, the Prime Minister's military secretary. Argov had flown into a rage, commanded him not to meet with the Russian, and to tell the whole story to Joel Morag, the head of Shin-Bet.

Morag had reacted equally violently and had officially forbidden Beer to see the Soviet diplomat again. "He's a spy," Morad said, "just like all the rest of his breed."

Iser felt the same way. He was well acquainted with the diplomat in question, who was involved in every bit of Soviet espionage in Israel and was doubtless one of the KGB's controllers. In forceful language Iser also forbade Beer to meet the Russian again. Beer slammed the door behind him, but Iser was sure that Beer would have no contact with the Russian for quite a while.

Iser's preventive measures may well have been the reason why up to October 29, 1956, the Sinai campaign was a well-kept secret.

Beer's file was laid on Iser's desk for the third time in mid-1960 in consequence of serious information of German origin.

The head of Mossad had not been at all pleased with the number of trips Beer had made to Germany, for he was well aware that in the struggle between East and West, Germany was a vulnerable spot and at the same time a starting point for Soviet strategy. The U.S.S.R. was profoundly fearful that Germany would attempt to recover the territories she had lost in the war, unite the two divisions of the country, and regain political and military supremacy in Europe.

It occurred to Iser that Beer, a potential danger to Israel's security, might well be working for the Soviets during his long stays in Germany, during which he repeatedly met with those responsible for that country's security and defense. And now he suddenly learned that in mid-1960, Beer had stayed in München-Gladbach and there had met General Reinhard Gehlen, the chief of the German Intelligence service!

Gehlen's organization occupied a highly privileged position in the West's strategical system because of the cold war. Even during World War II there had been fundamental differences of opinion between the United States and Great Britain as to what their policy should be toward the Soviet Union. Britain's Prime Minister Winston Churchill had a certain respect for the Russians, it is true, but he profoundly distrusted them and was very cautious with them, for he foresaw the conflict between East and West that was sure to arise after the defeat of Hitler.

Franklin D. Roosevelt, on the other hand, was spellbound by Stalin and his fine promises and almost naively made concessions to Stalin that gave the U.S.S.R. a distinct advantage over the United States and the other pillars of the West. Roosevelt had overlooked matters of information, and while Stalin was planting his spies in Europe, Asia, and even America, the United States never dreamed of conducting secret warfare against the Soviet Union.

America's awakening to the facts was painful. In the early 1950s cases of Soviet espionage came to light again and again in Canada, England, and the United States. The Americans suddenly discovered that their most closely guarded atomic secrets were traveling to Moscow. They also learned that right in the middle of the war, when they were swearing eternal devotion to their Soviet allies, the Russian spy Richard Sorge was in Japan, installing a network to spy on America.

Now, when Senator Joseph McCarthy was engaged in his witch hunt, and the CIA was incapable of meeting the urgent needs of the United States for all kinds of information on the Soviets, Reinhard Gehlen appeared on the scene.

During the war General Gehlen had been one of the chiefs of the Abwehr, the German military Intelligence, and headed a division that specialized in espionage against the Russians. Gehlen had extended his networks into Russia itself, had slipped his agents into the Red army, and had procured for his bureau a steady supply of important reports on top secret military subjects. Many of his networks were still intact after the war, and when the need for fresh information was felt in the West, Gehlen simply reactivated them. Either out of hatred for the communist regime, or out of greed, or even under threat of blackmail, many German spies resumed their activity behind the Iron Curtain, and precious information began to flow into the Federal Republic of West Germany. Gehlen also was able to create secret routes by which his agents could get into the Soviet bloc.

The Soviets were not slow in recognizing the serious danger that Gehlen's organization — the West's principal source of information on the U.S.S.R. — was to them, and they used all possible means to smash it. They tried to ruin Gehlen's reputation by accusing him of Nazi atrocities, and, of course, they tried to get their own agents into Gehlen's services. Soon Gehlen's organization became one of their principal targets in the cold war.

In the course of his interviews with Gehlen and his colleagues, with Defense Minister Franz Joseph Strauss, and with other high-placed persons, Beer expressed opinions almost identical with those of the most extreme circles in the German army. The German generals were delighted with this new friend and ally, who fully espoused the stubborn opposition to an organization that was urging young Germans to refuse military service by expounding, as an Israeli, the importance of young Germans joining their country's new army. He willingly spoke on this subject to many German youth groups.

Such was the message of Israel Beer, David Ben-Gurion's personal representative! He favored not only a rehabilitation of Germany, but was conducting a veritable campaign on behalf of the Jews for a revival of German military might.

In those activities of Beer's can be discerned the typical strategy of a Soviet agent protected by Israeli citizenship trying to insinuate himself into the German secret service with Gehlen's unconscious help. There could be no better disguise possible for a Russian spy who wanted to get inside Gehlen's sanctuary and tap the resources of his organization than to pose as an Israeli with a government post and Ben-Gurion's endorsement. If Beer played his cards well, he could work his way into the one place most carefully protected against Soviet infiltration and there have access to communications between Gehlen and Adenauer that would yield him data of inestimable value to Moscow.

On his return from Germany Beer let it be known far and wide that he was bringing a message from Gehlen to Ben-Gurion, but this announcement, it soon appeared, had no basis in fact.

Immediately Iser summoned Beer to account for his trip. He did not mince words in reproaching Beer to his face for what he considered a serious misuse of his official position. But without evidence, he could not accuse Beer of actual espionage, though he did warn him unambiguously: "You shall make no more trips to Germany. The foreign minister and the defense minister no longer authorize you to do so."

Beer's face grew purple with rage. "I demand," he shouted, "that you be called before the party to explain yourself!"

Beer's remark increased Iser's suspicions because, in the first place, there was no such procedure in Israel as "explaining before the party," and secondly, Iser was not an active member of Mapai. Beer's threat was clearly communist lingo.

By the end of the interview Beer had completely lost his self-control. Shaking, and so blinded by rage that he could scarcely see where he was going, he stumbled toward the door, bumped against the jamb, and had to grope for the knob.

On Iser's recommendation the government did forbid Beer to go abroad again, but Ben-Gurion's attitude toward him remained typical of the Old Man's candor. Since Beer had not seen any classified documents and had not been present at any closed sessions of the ministers, Ben-Gurion believed he could not know state secrets. Yet everyone else thought that Beer must know what went on behind the scenes in the government because, since he was one of Ben-Gurion's intimates, people spoke freely before him.

Not until later did it come to light that Beer used to walk up and down the Defense Ministry sidewalk, plucking by the sleeve every senior army officer he knew and getting information from him, then repeating what he had learned to another officer and then to a third. These, thinking that Beer already knew everything, would in all innocence disclose to him their own confidential information. This mode of gathering information earned Beer the nickname of *Hamosser* — the informer.

That's the way things went on until Beer was arrested — to the amazement of the whole country.

One of the first things the Shin-Bet agents seized in Beer's apartment was the black briefcase that the Soviet diplomat had given back to him after having photographed its contents. Inside were, among other papers, a bundle of black notebooks whose pages were covered with a well-known neat handwriting. They were Ben-Gurion's private diaries! Apparently Beer had borrowed them from the Old Man on the pretext that he wanted to study them for his book on the War of Independence. Another document in the briefcase was a report from the manager of one of Israel's top-secret armament factories, disclosing the nature and rate of its production. Later investigation revealed that one of the managers of that factory had given the document to Beer on his explicit request for it. It was also established that various high officials also had given Beer information in good faith, believing that he needed it for his Defense Ministry work. The briefcase contained several other documents of considerable importance.

Beer's arrest was not made public. On the bulletin board of the University of Tel Aviv was merely a notice that "Dr. Israel Beer's courses will not meet until further notice." His interrogation began in absolute secrecy.

Iser Harel was now convinced that Beer was a Soviet agent who had been installed in Israel over twenty years ago. Iser's case rested on the fact that Beer had fought in the International Brigade during the Spanish Civil War. Only a few officers of that brigade were still alive, the majority having either died during the war or been liquidated in Moscow or elsewhere on Stalin's orders. The few survivors had become faithful servants of the U.S.S.R., and before World War II several had been sent as spies into the West or, like Beer, into Palestine.

Iser questioned his prisoner in an isolated cell. "I know you are a Soviet Intelligence officer. If you admit it, we'll take your confession into consideration."

Beer merely shrugged.

"You've already lost the game, so confess. If you cooperate with us, your punishment will be less severe."

The prisoner still refused.

A physical examination of Beer revealed that he had not been circumcised. For a short time it was believed that Beer was not a Jew at all, but a Gentile passing for one. That easy conclusion had to be reconsidered, however, in the light of the fact that many Jewish families in Austria and Germany did not have their sons circumcised in order to make it easier for them to mingle in non-Jewish society. The question was finally abandoned after Shin-Bet's thorough investigation both in Israel and abroad produced the amazing truth about Beer.

First it was found that Israel Beer had never earned a doctoral degree and that his university career was a complete invention. Then it was established that Beer had never attended a military school in Vienna, or served in the ranks of the Republikanischer Schützbund, or fought against Dollfuss' fascists.

Stone by stone rose the tower of Beer's definitive biography, each level causing greater and greater astonishment. Beer, it turned out, had never served in the International Brigade or even set foot in Spain. While he was supposedly shedding his blood at Guadalajara and Teruel, he was actually a minor civil servant in Vienna's Zionist organization. The special plane that Polish Defense Minister Kummer was supposed to have sent for him was another of Beer's pathetic lies.

Beer now stood naked in the noonday sun — a compulsive liar and an impostor whose life story had been constructed out of his reading in order to dazzle his fellow men. Under the stress of the questioning Beer finally went to pieces and confessed his lies, but he steadfastly denied the charge of spying. He a spy? Quite the contrary, he protested, he had always been a loyal patriot. As for his relations with the Russians, Beer's explanation was that when he saw that Ben-Gurion and his associates were on the wrong road he made up his mind to act alone and work for the reconciliation of Israel with the Soviet Union and other communist nations. He had believed that if from time to time he could make his friends in those countries aware of his "opinions" on the situation in Israel and convince them that Israel was not a lost cause for them but a country whose cooperation would be to their advantage, everything would be for the best in the best of all possible worlds.

That intricate explanation appeared to the investigators merely Beer's feeble attempt to get himself out of a jam. Such might indeed have been Beer's philosophy, yet what had been found in the black briefcase was not an expression of Israel Beer's opinions, but classified papers of a political and military nature. It may well have been that Beer's first contacts with the Russians had taken the form of an exchange of views, but they had soon developed into orders to a docile servant. Ben-Gurion's diaries and the confidential military papers could hardly be classed as the opinions of a man bent on improving the relations between Israel and the Kremlin.

At this point in the investigation it also appeared that Beer

had regularly received considerable sums of money from the
Russians to "cover his expenses" in procuring the papers he furnished them.

Bit by bit Iser Harel reached the conclusion that Beer's motives were only vaguely connected with ideology. Such a man
would indeed have been a gift from heaven to Soviet espionage,
but basically Beer had acted as he did because he was a frustrated man who needed to realize his ambitions by achieving
lofty positions in which he could dominate others. His trips
abroad, his lectures to select audiences, his connections with
political and military leaders, his value to the Russians — all
were means to this one end. Similarly he wanted money not to
enrich himself but to spend lavishly in order to show off before
his friends. This morbid compulsion to achieve recognition was
what eventually destroyed him.

For years afterward imaginative writers crammed their readers with stories about Beer in which he would appear to have
been sent by the Russians into Israel in 1938, or else that he was
not a Jew but an ace spy for the Soviets who had assumed the
identity of a concentration camp victim and reached Palestine
with a martyr's papers. Such stories may make good reading, but they are fiction.

Beer became a spy for the Russians only after the Sinai War.
His first contacts with the KGB agent in Tel Aviv were made in
1956, at which time the Israeli Secret Service had given him a
severe warning. It is likely that his Russian friend then planted
in Beer's mind the service he could render Moscow by spying
for the Soviets, but it was not until 1957 that he agreed to do so.
Meanwhile the agent who had seduced him had gone back to
the U.S.S.R. On his own initiative Beer got in touch with that
man's successor in the Soviet Embassy and began to give him
information both oral and written.

Beer confessed that the kind of information he had furnished
the Russians consisted of diagrams and blueprints, classified
military plans, itemized lists of Israel's purchases of arms in

France and Germany as well as of the firms that supplied them. Owing to his frequent visits to Germany, he knew all about Israel's secret dealings with Germany, especially the well-nigh secret shipments of arms from Germany to Israel ordered by Adenauer and Strauss. His investigations had led him into the field of German-Israeli relations. His trips into NATO countries, especially France, had provided him with a source of information on the armed forces of those nations. It is also probable that the Russians sent him to see General Gehlen in order that he might report to them what he found at German secret service headquarters.

A few days after Beer was arrested, his friend the Soviet diplomat abruptly terminated his work in Israel and hurried aboard the first plane to Moscow.

When banner headlines brought the whole affair to public knowledge in mid-April 1961 the entire country reeled under and shock. Many journalists labeled Beer the "personal counselor" of Ben-Gurion and asserted that he had had access to all state secrets. Others called him "the Sorge of Israel." The government, on the other hand, tried to minimize the importance of the incident by assuring the public that whatever Beer might have given the Russians was of small value. The scandal, however, disclosed indubitable negligence on the part of the administration.

In the excitement Iser Harel was blamed for not having kept Beer under closer observation. Iser icily replied that he had considered Beer a threat to national security and had warned his superiors about him, but they had continued to have confidence in Beer. Shin-Bet, then, could do no more than warn him. The national defense administration was also bitterly attacked, for in spite of Iser's advice, Ben-Gurion and his close associates had continued to employ Beer and thus provide him with access to military information.

In the general elections of August 1961 Ben-Gurion's political opponents tried to make capital of the Beer scandal, but it
appeared that Mapai's principal rivals in the electoral campaign belonged to the left-wing parties, Mapam and Achdut
Ha'avoda. Consequently, before attacking Mapai, they had to
get the skeletons out of their own closets, for it was the leaders
of Mapam who had "discovered" Beer, linked him to their party,
and opened the way for him to the top.

On January 14, 1962, Israel Beer was sentenced to ten years'
imprisonment. An appeal to the Supreme Court resulted in the
sentence being increased to fifteen years. The Supreme Court's
decision read: "Certain things revealed in the trial of this man
are enough to make one's hair stand on end, for now no one can
tell the difference between a past danger and a present calam-
ity."

Israel Beer died in Shatta Prison on May 1, 1966, a few days
after he had finished his book *Israel's Security — Yesterday,
Today, and Tomorrow*. In its preface he tried once more to
whitewash his sins, pretending that all his confessions in court
were lies and repeating the fiction of his experiences in the
Spanish Civil War. His explanation of the stubborn fact that
official documents proved that all the while he was supposedly
in Spain he was a civil servant in Vienna was:

Before going to Spain I returned, as was customary, my identity
papers to the underground Socialist Party in Austria. Those documents permitted — also the custom — some communist refugee from
Germany to assume a new identity. It happened to be a young
Jewish intellectual from Berlin who somewhat resembled me. While
I was fighting in Spain under an assumed name, that young man,
who was now using my name, was working for the Zionist organizations in Vienna while awaiting his immigration visa for Palestine.

Once back in Vienna, however, the real Israel Beer found he
had a desperate need for his papers.

I undertook to find the fellow who had them in his possession, and my efforts were crowned with success. For him also the papers were a matter of life or death. With the help of some friends I took them from him by force. As a result, the young man in question disappeared from the land of the living.

These passages put the capstone on Beer's pyramid of lies. Apparently it meant nothing to him to embroider his yarn with a "double" and then convict himself of murder — for how else would the young man have "disappeared from the land of the living"? — all in an effort to protect his own reputation.

Israel Beer's political and military theories are also as fictitious as his "apology." His book attempts to outline an ideological-strategical study, but most of his basic theories and conclusions could not stand the test of actual events and completely collapsed as a result of the Six Day War.

His Leftist friends were loyal to him, however, even after his death. In the eulogy of Israel Beer that Raphael Benkler wrote for *Al Hamishmar* he called him "a magnificent fighter, a titan, one of this world's great people . . . He was a giant as a man, a giant as an authority on military subjects, a giant, indeed, even as a spy."

One of the directors of the Secret Service, on the other hand, said of Israel Beer: "He was an infamous human being, a repulsive liar. Of all the spies I have brought to justice the only one for whom I have never felt pity or regret was Israel Beer."

22

Secret Mission
to Cairo

Suppose that a high official of the government of Iraq is alarmed by the dictator Gen. Kassem's unqualified admiration for the communist party. The official is seriously worried over the possibility of a Soviet takeover in Iraq and the danger that the northern part of Kurdistan will be irretrievably lost. At the same time the State of Israel, struggling for survival, is trying hard to obtain as much information as possible on her Arab neighbors. The Iraqi official, loyal to his national cause, will never yield to the temptation of serving Israel, but because of his fear of the Russians, he will work for the Americans, who in his eyes are a counterpoise to Soviet influence in Iraq. The most simple solution is for the Israeli agent trying to recruit the Iraqi official to pass himself off as an American . . .

This passage from *A Short Course in the Secret War* by former CIA ace Christopher Felix throws a beam of light on the most secret, most dangerous, and at the same time most important aspect of Mossad's work — espionage in enemy countries.

Mossad directed a vast network of espionage in the Arab countries from the jumping-off places it had established in several European cities. Many were the Mossad agents who, equipped with passports "issued by" friendly or neutral countries, rushed right into the lion's mouth by entering Arab countries, established bases in their capitals, and planted cells of espionage. Other Israelis recruited Arab and foreign agents. After training them in secret centers in Europe and even in Israel, they sent them on missions to the enemy's nerve centers. Iser Harel also often organized highly complicated operations to confuse the enemy with false information about Israel.

The Mossad networks in the Arab countries brought Israel a constant flow of exhaustive information. The Arab lands, however, were not Mossad's only targets; it had to its credit achievements of global importance. According to Allen Dulles, former CIA chief, the Israeli espionage system was one of the best in the world, and one of his deputies added: "The Israelis are marvelously efficient, though we know even less about their operations than about the Russians'."

"Israel's Mossad has agents in seventy countries," the Russian magazine *Nieva* declared in July 1968. The German historian Gert Buchheit wrote that Mossad employs men and women originally from Arab countries who speak Arabic fluently and are capable of understanding the Arab mentality. Furthermore, he said, Mossad knows how to make the most of the knowledge its agents, originally from Eastern countries, possess, as well as that of the large number of Jews employed throughout the world in non-Israeli secret services. The American writer Paul Jacobs states that "the Israeli Secret Service has at its disposal men with Brooklyn, Detroit, Liverpool, Oxford, and London accents. Israel is brimming with men who know the alleys of Berlin, Warsaw, Prague, and Budapest as well as they know the streets of Tel Aviv." The *New York Times* stated: "Israel and the United States regularly exchange top-secret military information."

Perhaps. But it goes without saying that the greater part of the work devolved upon the Israeli agents themselves, and they had no rest from their labors.

*

From 1949 to 1950 fanatical Nazis kept leaving Europe by secret means. Settled in Cairo, these men banded together into a spy network that was never molested. For years they sent their contacts in Europe complete information on the Egyptian army and secret service, their motive being to strengthen the West against the "Bolshevik peril."

They had been persuaded to enter the service of Western espionage by an SS colonel, a real warhorse and a Prussian to his fingertips, who had recruited them in Europe with impassioned Nazi-type orations, heil Hitlers, and exultant tirades on the eventual victory of the West. Then he had arranged their flight into Egypt. They never knew that this spiritual father of theirs was named Jeruvam Ben-Nevat, that he was a star of Israeli espionage, and that he took pleasure in having those who had escaped the gas ovens of Auschwitz get some advantage out of their former executioners.

Most of the spies Mossad sent into enemy countries, however, were Israelis, and for years a major concern of the Secret Service was to provide an impenetrable cover for them. A solution was found after the rebirth of the State of Israel, when there were plenty of foreigners, especially Germans and Englishmen, working in the Arab capitals as specialists, military advisers, civil service counselors, and secret service experts. Others were engaged in private industry and the import trade.

As the years went on, however, matters grew more complicated. The Arab governments began to distrust all foreigners, especially if they were Jews. Jews who lived in Arab countries were suspected of having clandestine relations with Israel and so were fired from all jobs that might give them access to confidential information. They were, moreover, an easy prey, for no foreign country would take the responsibility of protecting them, and the Arab secret police could do as it liked with them. For that very reason the Israeli Secret Service resolved not to engage any more agents from the Jews of an Arab locality.

The foreigners, too, lost their privileged status. Egypt and Iraq expelled the English, which meant for Israel that she would have a hard time thereafter employing English or pseudo-English in her secret enterprises. The number of German specialists in the Arab armies decreased daily. The Nazi exiles in Egypt and Syria began to die of old age, and in 1955, when Soviet advisers began arriving in Egypt in quantity, the government quickly got rid of the last German experts.

In the early 1960s the Egyptians were suspicious of any foreigner, whether European or American. "The situation of an Israeli or European spy in an Arab country is worse than that of an American spy in the Soviet Union," wrote one expert on secret warfare. The Israeli agent Wolfgang Lotz, who carried a German passport, was able to operate in Egypt up until 1965 because from 1960 to 1965 there was a large German colony in the country making rockets and airplanes for Nasser, but Lotz was an exception.

After the Sinai War of 1956 the efforts of the Israeli Secret Service focused on two main targets: recruitment of Arab agents from Arab countries and planting Israelis disguised as Arabs in Arab capitals. Among the last was Eli Cohen.

Numerous secret services specialized in blackmail. In one European capital a ravishing blonde seduced a Western diplomat, then let herself be seduced, and took the Don Juan to her apartment for an unforgettable night. On the following day a stranger called on the diplomat and spread over his desk a dozen or so "art photographs" in which he appeared naked as a jaybird and in extremely compromising positions with his delectable companion of the night before. Too late did the flabbergasted diplomat comprehend that he had been the victim of the sexual blackmail the Soviet secret service had perfected.

The Russian secret agent wasted no time in empty words. "These pictures will be published," he said, "and copies will also be sent to your family and your government unless you agree to work for us."

Old-timers in the CIA tell how one of their agents extricated himself from a sex trap by presence of mind. When the master blackmailer appeared and showed him the photographs, he picked three of them up, examined them with interest, and then said with a wink: "These aren't bad at all. Please make me six copies of each."

Mossad did not use these tactics. In the first place its chiefs did not believe blackmail an effective means of recruitment. Then, sexual blackmail violated the rigid moral principles that Iser Harel imposed on his men. Lastly, the experts in Arab psychology knew very well that an Arab would not be frightened or embarrassed in the least by the publication of intimate snapshots of his frolics with a European beauty, but would use them as proof of his virility and his romantic triumphs in Europe and would not fail to show them to all his friends.

The principal human weakness the Israelis exploited was the most common, namely, greed for gold. But even after they had succeeded in catching a candidate in their net, they dared not relax. A critical examination of the Arab press demonstrated that an Arab spy's usefulness was limited by his character. First was his cowardice. In innumerable cases Arabs let themselves be seduced by the attractive offers of foreign secret services that contacted them in Europe, but before they reached their own country — especially if it was Egypt — they threw overboard all the instruction sheets, code books, writing implements, and invisible ink they had received, and even went so far as to confess everything to the police.

A Sorge or a Lonsdale was not to be picked up in the streets. Arab spies suffered from lack of training. It was almost impossible to train one for months or years before planting him in his own country, and in most cases the spy went on his mission ill-prepared.

Another character flaw that sent several Arab spies to the gallows was their incorrigible vanity. As soon as they started getting paid by a foreign secret agency they could not wait to buy a big automobile and flashy clothes and to become regular patrons of expensive nightclubs. They could not have found better means of attracting the attention of the authorities.

Israel, however, did succeed in putting into operation a huge organization of spies throughout the Arab world, where they were able to tap the army, high-level political and economic circles, and centers of journalism, industry, and scientific research. To judge from the Arab press, countless spy networks were annihilated and the spies themselves tried, condemned, shot, or hanged, but probably just as many were not discovered and destroyed.

Espionage in the Arab countries, the most ticklish procedure of all in Israel's Secret Service, was shrouded in secrecy. Even the Israelis kept their mouth tightly closed about it. It was so strictly taboo that the only source of information on it was the Arab press, which, of course, reported rather inaccurately. Between 1960 and 1962, for example, the Cairo newspapers printed full accounts of many acts of espionage, always alleging that they were due to the Israelis. Several spies were executed after sensational trials. Here are some headlines:

May 19, 1960. Egyptian Security has succeeded in capturing six networks working for Israel, one composed of Italian fascists, a second of Dutch nationals, a third of Air Force officers . . .

April 30, 1961. The most dangerous network of spies in all Egyptian history has been uncovered. It was directed by an Egyptian of Armenian extraction.

April 19, 1962. The arrest of a beautiful young Greek woman has led to the catpure of two Greek spy networks in the service of the Zionists.

May 8, 1962. A German woman spy has revealed a nest of fifteen agents in the pay of Israel.

July 8, 1962. A network of Ethiopian spies has been broken.

May 20, 1963. An Egyptian law student has been captured with all his partners in espionage.

Of all these stories one stands out — that of Jacques Léon Thomas, to which the Egyptian press gave whole pages of sensational reportage spiced up with a liberal dose of Oriental fantasy.

Jacques Léon Thomas was born in Cairo of Armenian parents. He was a handsome fellow with thick black hair, a disarming smile, and a quick wit, and he spoke perfect Arabic, English, French, and German. In 1956, when the intelligent, refined Thomas was twenty-four years old, Cairo proved too small for him, and he decided to try his luck elsewhere. He spent some months in Beirut, then went to Europe and settled in Cologne, where he worked for two years in an export firm. He loved fine clothes, and he made friends very easily in the bars, nightclubs, and discotheques where he spent most of his evenings.

Early in January 1958 he met a pleasant fellow in a bar who said in Lebanese-accented Arabic that his name was Emile. The two got into a typical conversation for young men of their age — money, business, trips, fast cars, and girls. They got along so well that soon they were spending every evening together, with Emile always picking up the checks.

Three months were enough for Emile to learn all he wanted to know about Jacques Léon Thomas — his finances, the story of his life, his love affairs, his political opinions. Jacques spoke freely about his hatred of the Nasser regime in Egypt, and so when Emile suggested that Jacques return to Egypt and set up a spy network for NATO there, he was sure he would get an affirmative answer.

When Jacques did say yes, Emile's friends rented an apartment in Cologne, in which they conducted a spy school for one pupil, Jacques Léon Thomas, teaching him, among other things, how to photograph documents and how to hide rolls of microfilm in tubes of toothpaste and similar places. At the end of his course Jacques signed a contract with his new employers by which he pledged himself to go to Cairo and "procure political, military, and economic information on the United Arab Republic." Emile provided him with a plane ticket and $1200 as an "advance on his salary and for expenses," and on June 5, 1958, Jacques Léon Thomas landed at Cairo's airport.

He wasted no time. Presently his controls in Europe were receiving full reports that he dispatched by a belly dancer and similar messengers. Soon he had recruited his first agent, a childhood friend named Mohammed Hassan, a civilian employed by the Egyptian artillery. Jacques offered him a monthly salary of one hundred dollars, which was more than the army was paying him, and promised him a bonus for every valuable piece of information he delivered, as well as a definite sum for every document he managed to photograph. He instructed Hassan to get information from the officers at his base, technical details of the arms the Russians were supplying, and the Egyptian army's training methods.

Every day Hassan would wait until his fellow workers left and then went from office to office collecting all the papers he could find, photographing them, and putting them back in place. His salary rose to dizzying heights; by the end of 1960 it was ten times larger than his official pay. He furnished Jacques Thomas with confidential military manuals, maps on which were marked the locations of secret military bases, and similar treasures.

In August 1958 Jacques went back to Germany at the request of his employers. Emile met him at Cologne, warmly congratulated him on his first triumphs, and gave him a bonus of one thousand dollars for having recruited Hassan. In a separate envelope was a bonus for Hassan himself. Emile then informed his friend that his monthly salary would henceforth be three hundred dollars.

Jacques Thomas had done so well that his friends decided he deserved their closer attention and began to perfect his training. Emile introduced him to a young man who said his name was Albert and added: "I am an executive with NATO. My specialty is the Middle East."

Albert and Jacques secluded themselves in an empty room over a bar on Cologne's Rudolfplatz, where Albert patiently instructed the Armenian in the use of invisible inks and the decoding of messages hidden in apparently innocuous letters and papers, and finally presented him with a Retina camera for use in his work.

Jacques was not alone on his return trip to Cairo. He had made the acquaintance of a beautiful blonde named Kathy Bendoff, who worked in an insurance company, had fallen madly in love with her, and married her. Since he could not keep his work a secret from her for long, he made her his accomplice. She performed several missions for her husband, especially as a bearer of letters and documents.

The Thomas network continued to grow, a recent recruit being another Armenian named Joseph Tanalian, a professional photographer whom Thomas paid a monthly salary for reproducing the hundreds of documents that Mohammed Hassan regularly brought in.

Jacques Thomas registered himself with the chamber of commerce as an exporter and organized a company for shipping abroad "souvenirs of Cairo" and "objets d'art." Cases of these were piled up in the courtyard of his spacious house in Cairo's Garden City. Among the souvenirs were usually several taborets with inlaid tops, in the slim legs of which Thomas and his old father secreted microfilms destined for the main office in Europe.

With astonishing speed Jacques Thomas established close

contacts with several government and army officials, conceived numerous operations that would bring him a harvest of precious information, and became the best foreign spy ever to have worked in Egypt. With his wife and Mohammed Hassan he went on frequent "business trips" to the Suez Canal Zone, photographed installations and military bases there, and marked on survey maps the positions of the various army units. These were then photographed, and the microfilms went to Europe, along with detailed reports on the Katusha rocket-launchers the Soviets had furnished the Egyptian army and the battalions that were being formed to use them. His instructions reached him on coded postcards.

About this time Thomas woke up to the fact that his employer was not NATO but Israel. That discovery did not bother him in the slightest, however; in fact, it made him an even more zealous worker. Later he was to state publicly that he was becoming more and more sympathetic with Israel's cause and even considered himself a loyal emissary of the Jewish State.

In July 1959 Jacques Thomas and his wife announced they were going to visit her family and left for Germany.

The stranger who met Jacques in Cologne said his name was John. "I am chief of the division of the Israeli Intelligence Agency concerned with the Middle East and Western Europe," he explained. Then he added that Israel was eager to have information on morale and public opinion in Egypt, even rumors. "We need," he said, "this information for the Arab language broadcasts of Voice of Israel."

Jacques Thomas now entered another grade of training. A man named Albert introduced him to a man of about thirty-five with a military bearing who spoke three Arabic dialects: Lebanese, Syrian, and Egyptian. Thomas was asked to test this stranger for his superiors. "His Egyptian accent is not perfect," Thomas reported. He gathered from the questions John and Albert put to him that the man was soon to be planted in Egypt, but he never saw him again.

In October 1959 Thomas returned to Egypt alone; Kathy was not to join him for several weeks because the Israelis had sent her to Amsterdam to learn radio broadcasting and coding. The code book she was given before she returned to Cairo was Pearl Buck's *The Good Earth*.

Shortly after Kathy reached Cairo she received the latest model transmitter-receiver from the Israelis. On scheduled days Kathy contacted Israel directly at seven A.M. in order to transmit urgent information or receive instructions. Frequently she would report to Israel that a state of emergency had been proclaimed in Egypt moments after the order had been given, for Mohammed Hassan saw to it that such news was immediately relayed to the Thomas establishment.

In 1960 Thomas's network reached a peak of efficiency. Taborets and other souvenirs stuffed with microfilm left regularly for Europe, and, thanks to her radio equipment, Kathy was in constant touch with Israel. The Thomases got another raise in salary, sent by a Belgian bank and described as "assistance from Kathy's family in Germany." The network was equipped with five cameras, a suitcase with a false bottom, an electric razor with an inner compartment for microfilm or thin rolls of paper, a hollow cigarette lighter for the transport of microfilm, and transceivers of the latest model. In the Thomases' bathroom was a cache of sympathetic inks and various instruments for decoding secret messages.

Then came the day when Kathy received a message from Israel requesting Thomas to find an Egyptian officer who could be recruited for the network. Thomas was warned, however, not to make any contact with his candidate or try to recruit him before he had sent a complete report on him to Israel and got

the green light. But Thomas had contracted the deadly disease
that has sent so many spies to the gallows — he had become too
self-confident.

At the end of July 1960 Captain Adib Hanna Carolos, a Copt,
decided that it was time for him to take a wife. After an elabo-
rate wedding ceremony he took his new spouse to a photographer in order that the happy occasion might be preserved for
their posterity. The photographer was none other than Tanalian, who rushed straight to Jacques Thomas's house and
breathlessly announced: "We've found the man we need."

As soon as Jacques had heard Tanalian's report on the Coptic
officer, he encouraged the photographer to establish friendly
relations with him. For some time the two Armenians tapped
Carolos for information without his knowing it. But that was not
enough for the ambitious Thomas. He made contact with the
Copt, laid his cards on the table, and suggested that he cooperate "for the good of Egypt." Carolos thought a moment, then
said: "I agree."

As soon as he was alone, however, Carolos hurried to Cairo's
Central Police Station, where he fully reported to the Special
Branch his talk with the Armenian. He was ordered to become
a double agent, cooperating with the network by supplying it
with information the Egyptian secret service would give him
and reporting his new employers' activities to the Egyptian police.

Adib Carolos soon carved out a place for himself in the heart
of the Thomas network, for which he became an inexhaustible
source of information, some of which was authentic. Thomas
deluged him with questions on details of the structure and organization of infantry units, tank divisions, the navy, the artillery, positions of military units, training methods, and alterations in the Egyptian and Syrian armies due to their adoption of
Soviet techniques. He even suggested that Carolos go to Syria,
then a member of the U.A.R., to get information on the Syrian

army. "If I could lay my hands on documents dealing with that," Thomas said, "I would pay you ten thousand Egyptian pounds for them."

In addition Thomas told Carolos that the Israeli Secret Service was offering a million Israeli pounds to every MIG pilot who deserted the Egyptian air force and landed his plane in either Cyprus or Israel. Thomas and Tanalian then taught Carolos the art of microphotography and gave him a monthly salary of $350.

Carolos, now an accepted member, learned rapidly and soon knew all the network's secrets, the names of its members, and the hiding places of its equipment. He even learned that the Israelis sent Thomas instructions inside the chocolate bars that supposedly came from Kathy's family in Germany. The Egyptian secret service was well pleased with its man.

At the end of December 1960, after five months of this double game, the Egyptians decided it was time to liquidate the network. Finding things getting rather hot for him, Thomas provided himself with a forged passport in order to escape. On Christmas Eve Kathy happened to detect that she was being watched by the Egyptians and took off for Germany "to spend the holidays with her family." From Germany she sent her husband a New Year's telegram, which was a desperate plea in code for him to get out of Egypt at once.

On the night of January 6, 1961, however, Jacques Thomas and all his accomplices were arrested. The Egyptian Secret Police questioned them for fifteen hundred hours. In the souvenirs packed for shipment were found a thousand microfilms bearing photographs of five thousand documents.

Thomas did not try to clear himself. "I have no regrets," he told the police. "If it had to be done again, I would do it."

Throughout his trial he was proud and dignified and expressed no remorse or repentance, as so many others did. "I am no traitor," he told his judges. "I have never thought of myself as an Egyptian. In Egypt we Armenians suffer from being a minority group." He also proclaimed his sympathies and admiration for the State of Israel.

Jacques Léon Thomas, Jacob Tanalian, and Mohammed Hassan were sentenced to death on July 20, 1961, and were hanged in Cairo on December 20, 1962.

The story of Thomas and his accomplices is only one of dozens, if not hundreds. On the gallows in Cairo, Damascus, and Baghdad died Arabs, Ethiopians, Copts, Greeks, and many others condemned for spying for Israel. Several years will pass before it can be accurately determined who of those wretches were actually in the pay of Israel.

Some had served Israel merely for money; others, for the sake of adventure; a few, both Israelis and foreigners, out of idealistic desire to work for a cause. Whether major or minor, cynical or brave, these mercenaries and adventurers nevertheless made an enormous contribution to the preservation of the State of Israel.

23

Israel Saves de Gaulle

THE DINNER SHOWS at the Don Camillo cabaret on Paris' Rue des Saints-Pères are well-known to lovers of the theater and good food. Less well-known is the private club in the same building, whose members, mostly army officers and veterans, had been General de Gaulle's followers and comrades since he broadcast his rallying call on June 18, 1940.

In September 1966 the Israeli journalist Ben-Porat was invited to luncheon at the club by one of de Gaulle's bodyguards, a huge, taciturn man, who astonished him by speaking Hebrew and Yiddish. He told Ben-Porat he was a Jew who had lived in Israel, fought in the War of Independence, and served as an Intelligence officer in the Israeli army from 1948 to 1951. Afterward he had returned to his native France.

The first Jew ever to become a President's bodyguard would never have revealed any professional secrets, but when he took leave of his new friend, he did make a strange remark: "I hope you know that General de Gaulle is deeply grateful to Israel for a personal favor. At an appropriate time he will acknowledge it."

Without another word the general's bodyguard turned and

went off, and it was only a year later that Ben-Porat managed
to solve the enigma of his parting words. His article, titled
"How Israel Helped Thwart an Attempt on de Gaulle's Life,"
told how the State of Israel had alerted the French secret service to an attack on de Gaulle that the OAS (Organisation de
l'Armée Secrète) had scheduled for February 1963. Israel had
got wind that a number of army officers who wanted Algeria to
remain French were plotting to assassinate de Gaulle while he
was on a visit to the military academy. Israel had warned the
French secret service, which made several arrests and foiled
the conspirators before they could act.

There is some truth in Ben-Porat's story, but there are several
versions of Israel's part in preventing de Gaulle's assassination.
Our version puts the date two years earlier, at a critical time
for the Fifth Republic.

When de Gaulle assumed power after the riots of May 13,
1958, there were many who thought he would crush the Algerian revolt, halt France's inclination to get out of Algeria, and
re-establish her hold on that country. Then, two years later, he
opened negotiations with the leaders of the rebellion. The
parleys in Melun, it is true, did not get very far, but those who
wanted France to retain Algeria were in no doubt that deep
in his heart de Gaulle had decided to give Algeria to the
Arabs.

Early in 1961 the core of what would become the OAS was
created, and on January 25, 1961, the barricades went up in
Algiers. De Gaulle firmly suppressed the insurrection and
ordered severe punishments for the high-ranking army officers
involved in it, a reaction that indicated he would not hesitate to
use the same tactics to smash the supporters of a French Algeria. His enemies began thinking their only hope was the permanent removal of General de Gaulle.

In the second half of March 1961 an Israeli staying in France was invited to the house of a Frenchman well known for his sympathy for the State of Israel although he was a devout Catholic. After a certain amount of small talk the Frenchman introduced the topic of assassination as a not wholly repugnant means of achieving political ends and hinted that though the death of de Gaulle was only a dream, if that dream came true, France would be saved.

As the hours passed, the Frenchman got down to his real intention. In December 1960, he said, there had been a plot to assassinate de Gaulle, but for various reasons it was never carried out, and a new attempt was scheduled for the summer or early fall. Then the Frenchman laid his cards on the table. "We want Israel," he said, "to assist certain right-wing and army circles in assassinating de Gaulle."

He then explained to his astonished guest that neither Frenchmen nor Israelis needed to be directly concerned with the plot. He and his friends had already prepared their plan: an Israeli Arab was to be trained for the job in the utmost secrecy. He would be brought to France as an Algerian Arab, and he was to assassinate de Gaulle according to a plan that had been worked out down to the last tiny detail. The public would think that the leaders of the FLN (Front de Libération Nationale) were the perpetrators of the murder. The real conspirators would thus avoid all suspicion. The assassination would release such fierce hatred against the Arabs and the self-determination of Algeria that the atmosphere would be favorable for a seizure of power by the partisans of "French Algeria" (Algerie Française).

"As a token of gratitude to Israel for her assistance," said the Frenchman, "my friends are ready to promise the Israeli government, that if they get control of France, they will furnish Israel all the arms she needs for her defense for years to come, and at no charge whatsoever."

The proposition sounded so fantastic that the Israeli could

not take his host seriously. All he said was that he would not advise such a procedure and took his leave. He attached no importance whatever to the talk.

A few days later the same Israeli was chatting with Walter Eytan, Israel's ambassador to France, when he suddenly remembered his evening with the Frenchman and reported it to the ambassador as a joke. Eytan, however, quickly grasped that here was an extremely serious situation. He immediately wrote a personal and confidential letter to Foreign Minister Golda Meir and entrusted it for delivery to an embassy counselor who was leaving that day for Israel.

The message so disturbed Golda Meir that she quickly called in some of her closest advisers and associates and gave them the gist of Eytan's letter. All agreed that Israel could by no means lend assistance to some extremist group that was plotting to assassinate de Gaulle, but should immediately warn the President of France of the danger that lay in wait for him.

That decision evolved from Israel's foreign policy of maintaining relations only with the legitimate chiefs of foreign states and never lending any aid to subversive movements against a legally constituted government. In the case at hand, however, that did not seem enough, for if Israel did not warn de Gaulle, it would appear that she was in on the plot against him.

The conferees examined the eventualities with the utmost care. It was possible that the officers' plot would fail, in which event they would be arrested and might well divulge that Israel had played a part in their conspiracy. Israel would then be suspected of having known about the conspiracy and by keeping still would be thought an indirect contributor to the attempted assassination of a friendly chief of state.

Another possibility had to be faced, namely, that the Frenchman's proposition represented a challenge on the part of French military circles, for at that time there were rumors in

Paris that Israel had secretly promised aid to the conservative wing of the French army out of her fear that if France granted independence to Algeria, the way would be paved for a reconciliation of France with the Arab states, which would lead to a cooling of the friendly relations between France and Israel. (In fact, that is exactly what did happen.)

There was also the possibility that those in France who distrusted Israel were trying to test her loyalty to de Gaulle's government, in which event it was imperative that Israel immediately inform the French of the plot in order to free herself from such unjustified suspicion.

Golda Meir decided to take the matter to Ben-Gurion, but since she was obliged to keep an important engagement elsewhere, she gave her advisers full authority to explain the situation to the Old Man and to recommend that he immediately get off a warning to Paris in his own name. Ben-Gurion asked the opinion of some of his own advisers, among them Iser Harel.

While Eytan's letter was being explained to Ben-Gurion and various points of view about it were being expressed, Iser glanced at the Old Man. Ben-Gurion was not even listening to his own advisers' opinions. His face was scarlet, and he seemed profoundly upset.

"Why didn't you tell me at once?" he yelled. Then, grabbing the telephone: "Get me Walter Eytan in Paris. And hurry!"

"Why haven't you done anything about this already?" he shouted at the group. "Why didn't Eytan immediately warn de Gaulle? Eytan is a man of sense, he should have gone to de Gaulle at once. There's not a moment to lose!"

The officials had a hard time calming Ben-Gurion down until a highly classified telegram could be composed with precise instructions to the ambassador to France.

On the following day, March 29, 1961, an Israeli diplomat was quietly admitted to the Elysée Palace, where he asked to see Colonel de Boissieu, the President's son-in-law and the head of his military council, on a matter of great importance. De Boissieu could not conceal his emotions as he listened to the diplomat's story. He thanked him warmly and immediately alerted the French secret service. Some days later the Israelis received through unofficial channels an oral expression of thanks on the part of de Gaulle, but they did not try to learn what use had been made of the names and the facts they had conveyed to the Elysée Palace.

Less than a month later, on April 22, 1961, the generals' abortive revolt in Algeria occurred. It appeared that the plan to assassinate de Gaulle had been part of that conspiracy, in which it would have been the first step and probably would have made the putsch succeed. (It is likely that the removal of the general had been planned by a small group of conspirators who were in touch with the Algerian generals but had not told them everything about the conspiracy.) Since the death of de Gaulle was essential for the plan's success, it can be assumed that Israel had foiled the entire plot by her timely warning.

After the failure of their coup, the conspirators were brought to justice. General Zeller testified in court that the rebel generals had counted on their regime being recognized by such countries as Portugal, South Africa, and Israel. This author was present in the courtroom when Israel was mentioned. The judges and the French authorities in general paid little attention to Zeller's statement, and the reference to Israel quickly disappeared from the front pages of the newspapers. France was quite right not to believe that testimony.

On June 5, 1961, when David Ben-Gurion was visiting France as the President's guest, de Gaulle offered this toast: "How good and pleasant it is for friends to meet once more! We assure you of our firm and lasting attachment, and I raise my glass to Israel, our friend and our ally."

It is said that one of the reasons for that warm expression of feeling was the secret message sent to the Elysée Palace on March 29, 1961, by the government of Israel.

24

Where Is Yossele?

"WHERE IS YOSSELE?"

In 1961 that question had all Israel in a frenzy. It aroused public opinion, split political parties, made front-page headlines, sparked violent arguments.

Yossele Schumacher was an eight-year-old who had been kidnaped in 1960 by a sect of religious fanatics aided by the child's grandfather, who wanted to bring him up an orthodox Jew. The police could not discover the slightest trace of the boy.

Early in March 1962 Ben-Gurion summoned Iser Harel, who had just returned from a trip abroad to handle some Mossad emergencies. As usual, Ben-Gurion was friendly and talked to Iser for quite a while about one subject or another. Iser, who knew the Old Man well enough to see that his mind was not fully on what he was saying, kept wondering when he would come to the point.

Then Ben-Gurion abruptly asked: "Can you find that child, do you think?"

He did not say exactly what child he had in mind, but Iser was well used to his way of playing the game.

"If you want me to, I will try."

He returned to his office and ordered an operational file opened. On its cover he lettered the title: "Operation Tiger."

Yossele was a lively, good-looking, dark-haired child, whose only mistake had been to choose the wrong set of parents. That, at least, was the opinion of his grandfather, the venerable Nahman Shtarkes, a fanatical orthodox Jew, whose experiences had made him hard and stubborn. Nothing could change his mind, neither persons, nor the persecution and the concentration camps of the Soviets, nor the harsh climate of Siberia, where he had spent a part of World War II and lost one eye and three toes from frostbite. His morale had not failed then, but his hatred of the Soviets had increased, and it reached the point of hysteria when his youngest son was murdered by a gang of Russian thugs. He still had two other sons, however, Shalom and Ovadiah, and one daughter, Ida. After long wanderings in Russia and Poland, the family finally got back to Lwów.

Shtarkes then decided to emigrate with his wife and Shalom to Israel. Since he was a member of the fanatical sect known as the Hassidim of Breslau, he settled in the fanatics' sector of Jerusalem, Mea Shearim.

In 1957, Ida, too, came to Israel with her husband Alter Schumacher, a tailor, and their two children, Zina and Joseph, who was nicknamed Yossele. They settled in the small seaside resort of Nahariya.

Fortune did not smile on the Schumachers. Since they could find no work and were obliged to sell their possessions, they left Nahariya and tried their luck elsewhere, but it was not until several months later that they found a means of livelihood in the Tel Aviv region, where the father hired himself out to a textile factory and the mother got a job with a photographer. They went deeply into debt to buy a small apartment in the suburbs, and in order to keep their expenses to a minimum sent Zina to a religious institution and Yossele to his grandfather.

Nahman Shtarkes was overjoyed to have his grandson with him, and the youngster quickly adapted himself to the unconventional way of life in Mea Shearim.

Ida and Alter Schumacher, who had not reached the end of their woes, wrote to their friends in Russia that maybe it would have been better for them not to have come to Israel. Old Shtarkes got his hands on some of the replies to those lamentations and concluded that his daughter and his son-in-law intended to return to Russia with their children. That's when he made up his mind not to give Yossele back to his parents.

The Schumachers' situation took a turn for the better, however, in late December 1959, and they were able to have their son with them again. Joyfully Ida went to Jerusalem to fetch Yossele, but neither her boy nor her father was at home.

"Yossele is at the synagogue with his grandfather," said her mother, "and you must not disturb them. Tomorrow your brother Shalom will bring Yossele to you."

On the next day, however, Shalom showed up at the Schumachers' alone. "Father has decided not to give you back the child," he said.

Ida rushed to Jerusalem. Her father was in his apartment, but Yossele was not. Ida burst into tears and begged her father to give her back her son. At first Shtarkes absolutely refused, but finally he promised her he would discuss the matter with her again at the end of the week, provided she came to Jerusalem with her husband.

Ida and Alter spent Friday night with her parents, and that time Yossele was at home. On Saturday evening, when the Schumachers were getting ready to take the boy with them, the grandmother protested.

"It's cold," she said, "and late. Let him sleep here, and tomorrow I'll bring him to you."

Ida consented. She tucked Yossele in, kissed him good-night, and left with her husband.

On the following day there was no sign of either the boy or

his grandmother. Ida and Alter went back to Jerusalem, but it was a futile trip. The child had vanished. Old Shtarkes would not utter a word in spite of their tears and supplications and appeals to his pity. Finally the Schumachers went to the police.

On January 15, 1960, the Court of Appeals ordered Nahman Shtarkes to return the child to his parents within thirty days. When the patriarch persisted in his refusal, the police opened a file, "Yossele Schumacher 720/60," and began a search for the boy.

Two months later the police had to report to the Supreme Court: "The child has disappeared. It is unlikely that either secret agents or informers can solve the mystery." Consequently the police asked the court to be relieved of the responsibility of a longer search. The court reprimanded the police for its strange confession of weakness and ordered old Shtarkes arrested and held in custody until the child was restored.

If anyone had thought imprisonment would break down Nahman Shtarkes' resolve, he was wrong. His passionate religious zeal kept him from revealing what he knew. The police were sure that he had not hidden the child all by himself, but had had the assistance of some extreme orthodox, yet who they were Shtarkes would not say. He was utterly convinced that in hiding the child he had saved Yossele's soul in obedience to the Divine Will. He was certain that his daughter would take Yossele to Russia, where he would be converted to Christianity, and his sacred duty was to prevent that blasphemy. Rabbi Frank, the grand rabbi of Jerusalem, approved old Shtarkes' attitude and urged every devout Jew to come to his aid.

Rabbi Frank died on December 10, 1960. On his deathbed he confessed to his daughter that he was remorseful over that endorsement, but it was too late. Old Shtarkes had long since lost control of the situation; the child was no longer in his hands, but in the power of some fanatics who would stop at

nothing in what they considered a sacred endeavor. They believed they were acting according to the Jewish command-
ment: "He who saves a single soul for Israel is the equal of him
who saves the whole world."

In May 1960 the question appeared for the first time on the
Knesset agenda. The press had got hold of the story, and the
public reaction to it boded no good. The first to sense these attitudes were the religious deputies. Shlomo Lorentz, the Knesset representative of an ultra-orthodox party, felt that the kidnaping could unleash a religious war in Israel, a country that
was very sensitive to the delicate balance between church and
state. His many personal efforts to find the child and return
him to his parents included arranging a meeting between
Shtarkes and the Schumachers, in the course of which Yossele's
parents signed an affidavit that they would give the boy an
orthodox education. With this document Lorentz went to the
orthodox Rabbi Meizish, who was involved with the kidnaping.
Meizish gave Lorentz to understand that the child would be
returned to his parents on the condition that his abductors
would not be harassed.

Lorentz reported this answer to Chief of Police Joseph Nahmias. "I consent," Nahmias said. "Take my car and go find the
kid. You have parliamentary immunity, and no one would follow my car anyway, so those involved will not be known."

In high spirits Lorentz returned to Meizish's house, but the
rabbi refused to honor his word and sent Lorentz away.

The police were powerless. Israel was literally strewn with
religious communities, Talmudic schools, and orthodox villages, all of which were closed worlds living according to their
own laws, a cardinal principle of which was silence. Somewhere among them Yossele must be hidden. How to find him,
however, was something else again.

On August 10, 1961, when the tension had considerably increased, the Supreme Court declared: "The kidnaping of Yossele is the most despicable crime ever to have been committed in the whole history of Israel."

The general anger now took on a disturbing quality. In August there was formed a National Committee for the Return of Yossele, which distributed pamphlets, circulated petitions that thousands signed, organized meetings, and supplied the press with detailed information on the progress of the search. The specter of a cultural war loomed on the horizon.

Early in August 1961, barely ten days before the general elections, the police staged a surprise raid on the orthodox village of Komemiut in the south and discovered, twenty months too late, that Yossele had been there in December 1959 in the home of one Zalman Kot. The child had been brought to Komemiut by his uncle Shalom Shtarkes and was called "Israel Hazak."

Shalom Shtarkes himself had left Israel in May 1960 and was living in Golders Green, London, where he was awaiting the birth of his first child. The Israeli police requested that he be extradited, and after much bureaucratic palaver the English police did arrest him. After the birth of a son, the whole Shalom Shtarkes family moved into Shalom's jail cell, where the ceremony of circumcision was performed.

Still, no Yossele. Old Shtarkes, who had been released from jail for reasons of health, was locked up again, and the people of Komemiut were arrested and questioned but with no results. Experts were of the opinion that the child was no longer in Israel and might well be dead of some disease contracted during his sequestration. The police were the laughingstock of the whole country. The indignation of nonreligious groups produced incidents in which students of rabbinical schools were insulted and injured. The authority of the government was at stake, for the general public had good reason to believe that the administration was being unduly considerate of the orthodox in order to avoid an explosion. In the spring of 1962 the tension reached its peak when violent arguments shook the Knesset.

That was the time when Ben-Gurion, fearing serious consequences, decided it was time to call in Little Iser.

When Iser agreed to take on the search for Yossele, he had no idea that it would prove to be the most complicated assignment of his entire career. It was also the first time he took Rivka into his confidence. "The prestige of the government is at stake," he told her.

First, he went to the police. All too happy to be rid of their thankless task, they gladly agreed to become mere auxiliaries. Joseph Nahmias took a rather skeptical tone, however, when he asked Iser: "Do you really and truly believe it is still possible to find that kid?"

Joel Morag, on the other hand, was far from pleased, and several of the Secret Service staff shared his feelings that the Yossele case was of a social and religious nature and no proper assignment for security officers. But Iser considered it a matter of safeguarding the prestige and authority of the state as well as a humane and national duty.

Operation Tiger eventually involved more than forty agents. The first group, which tried to penetrate the strange orthodox world within Israel itself, got nowhere, for its members stood out boldly among the fanatics, who had long black caftans, fur hats, long beards, and curled side locks. "I felt as if I had landed on Mars," said one of them, "and had to get lost in a crowd of little green men without being noticed."

Iser went through the file over and over again, patiently reading and rereading the documents that had accumulated in it over the years. His intuition led him to one conclusion only — the child must be outside the country, for there was no trace of him whatever in Israel.

Then a bizarre piece of news came to Iser's attention. In mid-

March a group of Swiss orthodox — men, women, and children — arrived in Israel with the coffin of the spiritual leader of their sect whom they wished to bury in the Holy Land. Perhaps, thought Iser, that mission is only an excuse, and the fanatics are here for the real purpose of spiriting Yossele away with them. Iser had Lod Airport carefully watched and sent agents to Zurich to keep an eye on the zealots after their return. But after a week his men reported that no one corresponding to Yossele had been mixed in with the Swiss orthodox children.

The incident only strengthened Iser's conviction that the boy was no longer in Israel and that he had to be looked for in ultra-orthodox centers throughout the world. He ordered operations started simultaneously in Italy, Austria, France, Switzerland, Great Britain, Belgium, South Africa, and the United States. Religious communities, Jewish orphanages, and Talmudic schools were gone over with a fine-toothed comb. No results.

Even Iser's most loyal associates began to complain and to urge him to call off the hunt, but Iser hung on like a bulldog. Come what may, he was going to find that child.

"The boy had become a fixation with him," said one of Iser's intimates. "At that time Iser was under considerable tension. He was the subject of attacks from Ben-Gurion's 'court' and was quarreling with Shimon Peres and other government officials. But he was determined to succeed at any cost."

25

The Mohel
and the Arab Prince

By April no one but Iser Harel any longer believed that Operation Tiger would succeed. In spite of all his disappointments and frustrations, Iser would not give up, but spent almost every night in his European office, examining reports and writing instructions to his widely scattered searchers. Then one fine morning a ray of light pierced his gloom.

This was a report from a young orthodox Jew named Meir, who was not a regular employee of the Secret Service but had volunteered his help to Operation Tiger and had been sent into many extremist religious centers in Europe. In due time he had met up with a group of orthodox Jews, all businessmen or bankers, who had a deep reverence for a local rabbi, a kind of Methuselah, whom they considered a holy man. This group, which even in the heart of modern Europe still observed the customs of ancient times, told Meir an extraordinary tale about a blond, blue-eyed French Catholic woman who had helped them during the Nazi occupation of France in their efforts to keep Jews out of the clutches of the Gestapo.

Her contacts with the venerated rabbi persuaded her to the Jewish faith, and after her conversion she became a priceless asset in the group's underground activities because she could and did go anywhere in the world on her French passport. She could also change her identity as easily as her gown, and she had a keen sense of what had to be done as well as great natural intelligence. She had been in Israel, and Claude, her son by her first marriage, had elected to continue at a Talmudic school in Jerusalem the education he had begun in similar institutions in Switzerland and Aix-les-Bains. The only trouble was that no one knew where she was now, and Meir had not even learned her name.

Unrelated to the Yossele case as this story seemed, it nevertheless kindled Iser's imagination. Here was the perfect woman of a hundred faces. If she was truly a frequenter of fanatic circles, who better than she would there be to help with the abduction of Yossele? Iser bet the limit on his intuition and decided to concentrate on this mysterious convert to Judaism. His telegram to headquarters in Israel requesting information on her brought a swift reply. Her name was originally Madeleine Féraille, but after her conversion she had taken the name of Ruth Ben-David.

The subsequent check on her that Mossad agents made in France showed several errors in the account given Meir. The college-educated Madeleine Féraille had fought for the French Resistance, which had brought her into contact with the orthodox group, and her postwar relations with them had vaguely involved her in their import-export business. In 1951 Madeleine Féraille divorced her first husband, a Catholic named Henri, because she had made the acquaintance of a young Zionist rabbi in a small Alsatian town who wanted to emigrate to Israel; regardless of the protests of the Jewish community, once in Israel they decided to get married. Hence her conversion to Judaism was not so much due to love for the religion itself as for one of its adherents. She then changed her son's name to Ariel, and took him with her to Israel, where, it appears, the young rabbi left her.

Ruth Ben-David reached Jerusalem depressed and disappointed. It was this frame of mind that brought her nearer to the most extreme religionists, and she made a close tie with fanatical Rabbi Meizish. She now dressed in the orthodox fashion, strictly observed all the precepts of her new religion, and won a great deal of merit for having — thanks to her French passport — crossed into the Jordanian sector of Jerusalem to pray at the Wailing Wall.

In the early 1950s Ruth went back to France, and between her several excursions around Europe and the rest of the world lived either in Aix-les-Bains or in a pension for devout Jewesses in a Paris suburb, but she had no permanent address. The Israeli Immigration Bureau's information that she had twice gone back to Israel confirmed Iser's belief that he was on the right track.

Iser gave his agents a full description of this woman and sent them searching for her in a small European city. On the outskirts of the town, they happened upon Madeleine Féraille, or Ruth Ben-David, thumbing a ride. They were so startled to find her — or any other woman so elegantly dressed — in this situation that they did not immediately stop to pick her up, and before they could turn around for her, another car had given her a lift.

Inside the town all they could learn about her was that she had some kind of permanent relationship with a rich London jewel merchant named Joseph Domb. Domb was no stranger to Iser and his agents; he had been on their blacklist for some time as a sworn enemy of the State of Israel. A hardened fanatic, Domb was a confidant of the rabbi of the Satmar sect* in New York City and also in touch with all its branches in Europe.

Soon Iser had the news that in London Domb frequently met Madeleine Féraille privately, usually in an automobile, quite

* So named for the village in Europe from which many of its members had emigrated — Translator.

contrary to the teachings of Judaism respecting the conduct of a married man and a father. This discovery persuaded Iser that his road led to London, for Shalom and Ovadiah Shtarkes were living there, and there, too, was a branch of the Satmar sect. Furthermore, letters that he intercepted from Ruth Ben-David to her son contained veiled references to the Yossele case.

Iser deduced that the Satmar sect had engineered the kidnaping and the concealment of the child under Domb's direction and with Ruth Ben-David's help. If only she could be apprehended and questioned, she might even reveal where Yossele now was, for her new religion had apparently not struck too deep, and, after all, she was a Frenchwoman. She alone, however, was not enough. Iser knew that Domb would not talk any more than old Shtarkes or any other fanatic. He needed someone connected with Domb or with the sect who would not be so close-mouthed. His search for such a person brought to the surface Rabbi Shai Freyer.

Freyer was a mohel — that is, a rabbi who specializes in circumcising newborn Jewish boys — and he entered the picture by means of a letter that reached Iser's desk in the middle of May, having been photographed by Shin-Bet agents during their investigation of a fanatical group in New York and its counterpart in Paris. The letter, expressed in a formally religious style, was a request for the name of a mohel in Italy, where there were few if any to be found.

Reading between the lines, Iser concluded that Freyer, a man who liked travel and new experiences, would be all too willing to go to Italy to teach his art to his coreligionists there. Freyer, Iser then learned, was an associate of Joseph Domb and, like him, hated Israel and Zionism. He was also known to be a chatterbox, who had frequently expressed the opinion that Yossele should by no means be returned to his parents, and an avaricious blackguard whose piety was a mask for his far from high principles, among which was adultery. Deducing from Freyer's character that if anyone in London knew where Yossele was, this rabbi did, Iser directed his agents to drop everything and concentrate on Freyer and Ruth Ben-David.

The thing to do was get Freyer to the continent on some pretext or other so that he and Ruth could be questioned simultaneously but separately. Iser spent long nights tossing on his office cot, which his associates called "Yossele's bed," thinking up a means whereby Freyer could not elude him and also by which he could be persuaded to talk. Little by little he put together a plan.

Early in June 1962 a mysterious stranger called on a Parisian mohel of Polish origin who was said to be one of the most extreme religionists in the city's Jewish community. The expensively dressed visitor looked like an Arab and spoke French with a North African accent. He seemed very nervous, and only after extracting from the mohel a promise that their conversation would be kept absolutely secret did he reveal his purpose in a deep, hesitant voice.

"I was a Muslim in Morocco," he said, displaying his credentials, "where my father is one of the most famous sherifs in the kingdom. About a year ago I fell in love with a Moroccan Jewess and decided to abduct her and force her to marry me."

The mohel was not surprised. The story was not an uncommon one for those changing times.

"I loved her so much," the son of the sherif went on, "that I converted to Judaism and had our marriage solemnized according to the Jewish ritual. We have managed to keep that a secret. If my father found out, he would kill both my wife and me. Together and alone, we strictly observe all the rules of our new religion, but in public I pose as a Muslim.

"A few weeks ago my wife was delivered of a son. I took her to London to have the baby, and she is still there. She insists that the baby be circumcised according to the teachings of our religion, and I have no objection whatever, except that the ceremony must be performed in the utmost secrecy. Otherwise the Muslims we know would find out and kill all three of us.

"I'm afraid to bring my wife and son to Paris because it is full of North Africans, and we would be quickly discovered. That's why I have come to you instead of to a North African rabbi. Will you come to London to circumcise my son? Naturally I will pay all expenses over and above your fee. I must warn you, however, that it is a dangerous undertaking."

Now it was the Polish mohel's turn to be nervous. "Why do I have to go to London?" he asked fearfully. "There are plenty of excellent mohels in London. Just wait a minute, and I will give you a letter of introduction to one of my colleagues there."

"Please," said the son of the sherif, "be sure to write the letter in very vague terms, and by no means say anything in it about what I have just told you. If it should fall into the wrong hands, it would mean death for me and my family."

"Of course."

The mohel then wrote a short note to Dr. Homa, the president of the association of orthodox mohels in London.

On the following day two dark-skinned men called on Dr. Homa. One was the sherif's son; the other, a "Moroccan Jew," an intimate friend of the Arab noble. After giving Dr. Homa the Polish mohel's letter, the prince told him a slightly different story from the one he had recited in Paris:

"My wife is now recovering from childbirth in Morocco, and I want to bring her and the baby to London or the continent for the circumcision. Or, of course, I could have the mohel go to Morocco with all expenses paid and a handsomely increased honorarium. Could you possibly tell me of someone who might be willing to undertake this trip?"

"I know just the man for you," Dr. Homa said. "He is a man of the world, and he is used to travel."

At once he wrote a letter of introduction addressed to Mohel Shai Freyer.

Freyer warmly welcomed the Arab prince and his Jewish friend, listened to their story, and unhesitatingly agreed to circumcise the child.

His visitors then said that there were three places possible for the ceremony: London, Marrakesh, or some large city on the continent. They stressed the hazards of bringing the mother and her son to London and strongly hinted that if Freyer would go to Morocco or to the continent, he would be well rewarded.

Freyer did not miss their implications and said he would be willing to go anywhere they chose.

"In that event," said his visitors, "there are many reasons why a European city would be best."

The hook now firmly in his greedy mouth, Freyer agreed, and within a few hours was in possession of a plane ticket for a continental city. When he presented it to the mohel, the Arab prince said that he himself had to go back to Morocco at once, but would return a few days later with his wife and son and would meet Freyer at the apartment he would have rented for the ceremony on June 20, 1962.

While the net was closing in on Freyer, Iser's men laid a trap for Ruth Ben-David. After many discouragements, luck finally favored them by bringing into their hands some letters addressed to the beautiful convert. One of these, a reply to a newspaper advertisement offering her country house for sale, solved the problem for them. They immediately wrote to the box number given and offered Ruth more than she was asking on the grounds that they were businessmen looking for a permanent spot for their annual vacation.

As soon as Ruth answered, giving the address of the house, they went to inspect it. When they returned, they wrote that they would buy it and requested a meeting to settle the deal on June 21, 1962, in the lobby of a big commercial hotel, in the same city where Mohel Shai Freyer would be met by his Arab prince on the same day.

A few days beforehand Iser Harel and his men descended one by one on the city in question. They rented several cars and two houses in a quiet suburb and reserved a few apartments — all with quick and easy means of exit in case of need. Then Iser summoned one of his experts from Israel to set up a system of communication among these abodes and his own headquarters in the city center, which were also to have permanent contact with headquarters in Tel Aviv.

Iser had already decided that the best means to get Ruth Ben-David's secret out of her was through her son Ariel, who he was sure knew a lot about Yossele. Ariel, less a fanatic than his mother, had put down roots in Israel. Consequently Iser also ordered a system of communication that would permit him to synchronize his questioning of Ruth with that of her son in Israel, in order to be able to use the answers of the son for the questioning of the mother.

On June 20, Shai Freyer landed at the airport in the best of moods and was met by his North African friend in a car.

"We'll go straight to the apartment," said the prince. "Mother and son are waiting for us there."

Neither a mother nor a baby greeted Freyer, however, but several strangers who said they were friends of the Moroccan. The mohel was setting out his instruments on a table in the corner when, to his considerable surprise, the prince's friends started asking him questions about the kidnaping of Yossele.

Freyer shrugged. "I don't know a thing about it."

Just as he was about to begin the ancient rite of circumcision it dawned on him that the whole situation was a fake and that the prince and his friends were Israelis determined to drag out of him the place where the kidnaped boy was hidden.

Freyer raised his hands to heaven. "I am dreadfully sorry," he said, "but I do not know a thing."

On the next morning, June 21, Ruth Ben-David arrived in the hotel lobby where the two "businessmen" were waiting. But it was not actually Ruth Ben-David, rather Madeleine Féraille, for when she was not out with pious Jews she resumed her original costume and appearance. The two men who rose to greet her found themselves in the company of a fashionably dressed, tall, slim woman of ravishing beauty — a real Frenchwoman.

The business part of their talk, conducted in English, proceeded perfectly, and Madeleine never suspected the identity of her two buyers. But when they called their lawyer, who had promised to attend the conference, he said he had been detained by an emergency and suggested they all come to his house, where the papers could be signed more quickly than at the hotel.

Off went the three of them to the suburb where the lawyer lived, but in driving through the midcity traffic, the agent at the wheel got so entranced by Madeleine that he went through a red light and was stopped by a policeman. Madeleine rose to the occasion, gave the policeman the business, and got the panic-stricken agents off without arrest.

Presently they stopped before a pretty house, whose door opened and closed on Madeleine Féraille. Only then did she learn that she was in the power of Mossad.

At Beer Yaakov in Israel, at exactly the same time, policemen and Shin-Bet agents arrested Ariel Ben-David.

26

Madeleine's Secret

THE FIRST REPORTS of the interrogations that Iser received could be summed up in one word — frustration.

The conception Iser had formed of Freyer corresponded exactly to reality with one exception. Iser had overlooked the possibility that Freyer might know absolutely nothing about where Yossele was hidden. That was what Freyer kept saying until the agents questioning him concluded that he was telling the truth. Then they told him that there never was to be a circumcision ceremony, but they would not grant him permission to return to London.

There could be no question of releasing Freyer before the question of Ruth Ben-David was over, for otherwise Freyer would warn Domb, and Yossele would be immediately transferred to another hiding place. The agents who kept Freyer in custody got on so well with him that on his fervent request they even took him to the red light district of the city.

Quite a different atmosphere prevailed in the isolated suburban house where Ruth Ben-David was being detained. At first paralyzed with fear, she relaxed somewhat when she learned she was in the hands of good Israelis, but she never wavered under the direct questions the agents kept flinging at her.

"Madame, we know you were mixed up in the Yossele affair. We want the child!"

"I do not know anything about it, and I have nothing to tell you about it."

Still, she was Iser's only hope of success.

The Israelis treated her well, providing her with prayer books, kosher food, and candles for the Sabbath. The agents kept out of the wing where she was lodged, and the room next to hers was occupied by a trained nurse in case of emergency. The agents tried day and night, however, to get her to talk, but although she stopped denying that she had anything to do with the kidnaping, she kept repeating: "I will tell you nothing."

The interrogation of her son in Israel, however, was beginning to produce results. His questioners kept telling him things they said had come straight from his mother's lips. "Your mother has confessed to everything," they said. "Your lies will get you nowhere. Tell the truth!"

Ariel finally admitted that his mother had played a part in the kidnaping. The agents immediately confronted Ruth with Ariel's statement. "We've got your son," they told her. "He is likely to get a stiff punishment. He has confessed everything. Don't you care what happens to him?"

Ruth Ben-David even then refused to talk.

Finally Iser decided the time had come for him to take over.

Iser Harel and Ruth Ben-David sat facing each other across a table. Beside each of them sat an interpreter. Behind them stood the Mossad agents.

Iser knew well that this fiercely determined woman would not yield to any argument whatever or to any threats. He would have to wheedle her into acknowledging that her secret was out, that her son had betrayed her, and that what she had done would haunt her all the days of her life. He would have to appeal to her moral instincts. Since she had not been a Jew all her life, nor her forebears, she might eventually listen to reason.

"I represent the Israeli government," Iser said slowly. "Your son has told us everything, and we have lots of other information about you. Most of your secrets are known to us. You have no defense against us. We are sorry that we had to bring you here by force. You converted to Judaism, and Judaism means Israel. Without Israel, Judaism could not survive. The kidnaping of Yossele has dealt a terrible blow to the religious in Israel. It may mean a divided nation. You could be the cause of shedding the blood of brothers in a civil war. Just think what might happen to that child! He could get sick, even die. How could you and your accomplices face his parents then? You are a woman, and a mother. If someone disapproved of the way you were bringing up your son and took him away from you, how would you feel? Could you sleep at night? We are not fighting against religion, you must understand. Our only purpose is to find that child. As soon as we have him in our hands, you may go free, and your son also. Yossele will find his parents again, and Israel will be united once more."

Before Iser finished, Ruth's face had begun to show her inner conflict. She was clearly in a state of high tension, fighting against herself as only a strong person can before an uncompromising dilemma. Iser could not help thinking that she was trying to pry herself loose from the vise by placing upon him some of the burden she found too great to bear herself.

The Israeli agents were motionless as statues. They too believed the moment of truth was at hand.

Finally Ruth raised her head. "How do I know that you are a bona fide representative of the State of Israel? How can I trust you?"

Iser pulled out his diplomatic passport, issued in his true name, and handed it to Ruth Ben-David. His associates were dumfounded. How could he tell her his right name? He must be mad!

Iser, however, knew that the only chance he had of success with her was to show he was sincere and had confidence in her.

For a long moment Ruth gazed at the seal of Israel embossed on the passport. She bit her lips until the blood came. Finally she murmured: "I can't take any more. I'm going to crack . . ." Then suddenly, without raising her eyes, she said all in one breath: "The child is with the Gertner family, 126 Penn Street, Brooklyn, New York. They call him Yankele."

Iser shook her hand and left the room.

That night Iser, certain that Ruth Ben-David had told him the truth, wired Israel. Jerusalem alerted New York and ordered the security officer of the Israeli Consulate to check on the Brooklyn address. A few hours later the officer cabled back that the address was correct and that the Gertners lived in the Satmar district. Should he try to get the child?

"No," Iser cabled back. He was afraid that the presence of an Israeli in that ultra-orthodox section of New York might arouse the suspicions of the fanatics and cause them to hide the child elsewhere.

Iser decided to approach the Americans through the proper channels. Ambassador Avraham Harman in Washington could surely put him in touch with the FBI, which he would ask to find the child at the address given and send him to Israel.

Then disquieting telegrams began pouring into Iser's headquarters. The representatives of Israel in Washington were reporting that the Americans wanted to be absolutely sure the child was at that address. The Americans' reticence was due to the coming congressional elections. The Satmar sect controlled almost one hundred thousand votes, which the administration did not wish to risk losing. At midnight Iser lost patience. Picking up the telephone, he shouted: "Get me Harman in Washington.

"Good evening, Harman. Iser Harel speaking. I want you to go straight to Attorney General Robert Kennedy and tell him for me that the FBI must go after that boy at once. An Israeli child has the same rights as an American child. Tell him to get on the ball."

Flabbergasted, Harman replied: "Iser, how can you talk like that?" Then he indirectly let Iser know that the FBI was undoubtedly monitoring their conversation.

"So much the better," said Iser, hoping that if the Americans were indeed listening in, his firm words might rouse them to action.

Harman said he feared there would be both diplomatic and legal complications.

"I didn't ask your opinion," Iser said. "Tell them that if they don't act immediately they will be held responsible for anything that happens. I absolutely demand that you go at once to Kennedy and do what I tell you."

A few hours later Iser was called to the telephone. New York informed him that Robert Kennedy had taken immediate action. A team of FBI agents, accompanied by the Israeli security officer, had already gone to Brooklyn. The child had been found, and he was indeed Yossele. He was now in a safe place, and everything was being prepared for his transfer to Israel.

The fourth of July 1962 was like a national holiday in Israel as a cheering crowd surged toward the plane that was landing at Lod Airport bearing Yossele, "the child of discord." Two hours earlier, Nahman Shtarkes had been freed from jail, and he too had come to the airport, but he was not allowed to approach his grandson.

The press let itself go in its praise of the dedicated efficiency of the Secret Service. Israel was fast becoming the only country in the world where that body was loved and admired by the whole nation.

Ruth Ben-David, however, did not share in the enthusiasm. For her the day of rejoicing was a night of tears. As had been promised, she was set free on the day Yossele was found. So was Freyer, who hastened back to London to tell Domb and his other friends about the vicissitudes of his captivity with the Zionist infidels.

Ruth, her spirit broken, went to the fanatic Jews of Paris to make her confession. "I am guilty," she sobbed. "I betrayed our cause. I can never forgive myself. I had a precious treasure entrusted to me, and I could not keep it."

Only after this happy ending did the whole truth come to light.

It had all begun with a telegram. In the spring of 1960, while Yossele was still wandering clandestinely in Israel, Ruth's old friend Rabbi Meizish had cabled her in Paris: "Come immediately to Jerusalem. I have a good match for you."

Ruth took the first plane. In Jerusalem, Rabbi Meizish translated his "good match" as his intention to give her Yossele to smuggle out of Israel and thus save him from the blasphemy of his parents. Ruth agreed enthusiastically. Thanks to her work in the French Resistance, it took her only twenty-four hours to think up a way to execute her mission.

With some trouble Ruth managed to procure the means to alter her passport, changing the name of her son from Claude to Claudine and the date of his birth from 1943 to 1953. Then she boarded a plane for Genoa, where she bought a ticket for Haifa on one of the ships that regularly left Genoa with immigrants to Israel.

On the dock she began to play, as if by chance, with the eight-year-old daughter of some immigrants, and at the hour of departure, while the girl's parents were struggling with their luggage, she led the child up to the deck with her. The Italian immigration officers looked at Madeleine Féraille's passport

254 Spies in the Promised Land

and confirmed that she was indeed a Frenchwoman traveling with a little girl. Once in Israel, Ruth Ben-David went through the same procedure and was successful again.

A few days later she appeared at Lod Airport to take the plane for Zurich with her "daughter Claudine," who was none other than Yossele Schumacher, unrecognizable in a dress and patent leather pumps.

In Switzerland, Yossele spent a year in Rabbi Soloveitchik's boarding school for religious Jewish children. No one suspected his true identity, but Ruth Ben-David kept on guard. When the excitement began in Israel and the search for Yossele reached a large scale, she showed up at the boarding school, dressed Yossele in girl's clothes once again, and, thanks to her miracle-working passport, got him into France. There, under the guise of "Menachem, an orphan of Swiss parentage," he was enrolled in a school for religious children in Meaux, where he stayed for one year.

Ruth Ben-David did not have to worry about money, for she had a fortune of her own in France, and before she left Israel with Yossele-Claudine, the rabbi of a fanatical sect had given her a to-whom-it-may-concern letter specifying that she was soliciting funds for a religious school in Jerusalem. The sums she collected, however, were devoted exclusively to Operation Yossele.

In March 1962, when the Israeli Secret Service mounted Operation Tiger, Ruth smelled danger. For the third time she got Yossele into female attire and flew with him to America as his mother. There she went to the head of the Satmar sect, Rabbi Joelish Teitlebaum, who immediately directed the Gertners to take "Yankele" in and pass him off as a cousin who had come for a long visit. According to one version of the story, Joseph Domb and his friend Meir Lifschitz, both of whom had also been involved in the kidnaping, met the Satmar rabbi on the same day.

Madeleine Féraille–Ruth Ben-David had so admirably demonstrated all the qualities desirable for a secret agent that it is not surprising Mossad offered her a job. But by then it was too late. In Jerusalem she took refuge in the closed world of Mea Shearim, and three years later she married Rabbi Amram Bloi, the seventy-two-year-old head of the most fanatical of all the sects, Neture Karta.

Iser attended none of the receptions and banquets given in celebration of Yossele's safe return by various prominent persons who acted as if they themselves had found the boy. He spent a few more days in a European capital, where his associates gave a small party in his honor at which a Mossad agent made the following toast: "To the child returned to his fatherland, to the iron-willed man who found him, to the state that knows so well how to protect its citizens."

Iser's associates presented him with a plush tiger cub as a souvenir of the operation and shipped to Iser's house in Zahal "Yossele's bed," on which he had passed so many sleepless nights laying plans.

Iser Harel never laid eyes on Yossele Schumacher either during or after Operation Tiger until nine years later, when the author of this book invited Yossele — by then a first-class soldier in a tank division — to a party in Iser Harel's honor. The two heroes of Operation Tiger shook hands for the first time. Yossele then declared: "I must say I am deeply touched. Iser Harel has been the most important person in my life. Without him I would not be here among you."

27

Nasser's Secret Weapons

THE DIRECTORS AND THE AGENTS of the Secret Service were unanimous in their opinion that without Iser Harel's dedicated zeal Yossele would never have seen his parents again. There were many others, however, who criticized the Service for having done practically nothing for months but search for Yossele. Some added that the Yossele affair was not the province of the Secret Service and certainly did not merit such a deployment of men, effort, and money.

Those who found fault with Iser had heard his opinion on the moral and national importance of Operation Tiger at a time when a religious war was threatening the Jewish State, but they had not been convinced he was right. They kept repeating that all the resources and all the efforts of the Service should never be devoted to one particular affair unless the result would bring it unusual distinction.

The Mossad agents kept these criticisms from reaching Iser's ears, but shortly after the happy conclusion of Operation Tiger similar reproaches were hurled in his face. Several important persons who had never shown much affection for Iser began to accuse him of neglecting dangers that threatened Israel's survival as a nation while he was trying to find "his" Yossele.

Those dangers exploded with a fearful din in the skies of the Middle East only two weeks after Yossele was restored to his parents. On July 21, 1962, Egypt surprised the world by successfully launching four rockets. Two were of the Al Zafir (Victory) type, with a range of 175 miles, and two of the Al Kahir (Conqueror) type, with a range of 350 miles. In Cairo, Gamal Abdel Nasser proudly proclaimed to an ecstatic crowd that the rockets were capable of destroying any and every target "south of Beirut."

Being "south of Beirut," the administration of Israel were smitten not only with astonishment but with grave anxiety.

Israel herself had started the rocket race in the Middle East one year earlier, when, on July 6, 1961, at 4:41 A.M., the scientists of the Defense Ministry launched Shavit 2, a solid-fuel rocket that soared to a height of sixty miles. Official releases informed the nation and the world that it was merely an experimental rocket intended for meteorological research, but commentators pointed out that the date had been chosen for political reasons, namely, that the Egyptians had bought exploratory rockets from the United States with the intention of launching them on July 23, Egypt's national holiday. Israel had therefore decided to launch her own rocket in order to pre-empt Egypt's show of prestige.

These explanations seemed a little far-fetched inasmuch as the Egyptians did not proceed to any launching on the anniversary of their revolution, and many Israelis were inclined to believe that Shavit 2 was an "election rocket" designed to influence the voters who would go to the polls on August 15, 1962.

The Israelis, however, were too busy congratulating themselves on having made the space club to heed the warnings that began to appear in the press. "The rocket race has begun," announced Uri Dan in *Ma'ariv* on July 9, and he predicted a great influx of Soviet guided missiles into the U.A.R. On November 7, Ze'ev Shiff wrote in *Ha'aretz* that German experts were working on rockets for Egypt.

On the same day it was learned that Dr. Eugen Sänger, one of the most famous of German rocket specialists, had resigned as director of the Institute of Research on Jet-Propulsion in Stuttgart because the Bonn government had opposed his activities as adviser to the Nasser regime. German newspapers stated that Professor Sänger had already recruited several department heads from the Institute as his associates for the Egyptian project, among them Professors Wolfgang Pilz and Paul Goerke and Drs. Ermin Dadieu and Heinz Krug. A debate in the regional parliament of Baden-Württemberg revealed that Cairo had promised the German scientists a bonus of two million marks, of which six hundred thousand were to go to Professor Sänger, and that half of that sum had already been paid him.

The Israelis and their government did not worry unduly about this news. It was only when Nasser's four rockets went up on July 21 that a wave of anxiety began to sweep over Israel. Deputy Defense Minister Shimon Peres declared: "The rockets the Egyptians have launched constitute a serious threat to Israel. They have inaugurated a new era in the Middle East. The advent of these modern weapons has radically changed the nature of the danger that lies in wait for us and the measures we have to take to protect ourselves from it."

"Has Israel taken the proper measures?" asked many different figures in the army and in politics. "What is known about the Egyptian projects, and what have we done since Shavit Two to perfect our own rockets?"

It was quickly ascertained that very little had been done in either area. When Iser was being blamed for having "run after Yossele" instead of procuring information on the Egyptian rockets, he reminded his critics, citing chapter and verse, that he had long ago called their attention to the fact that the Egyptians were building a plant for the manufacture of rocket-planes with the help of German scientists.

Early in 1961 a Swiss firm in Emmen was testing rockets in an aerodynamic tunnel for the benefit of the Egyptians. But Israel's specialists had thought Egypt would need at least five years to perfect her missiles. In January 1962, in the wake of Sänger's resignation, there had come to light the existence of a company in Stuttgart called Intra-Handel, which was probably connected with the Egyptians' plans. Yet, ever since then, the Egyptian rockets had apparently been forgotten.

Now, however, it was clear that for at least two years hundreds of experts, technicians, and laborers had been working in completely up-to-date factories on the construction of long-range rockets in Egypt. It had to be admitted that no one knew these factories existed or what they were making or where they were located. Nor did anyone know the details of the Egyptian project, or how it stood at the moment, or what type of rockets it involved, or when the first tests had taken place and with what results. The launching of the four rockets had taken Israel completely by surprise.

The Defense Ministry's scientists were just as much to blame, for since little Shavit 2, which weighed only five hundred pounds, they had made no progress.

With no time to lose, Israel committed large sums of money for the acquisition of rockets abroad. (In 1965 the American press revealed that Israel had bought Diamant three-stage rockets from France and was also contributing to their further development.)

As to the Egyptian rockets, Iser said to Ben-Gurion: "I will undertake to gather all the information necessary and will have it in a few months."

The value of a secret service is best measured in a time of crisis, when the missions it undertakes are complicated and risky, when time is a factor and the target seems out of range as well as protected by all the enemy's security measures, **and** when the nation is anxious and the government is demanding instant results. In such circumstances a secret service has to prove its worth by tackling the situation boldly with all its resources. The rocket crisis confronted Israel's Secret Service with the severest test of its career.

On August 16, 1962, Iser Harel went to the Prime Minister's office to report that — less than a month since the launching of the Egyptian rockets — he had the story on them.

In mid-1959 the Commander in Chief of the Egyptian army, Marshal Abdel Hakim Amer, called in General Mahmoud Khalil, the former head of the Intelligence Bureau of the air force, who had Nasser's complete confidence. Some years earlier, when several superior officers were contriving a plot to overthrow the regime, Khalil, a member of the conspiracy, had seen which way the wind was blowing and had turned in his fellow conspirators to the police. Ever since, Nasser had heaped favors on him.

Amer told Khalil that Nasser had decided to create a special section in the Egyptian army to be called the Bureau of Special Military Programs, which would be responsible for perfecting ultrasecret modern weapons — jet fighters, rockets, and other latest-model missiles. The bureau was to have an almost unlimited budget and the best possible equipment and staff. Amer himself was to head it, and he was to have free and immediate access to Nasser at any time.

Since it was impossible to recruit qualified technical or scientific personnel in Egypt, a search for them would have to be made abroad, especially in Germany, for it was German scientists who had invented rockets and jet planes. At that time, however, the laws of Germany and also of the Occupation Powers forbade the manufacture of jets and rockets in the Federal

Republic of West Germany, and so these scientists had had to seek their fortunes elsewhere. They were now working in the United States, South Africa, India, Latin America, Spain, and several Eastern countries. A number of them, however, were still living in Germany, hoping that some foreign country would finally discover them and invite them to perfect on its own soil the complicated weapons they knew how to make. Egypt, therefore, had a good chance of attracting some of these retired scientists because several were still Nazis and anti-Semites and would find Egypt a congenial place to work.

In November 1959 Mahmoud Khalil went hunting for scientists in the Federal Republic. By November 29 he had signed a contract with Willy Messerschmitt, the inventor of the famous fighter planes that bear his name and one of the giants of aerial navigation. Messerschmitt pledged himself to establish an airplane plant in Egypt that would draw upon the expertise and experience of another factory he owned in Spain.

Through Dr. Eckart, one of the directors of Daimler-Benz, Khalil got in touch with aeronautics engineer Ferdinand Brandner, who had recently returned from Russia. Brandner undertook to build a jet-engine factory in Egypt to supply Messerschmitt's airframes. Hassan Kamil, an Egyptian millionaire living in Switzerland, was also enlisted as a façade and liaison man. Some months later the Egyptians organized two dummy companies in Switzerland, MECO (Mechanical Corporation) and MTP (Motors, Turbines, and Pumps), which were to purchase basic materials, instruments, electrical apparatus, and precision tools and also to recruit workers. The three directors of these companies were Messerschmitt, Brandner, and Kamil.

Early in 1960 the Bureau of Special Military Programs began to take form. Messerschmitt's factory was under construction near Cairo with the code name of "36." About fifteen miles from the capital was Brandner's engine factory, "135." In Heliopolis Khalil's men were building the most secret plant of all,

"333," to manufacture the rockets with which Nasser intended to fulfill his dream of destroying Israel and becoming sole master of the Arab world.

Mahmoud Khalil was very much at home with German scientists. Between 1951 and 1956 several German specialists had worked in Egypt, but all their enterprises had fallen through, and they had left after the Sinai War. Mahmoud Khalil had been the liaison with these German miracle workers during their stay in Egypt and knew how to argue with them.

Only a few persons knew that during his trip to Germany in 1959 Mahmoud Khalil had stopped off in Stuttgart, where he had found just what he was looking for — a greenhouse of bitter, frustrated scientists headed by Eugen Sänger.

Sänger had good reason to feel frustrated, for during the Second World War he had been one of the titans of German military science and had conceived a rocket-plane that could circle the earth in two hours. After the war several of Sänger's secret designs had fallen into the hands of the Russians, who had subsequently chased the scientist all over Europe in order to get him to work for them. Unfortunately for him, Sänger had already been captured by the French, who put him to work on minor projects. In 1954 he had returned to Germany, where no one was much interested in him. Whereas other German scientists like Wernher von Braun had covered themselves with glory in the eyes of the world by launching rockets, satellites, and spaceships, Sänger had had to content himself with the directorship of the third-rate Stuttgart Institute.

Sänger's associates there had never achieved much reputation even in their own country. Wolfgang Pilz, a second-rate engineer at Peenemünde, the launching base of the V–2, had been taken to France after the war, where he helped perfect the Véronique rocket. After he returned to Germany he submitted a plan to the Bonn government for a three-stage rocket, but it was rejected. He had no alternative to abandoning his ambition and becoming director of the Engine Department at the Stuttgart Institute.

The head of the Electronics Department was Professor Paul Goerke, who had worked in Egypt in the early 1950s. Another electronics expert was Dr. Hans Kleinwachter. The Chemistry Department was headed by Dr. Ermin Dadieu, a former SS officer. Dr. Heinz Krug was the administrative director of the Stuttgart Institute.

The Bonn government controlled that Institute and supplied most of its budget, and German law strictly forbade its staff to do research on weapons for a foreign country. But that was no obstacle to Mahmoud Khalil, who quickly perceived the enormous advantages of the Institute to Egypt. He signed secret contracts with Sänger, Pilz, Kleinwachter, Goerke, Krug, Dadieu, and some twenty of their associates, whereby they would create in Egypt a whole rocket industry in exchange for high salaries and large bonuses.

In order to be sure of a regular supply of parts, metals, guidance fittings, and various other kinds of instruments — and also to keep everything completely under wraps — the Egyptians created several companies in Europe to conceal their activities. The most important was Intra-Handel, with branches in Munich, Stuttgart, and other cities. Its offices were on the premises of the Egyptian Airline Company, and the materials it purchased were sent to that company's address in Egypt, labeled "technical equipment for airplane maintenance." Dr. Krug was made director of Intra. Other companies camouflaged by innocent façades were Linda and Patwag. Lastly, an ultramodern laboratory was established in Lörrach in southern Germany, where Kleinwachter was to perfect a control system for the rockets destined to destroy targets situated "south of Beirut."

This infrastructure having been completed, both Egyptians and Germans got down to work. Sänger, Pilz, and their associates went to Egypt to direct the construction of Factory 333. Intra supplied enormous quantities of parts. The German scientists had brought in their personal luggage designs for liquid-fuel rockets that were to be modified versions of the Véronique and the V–2, weighing from four to twenty tons.

Early in 1961 the Germans began building their engines. The work progressed according to schedule until, toward the end of the year, the Bonn government suddenly discovered the connection between the Stuttgart Institute and Egypt's Special Military Program. The authorities, learning that for two years the Institute had been a bottomless source of supply for knowledge, for scientists, and for the basic needs of Factory 333, forced Eugen Sänger to resign, return to Germany, and cease all activity. Pilz succeeded him as head of the Egyptian project.

Eighteen months later, in July 1962, Factory 333 had produced about thirty rockets. Four of them were launched with great pomp and ceremony before a huge crowd that included guests of the government and journalists; twenty others, draped with the Egyptian flag, were paraded through the streets of Cairo on the anniversary of the revolution.

During the meeting in Ben-Gurion's office Iser Harel produced a document that told of the expanse of the Egyptian project. This was a letter from Professor Pilz to Kamil Azzab, the Egyptian director of Factory 333, dated March 24, 1962. In it Pilz asked the government to put at his and Dr. Krug's use the sum of 3,700,000 Swiss francs for the purchase of machine parts and other equipment for the five hundred rockets of Type 2 and four hundred of Type 5 that he intended to construct.

Israel was faced with two questions: What real threat did these rockets present, and what was the best way to neutralize it?

The experts said that in all probability the Egyptians had no intention of loading the nose cones with conventional explosives, for they would not have spent hundreds of thousands of dollars on their construction merely for them to carry a half-ton or even a ton of dynamite. A bomber could do that with more precision. Their belief was that Egypt would load the cones with atomic bombs or some other device forbidden by international law, such as poison gas, microbiotic cultures, or deadly radioactive waste. Egypt's interest in nuclear research for military purposes had been known in Israel for some time.

There could be no doubt that if the Egyptians managed to get hold of such forbidden weapons they would indeed be a serious threat to the security and even the survival of Israel. But there was a weak spot in the Egyptian rockets; for the time being they had no guidance system, and all the efforts of the German scientists to perfect one had so far failed. Since they could not direct their rockets to the targets, the Egyptians could hardly use them for military ends for the time being.

Iser was of the opinion that Ben-Gurion should immediately give Chancellor Konrad Adenauer proof that German citizens were participating in the manufacture of illicit weapons in Egypt and demand that the Bonn government take strong measures to put an end to their activities. Ben-Gurion, however, preferred the recommendation of his deputy Shimon Peres, who proposed to write German Defense Minister Franz Joseph Strauss, informing him of the serious situation that had arisen and requesting him to take the proper action. On the following day, August 17, 1962, therefore, Peres sent a cable to the Israeli Trade Mission in Germany asking that this message be transmitted orally to Strauss.

Peres' message emphasized that the July launching of the Egyptian rockets had produced great anxiety in Israel and that investigation had shown they had been manufactured with the aid of German scientists. He also included a detailed report on the activities of those scientists and stated his conviction that Strauss and Adenauer must be embarrassed by the thought that Germany at that time could be participating directly or indirectly in Russian and Egyptian attempts to destroy Israel.

Peres also asked how it happened that the German secret service had been unaware of the work of the scientists in

Egypt. Had German citizens a right to indulge in the manufacture of weapons in so explosive a region? It surprised him that the German Embassy in Cairo had not advised its government. Peres also stressed the fact that the German scientists were acting in flagrant opposition to the Bonn government's efforts to open a new chapter in its relations with the Jews, and he hoped that West Germany would put an immediate end to the activities of her citizens in Egypt. He clearly implied that this particular crisis might well reopen the wounds the Germans had inflicted on the Jewish people and provoke another frightful tragedy. He ended by expressing his hope that Germany would do everything possible to recall the scientists.

In a parallel action Foreign Minister Golda Meir and Shimon Peres got in touch with President John F. Kennedy through one of his close advisers. They described the rocket project to him in detail, adding that Israel was seriously worried and asking the United States to use its influence with the Federal Republic of West Germany.

Unfortunately, those diplomatic measures brought no results.

28

The Affair
of the German Scientists

AT 10:30 A.M. on September 11, 1962, a swarthy stranger with
an Oriental cast of features entered the Intra offices on Munich's Schillerstrasse and left the building a little later with
Heinz Krug. Half an hour later a United Arab Airlines stew-
ardess saw the two go by outside the ticket office. She was the
last person to see Krug.

On the following day Frau Krug telephoned the police that
her husband was missing.

Two days later Krug's mud-spattered car was found outside
the city, its tank empty. Then an anonymous phone call to the
police announced that Dr. Krug was dead.

To this day no one knows what happened to him.

On the morning of November 27 Hannelore Wende, Wolfgang Pilz's secretary at Factory 333, was opening the mail as
usual when she came to a thick package that, according to the
address on the wrapping, had come from a well-known Hamburg lawyer. As soon as she started to open it, a terrible explosion shook the office. Hannelore had to spend several months in
a Cairo hospital. She emerged with one eye gone, her hearing
impaired, and her face badly scarred.

On November 28 a large package marked "special book rate" and addressed to Factory 333 arrived by surface mail from Hamburg. As an Egyptian civil servant was opening it, the package exploded, killing five persons. Investigation revealed that the name of the sender, a publisher in Stuttgart, was false.

On the next day two more packages arrived with the same description of contents. By now the Egyptians were wary enough to have them examined by experts. Inside were books stuffed with explosives.

On February 23, 1963, Dr. Hans Kleinwachter, who had been in Europe for several weeks, left his laboratory in Lörrach to drive home. He had just turned into the dead end street he lived on when another car, with a great screeching of brakes, blocked his way. One man was at its wheel; another jumped out and approached Kleinwachter. The scientist glimpsed a third man in the car.

"Where does Dr. Shenker live?" asked the man who had got out. Then without waiting for an answer, he pulled out a revolver equipped with a silencer and fired, shattering Kleinwachter's windshield. The bullet lodged in the scientist's thick woolen muffler.

While Kleinwachter was trying to get his own pistol out of the glove compartment, his assailant and his accomplices fled. The police found their abandoned car about one hundred yards from the spot. The three had made their escape in another car, but they had dropped a passport made out to one of the heads of the Egyptian secret service, Ali Samir. Samir, however, could not himself have been involved in the ambuscade, for investigation proved that at the time it took place he was having his photograph taken with a German journalist in Cairo.

Neither the Egyptians nor the German police ever found any of the men who had attacked Kleinwachter.

In posts all over the world Mossad agents kept searching for information on the Egyptians' secret weapons. Presently they added two more names to their lists — Ibis and Cleopatra, which stood for two of Mahmoud Khalil's top-secret projects being executed by a very select group of scientists and army men.

Ibis was to supply Egypt with radioactive weapons capable of destroying all living things. Khalil wanted to get hold of the deadly cobalt 60 isotopes and ship them to Egypt for his experiments. If they were successful, Egypt would then purchase large quantities of cobalt for the nose cones of her rockets.

Cleopatra was a more ambitious project — the production of Hiroshima-type atomic bombs. Since Egypt had no nuclear reactors, the directors of the Special Military Program were seeking low-grade uranium, which they planned to improve with special centrifuges being perfected in the Netherlands and Germany.

The Egyptians had allocated fabulous sums for these two projects. Their emissaries, who were combing Europe for the deadly minerals, succeeded in buying a certain amount of cobalt 60, which the Egyptian Airline Company forwarded to the address of a Cairo gynecologist who presumably needed it for her medical work. That might have been believed had not the gynecologist been found to be Mahmoud Khalil's sister.

Presently another incident, which occurred far from Israel's borders, increased her anxiety. An international inquest came up with official proof that during the civil war in Yemen Egyptian planes had bombed villages with poison gas. From that report Israel deduced that the scientists in Egypt were involved in the manufacture of devices to be used in bacteriological and chemical warfare.

Toward the end of October 1962 the affair of the German scientists took a dramatic turn when a stranger came to one of Israel's European embassies and asked to see the security officer. "My name is Otto Joklik," he said, "and I can give you information on the work I have been doing for the Egyptian military projects."

Joklik, it appeared, had been hired by the Egyptians to perfect their forbidden weapons. "I have just come from Cairo," he said, "with proof that the scientists working in Egypt are manufacturing nose cones to be loaded with radioactive waste composed of cobalt sixty and strontium ninety; other cones are to be loaded with what's known as the poor man's atom bomb. When these rockets land on Israeli soil they will spread deadly rays that will infect the whole region for months, if not years."

Joklik himself, so he said, had been ordered to procure a large quantity of radioactive substances for Pilz and his colleagues.

The Israeli government did not let the people know how worried it was. The only hope was that the deadly rockets could not be put into use until the Egyptians had developed a guidance system for them. Israel reached the conclusion that something had to be done to prevent the scientists working on that problem from completing their infamous task.

As a matter of fact, at that time the Israelis were being accused of conducting a campaign of intimidation against the Germans working in Egypt and their families. Nasser's scientists kept getting threatening letters and telephone calls, sometimes directed to them personally and sometimes to their relatives. Also, their friends were urged to persuade them to get out of Egypt on the premise that if they went back to Germany nothing bad would happen to them. Otto Joklik himself undertook to persuade some of his colleagues to wind up their work and went to Europe with an Israeli companion named Yoseph Ben-Gal in order to get in touch with Professor Paul Goerke's daughter.

Goerke's assignment of developing a guidance system at Factory 333 made him extremely valuable to the Egyptians. Heidi, his daughter, lived in Freiburg, a small German city near the

Swiss border. Joklik told her that he knew her father in Egypt, where he was working on the manufacture of outlawed weapons designed for the destruction of Israel, and gave her to understand that if her father did not cease those activities he would run the risk of dire reprisals. If, on the other hand, he were to leave Egypt and return to Germany, he would not be molested, for Israel would guarantee his safety.

"If you love your father," Joklik said, "come on Saturday, March second, to the Three Kings Hotel in Basel at four P.M., and I will introduce you to my friends."

Panic-stricken, Heidi notified a former German army officer with a Nazi past whom the Egyptians had engaged to protect the scientists' families. The officer went to the Freiburg police, who notified the authorities in Basel. The Swiss police laid an ambush for Joklik and Ben-Gal, ordering several police cars to wait behind the Three Kings Hotel, stationing detectives in its lobby, and hiding microphones and tape recorders near the table Heidi Goerke would take.

Joklik and Ben-Gal arrived on schedule — and fell right into the trap. Suspecting nothing, they talked with Heidi Goerke for an hour in guarded terms, explaining to her why the weapons her father was making were an atrocity and what terrible damage they would cause if used against Israel. They also alluded to the frightful risk Professor Goerke was running, but they refrained from mentioning any explicit threats to him and his family. They offered Heidi a plane ticket to Cairo so that she could visit her father to try to persuade him to go back with her to Germany, where, they assured her, no harm would come to either of them.

After the interview Joklik and Ben-Gal left the hotel and took the six o'clock train to Zurich, where they parted company — but not for long. While Joklik was waiting for another train on the station platform, plainclothes men surrounded him and asked him to follow them. Ben-Gal was arrested near the Israeli Consulate.

That evening the German police requested the Swiss to extradite the two men on the grounds that they had threatened Heidi Goerke and were also suspected of having tried to kill Dr. Hans Kleinwachter two weeks earlier in Lörrach.

As soon as the Israeli authorities were notified of the arrest of Joklik and Ben-Gal, they put great effort into persuading the Swiss to free the men, but the Swiss refused on the grounds that Germany had demanded their extradition. All Iser Harel's attempts in that direction having failed, he went to Golda Meir and informed her of the situation. She suggested that Israel should approach Adenauer and demand that Germany withdraw the request for extradition.

Iser left at once for Tiberias, where Ben-Gurion was on vacation, and, following Golda Meir's suggestion, urged the Old Man to send a special envoy to Bonn at once in order to present Adenauer with concrete proof of the German scientists' activities in Egypt and persuade him to withdraw the demand that Joklik and Ben-Gal be taken to Germany.

Ben-Gurion refused.

Iser insisted. "Try to foresee what will happen when the public finds out."

"Well, what will happen?" said Ben-Gurion.

"As soon as Ben-Gal's arrest becomes known, the secret of the German scientists will be known also, and all their work in Egypt disclosed in complete detail. Israel will have to explain why Ben-Gal acted as he did. We shall also have to disclose that the Egyptians have been buying equipment for their rockets and other military projects from Germany."

Ben-Gurion thought a moment. "Well," he said, "so be it."

That answer seems to have marked the beginning of the rift between the two men.

29

Iser Resigns

THE ISSUE of the German scientists in Egypt did not provide the first occasion for Iser Harel to ask Ben-Gurion to take the matter up with Adenauer, and it was not the first time Iser had met with a refusal from the Old Man.

Ever since the question had arisen there had been rumors that the diplomats of the German Embassy in Cairo and also high officials in various German ministries were aware of their fellow countrymen's activities in Egypt. Iser believed that the Bonn government should be required to take strong action against them, as German law provided, and that Israel should make known all the information she had on their activities. Howls of protest from all quarters of the globe would then force the German government to act at once.

Ben-Gurion, on the other hand, consistently refused to appeal to Adenauer, preferring the campaign against the scientists to be handled by other methods. In his letters to the chancellor of the West German Republic in 1962 and 1963 there occurred not the slightest reference to the matter. He had indeed authorized Peres to write to Strauss, but when he saw that there were no sequels to that correspondence he had determined to oppose any further official intervention.

The difference of opinion between Iser and Ben-Gurion in this connection went deep. They were divided about the whole German question. Ben-Gurion had created in Israel the concept of "the new Germany," for he firmly believed that Adenauer's Germany was sincerely trying to expiate the sins of Hitler's. He also thought that France's recent alliance with Germany obliged Israel to keep on good terms with Bonn if she wished to continue working closely with France.

There were other reasons for thinking that this policy would have good results. After Germany had paid the last penny of reparations, Adenauer's government had been pouring tens of millions of dollars into the Israeli treasury according to the terms of a loan of five hundred million dollars that the chancellor had secretly promised Ben-Gurion when the two met in New York in 1960. Furthermore, Germany was very secretly furnishing Israel with ultramodern armaments on incredibly low terms — only 10 percent of their value — and delivering other costly items free.

Ben-Gurion believed that this arrangement was extremely important to the survival of his country and did not wish to endanger it by pointing an accusing finger at Adenauer in demanding that he take action against the scientists. Ben-Gurion apparently feared that Adenauer would not grant such a demand, and so why ask only to be refused and at the same time create tension between Bonn and Jerusalem?

Iser, however, had no love for Germany. He had, of course, approved of the reparations payment and had even gone so far as to speak out in favor of it, but he had also reacted violently against Israel's sale of machine pistols to Germany, a transaction that had raised a storm of protest in 1959. Iser thought that Israel ought to establish standard diplomatic relations with Germany only if Germany made the first gesture in that direction, but he had absolutely no use for the concept of "the new Germany," and he never overlooked an opportunity to point out at high-level conferences that Nazis still held important posts in it. In short, he was in entire disagreement with Ben-Gurion on the whole subject of Germany and wanted to take a hard line. Iser's friends had noticed that since the capture of Eichmann in 1960 he had become more hostile than ever to Germany, to the point of real hatred.

Foreign Minister Golda Meir had no love for Germany either and felt exactly as Iser did. Deputy Defense Minister Shimon Peres, however, loyally supported Ben-Gurion's policy. At this time relations between Golda Meir and Shimon Peres on the one hand, and between Iser and Peres on the other hand, were quite strained, and their differences of opinion added a personal and emotional as well as a political dimension to the German question.

Ben-Gurion's policy toward Germany was criticized by several political parties, in the government coalition as well as in the opposition. Herut (the extreme Right), Achdut Ha'avoda (workers' Left), Mapam, and the communist party, as well as some factions of Mapai itself, strongly opposed the Old Man. The Prime Minister, who had so patiently and energetically nourished the relations between Israel and his "new Germany," and who had also gradually caused the nation to understand the necessity of maintaining them, now was in fear that a tiny slip or a hasty and unwise decision might revive the Jewish people's bitter resentment and destroy the structure he had labored over for fifteen years.

Early in the evening of Thursday, March 15, 1963, United Press International announced the arrest of Joklik and Ben-Gal "on suspicion of having threatened the daughter of a German scientist in the employ of Egypt." The same evening Iser Harel and Golda Meir discussed the answer the Israeli government should make. On the next day Iser went to Tiberias.

Iser laid Golda Meir's proposals for Israel's answer before Ben-Gurion, who decided that there was no need for any reply at all. As to what the press should be told, he said: "We shouldn't raise the question of the rockets, just explain the arrest."

On his return to Tel Aviv, Iser called a secret meeting of the chief editors of the Israeli daily papers at which he sketched the whole Ben-Gal affair. He particularly emphasized Joklik's part in the affair, the kind of work Joklik had been doing for the Egyptians, and the fact that Joklik had changed sides voluntarily in order to do his best to repair the damage already done to Israel.

During the next few days Iser's associates secretly called in three Israeli journalists: Naftali Lavi of *Ha'aretz,* Samuel Segev of *Ma'ariv,* and Ben-Porat of *Yedioth Acharonot.* They were given all the facts and the figures, and the addresses of Intra, Patwag, and the Stuttgart Institute. The three reporters then took off for Europe to gather data on the activities of the German scientists. Others were hurried off to "enlighten" pro-Israeli journalists abroad and provide them with details on the Egyptian rocket project.

In itself it seemed a good idea to give both the Israeli and the foreign press the facts as to why Israel had sent agents to Switzerland to put pressure on Heidi Goerke. The men who start the wheels of public opinion rolling, however, do not necessarily take into account just what the public's feelings are, and in this particular case they forgot the Israelis' sensitivity toward Germany. Probably they intended only to produce the evidence, but they succeeded in starting an avalanche of charges against Germany, some well-founded and others imaginary, that provoked a panic in Israel.

After March 17 both the Israeli and the foreign press got to floundering in a sea of headlines proclaiming the sensational news that German scientists, former Nazis for the most part, had been hired by the Egyptians to produce outlawed weapons and were preparing Egypt to wage biological, chemical, nuclear, and radioactive warfare. They were making poison gases, developing fatal microbes, death rays, and probably atom bombs to boot. The Egyptian rockets, capable of destroying every target within Israel, were to be loaded with deadly substances.

The press campaign was supported with references and even evidence designed to prove that the German government was doing nothing to prevent its citizens abroad from pursuing their criminal activities, the end of which was the annihilation of the Jewish people. The journalists who had gone to Germany and Switzerland added a personal touch by "discovering" every day new details of the diabolical plot being woven by the Egyptians and the German scientists.

The campaign quickly snowballed, and all sense of proportion and all faculties of reason were submerged in generalizations and exaggeration. The press, public opinion, and a large number of prominent leaders and Knesset members made no effort to distinguish between the scientists working in Egypt and the Bonn government. In fact, either for political reasons or because of painful memories, newspapers, parties, and individuals accused the Federal Republic of West Germany of following in Hitler's footsteps. Shrieking headlines, editorials, caricatures, and even poems proclaimed that the Germany of 1963 was no different from the Germany of 1933, and that the same Germany which had massacred Jews was now helping Egypt obliterate Israel.

Ben-Gurion's "new Germany" came in for its share of violent, ill-tempered abuse, as might have been expected in a nation largely composed of escapees from the Nazi holocaust. The delicate bridge that Ben-Gurion had thrown across the chasm separating Germany and Israel seemed ready to crash into an abyss of hatred.

In the midst of this anti-German campaign of unprecedented violence the government decided to make a statement of policy before the Knesset. Since Ben-Gurion was still vacationing in Tiberias, the task was handed to Golda Meir. For once the parliamentary committee of Defense and Foreign Affairs assumed the initiative, and in view of the serious danger threatening the nation, all parties represented on the committee decided to submit a unanimous resolution to the Knesset which would show the world that the State of Israel had firmly decided to demand that an end be put to the activities of the German scientists. Ben-Gurion approved this plan.

On March 20 Golda Meir mounted the Knesset tribune and declared: "The activity of the German scientists and experts in producing weapons for Egypt that she intends to use for the destruction of Israel and her people constitutes a serious threat to our survival. If that criminal activity continues, the German people must accept responsibility for it. The German government has a duty to cause the wicked pursuits of its citizens to cease, and to terminate their service to the Egyptian government."

Golda Meir refrained from specifying what types of weapons the Germans were making in Egypt, but she emphasized that they "were involved in the production of rockets and also of weapons forbidden by international conventions, whose sole aim was to destroy all living things." She also made reference to the radioactive weapons Otto Joklik had indicated were in the process of manufacture.

Her restrained and dignified tone was in sharp contrast to the frenzied debate that followed her speech. The representatives of the communist party proposed a "settling of accounts" with Germany. A Mapam deputy spoke in apocalyptic terms of the "German death ray." The leader of a religious party exclaimed in a doleful tone: "We have been led astray and gravely deceived by Germany's statements and promises." Most of the speakers violently attacked Ben-Gurion's German policy, the most unrestrained of all being the leader of Herut, Menachem Begin, who in an inflammatory tirade accused Ben-Gurion of "giving the Germans an alibi. You sent machine pistols to the Germans," he declared, "and now the Germans are sending microbes to our enemies."

In bringing the debate to an end, Golda Meir rebuked Begin: "Seldom has the whole Knesset been so shocked as when Mr. Begin allowed himself to speak in such a way . . . I shall not reply to him, for I have too much respect for this chamber, which has met to debate a crucial problem for the nation and its government."

That is how the session had changed into a trial of Ben-Gurion's German policy, which no one rose to defend. The Israeli journalist Natan Yanai wrote: "It is very significant that Golda Meir refrained from explaining Ben-Gurion's policy. She is known to oppose a policy of friendship with Germany and even to be actually hostile to some of its aspects."

After the debate in the Knesset, the anti-German campaign gathered strength, and it was not until a week later, on March 24, 1963, that Ben-Gurion acknowledged his mistake.

The Old Man's error was not to have taken the issue of the German scientists in hand as soon as it came to light. Even after the newspaper campaign began and the debate in the Knesset, Ben-Gurion's attitude had been to wait, shocked though he was by the mounting hysteria. He had not foreseen the danger lurking in the press campaign. By authorizing Iser Harel to "explain the arrest of Ben-Gal" he had probably thought of an information operation much more discreet than that conducted by the newspapers. He could have intervened in time to prevent some of the worst damage, but he had not done so; rather he had entrusted the direction of the campaign and of Israel's policy toward Germany to persons whose opinions were diametrically opposed to his own. Shimon Peres was abroad at the time, and so there was no one in the government who could restore a balance and subdue the violence of the anti-German manifestations. As a result of Ben-Gurion's silence, his German policy was on the verge of foundering.

But did the German scientists in Egypt really constitute such a serious threat to Israel's survival?

This author is convinced that the charges leveled at Germany and the scientists were only partly justified. Dr. Otto Joklik, whose testimony played a basic part in the whole business, was no more than an adventurer who had forged his scientific degrees. Later it was discovered that only an infinitesimal amount of cobalt had reached Egypt. Even though the Israeli and the foreign press published copies of orders for hundreds of thousands of curies of radium — not enough to produce deadly radiations anyway — it was ascertained that only forty curies had been sent to Egypt. Even if much larger quantities had been imported, it would have been impossible to manufacture fatal nose cones, and the danger they represented would have been very minor.

Neither can there be any doubt that the importance then being given to the Ibis and Cleopatra projects was greatly exaggerated. Cleopatra — the manufacture of inexpensive atom bombs — now seems ludicrous. Had any expert been consulted even then, he could hardly have taken the project seriously. As for Ibis — radioactive nose cones — the destruction they might have caused would not have surpassed that of ordinary bombs. Israel's state of mind greatly inflated the peril of the Egyptian projects.

The German scientists themselves were mediocre. The rockets they were perfecting were already almost obsolete. Their activities were, indeed, pernicious, but the panic that swept over the Israeli government was certainly out of all proportion. The affair did justify a firm warning to Bonn to recall the scientists, but in no respect did it justify the general attitude of hostility toward Germany or the charge that Germany was positively aiding Egypt to destroy Israel.

In the midst of the crisis, the journalist Shabtai Tevet wrote in *Ha'aretz:*

The mobilization of public opinion has gone hand in hand with disgraceful manifestations. The worst of all is the panic that has seized Israel, and which now appears ridiculous. The description given in the Knesset of the Egyptian death ray, hissing and devouring everything in its path, seems borrowed from the adventures of Flash Gordon. The peregrinations of the Israeli reporter-detectives in Switzerland and Germany have a certain amusing absurdity about them. In the outside world everyone is wondering why the Israelis should be so horrified over the arrest of one of their spies.

In another editorial Avraham Schweitzer wrote:

Judging the matter by the information published, not without the aid of the authorities, it is impossible to maintain the theory that Germany was connected with the production of outlawed weapons in Egypt . . . As for the nose cones, it is possible that Egypt was trying to equip her forces with weapons of chemical warfare, bacteriological or whatever, but it does not appear that Germany had any part in that project.

Several days after the stormy session in the Knesset Ben-Gurion emerged from his isolation. On March 24 he returned to Tel Aviv. Too late, he decided to stop the snowball that was already halfway down the hill.

Late in the evening of March 24 Iser Harel was called to the Prime Minister's house. At the beginning of their talk Ben-Gurion told him that the data published in the newspapers on his instigation had had a shameful effect. When he asked Iser if Mossad had given any directives to the reporters, Iser confirmed that three special writers had indeed been briefed. The Old Man then expressed his indignation over the way in which the papers had treated the whole question.

About midnight the two men parted in a proper manner but in a charged atmosphere. On the following day Iser was summoned to Ben-Gurion again. The Old Man seemed tense and sullen. Iser vigorously attacked those who had discounted the danger. He refuted Ben-Gurion's theories and directly contradicted his arguments.

Their conversation, which had begun with a confrontation on the affair of the scientists, shifted rapidly to a lively discussion of how to deal with the German problem on the political level. Iser stressed the German government's moral obligation to put an end to the activities of the scientists in Egypt, maintaining that pressure exercised by Israel on the diplomatic level would have a considerable effect internationally.

Ben-Gurion was not of that opinion. He was frankly skeptical of the efficacy of a program of pressure. He emphasized the importance of Germany on the European and the world scene, citing it as a reason why the friends of Germany were not interfering and recapitulating the great assistance Germany had given Israel, which required that good relations be maintained between them.

"The action we took against the scientists, in Switzerland and elsewhere, has turned public opinion against us," Ben-Gurion stated.

"Then why did you authorize it?" replied Iser.

Ben-Gurion then said that during the recent visit to Israel of Dr. Gerstenmayer, President of the West German Bundestag, Gerstenmayer had promised that when he returned to Germany he would settle the question of diplomatic relations between the two countries. Iser did not believe that. He said he had information that proved Gerstenmayer was opposed to any standardization of relations between Germany and Israel. Ben-Gurion said he put no faith in the sources of that information or in the information itself. (Two months later Gerstenmayer publicly stated that he and the majority of the Bundestag favored full diplomatic relations with Israel, but his recommendation was not followed.)

At the end of their talk the Old Man told Iser that he intended to convoke the parliamentary committee of Defense and Foreign Affairs and demonstrate to it that the threat of the Egyptian rockets was far from being so terrible as the newspapers and the Knesset orators had claimed. Iser tried to talk him out of it but failed.

He took leave of the Old Man and went back to his own office, where he was to receive a delegation from abroad. As soon as his guests had left, he called in his secretary and dictated:

MR. PRIME MINISTER:
Because of our fundamental difference of opinion on the matter of the German scientists in the service of the Egyptian war effort and all that it implies, I believe it my duty to resign my position as head of the Central Bureau of Intelligence and Security (Mossad) and as the director of the Secret Services.

> Respectfully,
> ISER HAREL

Iser left his office and went home, where his outwardly calm and detached manner did not fool Rivka. The telephone rang, but he did not answer it. After it had rung again two, three, and four times, Rivka said: "Iser, that's the telephone."

"Don't answer it," Iser shouted.

The telephone kept ringing all through the evening, but Iser would not let it be answered. Rivka knew that when he thought himself unjustly treated he would not think it over, he would just get up and leave.

Late in the evening a messenger brought Iser a letter in the Old Man's handwriting:

TO ISER HAREL:
I cannot accept your resignation. In any event you ought to stay on until the government and the Knesset decide what policy to adopt on the matter we discussed. Perhaps your opinion will prevail in

either the government or the Knesset, and in that event you can continue your work as you see fit under the orders of a new Prime Minister.

Cordially,
DAVID BEN-GURION

Iser read the letter without saying anything. Rivka asked no questions, but on the following morning she was delighted to see her husband go to his office as usual.

At ten o'clock Iser got another letter from Ben-Gurion, asking him to reply in writing that same day to several questions: What did he know about the work of the German scientists in Egypt in the area of nonconventional weapons (radioactive, biological, chemical)? Did he have in his possession information on the German industrial firms that were supplying Egypt with basic materials and machines for the manufacture of such weapons? What sources had furnished him with that information?

Iser did not answer the letter. He picked up the telephone and called in Haim Israeli, Director of the Defense Minister's office. When Haim arrived, Iser was in a towering rage.

"You can tell Ben-Gurion," Iser said, "that if he wants answers to his questions, he can get them from whoever replaces me. If human lives were not at stake, and if our men were not in jail in Switzerland, I would not stay here one second longer. Send someone right away to take over and pick up the keys."

Haim reported the scene to an astonished Ben-Gurion.

"Perhaps we can manage to persuade him . . ."

"He seemed firmly resolved to quit," Haim said, "and demanded we send someone to succeed him immediately."

"All right," Ben-Gurion said resignedly. "But who is there to send? Get me Joel Morag."

His secretaries could not reach Morag by telephone, for at that moment he was on his way to the Maagan kibbutz in the Jordan valley to visit his relatives.

"Then get me Meir," said Ben-Gurion.

General Meir Amit, the head of Aman, was on a tour of inspection in the Negev near the Dead Sea, but was reached by radio and called back urgently to Tel Aviv. A brief letter from Ben-Gurion greeted him on his arrival and explained the situation. It ended with Ben-Gurion's request that Meir Amit assume direction of Mossad until a new chief was appointed and immediately take the necessary measures for a transfer of authority.

At eleven o'clock Iser went home. "I have resigned," he told Rivka. He telephoned his office and asked for a driver to take back his car. "I won't be needing it," he said.

A few days later he sold his wife's Volkswagen because he did not want to own any German product. His friends tried to get him to reconsider his decision, but he would not.

On April 1, 1963, the Israeli press announced the astonishing resignation of the director of the Secret Services.

"Faithful Guardian of the State's Security, Its Honor, and Its Secrets"

Iser Harel explained his resignation as follows:

"Ben-Gurion wanted to convene the parliamentary committee of Defense and Foreign Affairs and tell it that the Egyptian rockets were no threat to Israel. If he had done so, I would have been the first to testify before the committee, and I would have been obliged to contradict Ben-Gurion, for, to the best of my knowledge, the rockets were very much a threat indeed. Ben-Gurion would have lost face; his colleagues in the coalition government would have rebelled against his authority; he would have been forced to resign. I myself resigned in order to prevent his calling the committee . . .

"Furthermore," Iser added, "we can't go backward. From the time when both the government and the Knesset defined and approved the policy to be taken toward the scientists and toward Germany herself, it was inconceivable that we should renege or retreat. You can't go back on resolutions that have been officially adopted."

Iser's reasoning is not very convincing. As indicated previously, time proved the Egyptian rockets relatively harmless, and the lofty plans and projects of the Egyptians came to nothing. It is possible, of course, that the preventive measures Israel took had something to do with rendering the Egyptian Special Military Program innocuous, but even if Iser had testified before the committee, he would have been unable to prove that the German scientists in Egypt were working to perfect outlawed weapons.

The same is true as to his reasoning about resigning in order to keep Ben-Gurion from defeat. On March 26 Ben-Gurion assured the committee — as he had intended to do from the first — that the rockets did not constitute a danger to Israel, and the committee did not "rebel" against him.

Iser's resignation, however, coming at the height of the crisis, was a blow to the Old Man's authority. One needs only to read the newspapers of the time to grasp how much Ben-Gurion's position was weakened by the departure of the head of the Secret Services.

Neither does Iser's argument that "we can't go backward" stand up, for in politics a backward step is not only possible but sometimes even desirable. Many nations have had to change their policy radically because of a change in circumstances or a fresh analysis of the situation. Ben-Gurion was wrong to let the crisis over the scientists get worse and endanger his whole policy toward Germany, but from the time he acknowledged that his policy was threatened he had a perfect right to abandon the line he had previously taken. If he wanted to tangle with a section of his coalition government in order to have his point of view accepted, that was his business and his alone. Iser had been prompted by his own short-term policy toward the German scientists. Ben-Gurion took a longer view of the whole matter of German-Israeli relations. Consequently he had to take a different attitude from Iser's even if his approach to the problem did weaken the efficiency of the operations against the scientists.

Iser would say that things had not been explained to him that way and would let it be more or less understood that if Ben-

Gurion had let him in on his plans he would have acted differently. It appears, however, that the abrupt turn his last conversation with Ben-Gurion took, as well as their divergence of opinion on other matters, induced him to resign.

Iser's friends were dumfounded by his action. A few thought he was right, but most still believe his behavior was a serious mistake.

Some journalists have tried to explain Iser's action. In *Ha'aretz* Ze'ev Schiff wrote:

Iser Harel and Ben-Gurion are very much alike; hence their close friendship and mutual confidence over the past fifteen years. But it is also the reason why their first disagreement produced such a shock . . . Iser's resignation was a model of democratic action. Instead of insisting on holding the line his powerful organization had taken, he preferred to leave so that his elected superior might maintain his own position. If this quarrel had not been connected with a matter of conscience and if interference with another power had not been involved, Iser perhaps would have accepted Ben-Gurion's judgment and stayed at his post.

One of Iser's closest friends said: "If the German problem hadn't come into it, he would not have resigned, but he was completely intransigent about Germany." Another said: "Ben-Gurion spoiled Iser by so often adopting his opinion and following his advice. Iser got a slap in the face, but it was not intended for him personally. Ben-Gurion never doubted his ability, his intelligence, or his remarkable talents. But Iser was insulted, and he resigned without thinking things through." One other friend said: "Iser acted like a man whose job is to conceive and formulate a policy, and not as a civil servant whose job is to execute a policy once it has been taken."

As a matter of fact, for a long, long time, Iser had not been the mere civil servant his job description listed him as, but had held a position equal to a minister's or even a superminister's.

His powers, his influence, and his opinions carried much more weight than most of the cabinet members. Ben-Gurion's door was always open to him, and in the majority of cases his judgment was heeded. He directed a powerful organization, and in the area of Intelligence he had become a kind of foreign minister. There is no doubt that during his last years in office Iser reached a much higher position in the state than any other head of a secret service in a democratic nation. His resignation was not that of a civil servant but of a political leader.

The author believes Iser's resignation a mistake. He seems to have acted on impulse, much as he did when he quit the kibbutz twenty-five years earlier. But Iser was Iser, and deep down inside, the stubborn, tough little pioneer had not changed.

Iser never lost Ben-Gurion's high opinion. On the day after Iser's resignation, the Old Man wrote him:

In spite of all that has happened since you offered your resignation, I want you to be assured of the high regard I have for the important services you have rendered during your term of office. My high admiration of your abilities, your devotion to your duty, and your loyalty has not altered.

You are leaving against my wishes, and you did not acknowledge my refusal to accept your resignation, but that is your own affair, and I have no right to pass judgment on you for it.

By his departure Iser inflicted an injury on Ben-Gurion, on the State of Israel, and, above all, on himself. With his own hands he wrecked a brilliant career that he might have followed for long years to come.

Throughout the world front-page headlines announced Iser's departure from office, and there were long editorials about it in the major newspapers. Up until then he had been somewhat unknown, but now he appeared as having established and run one of the best secret services of our times. Rarely has the resignation of a man in a similar position created such a stir.

The German scientists continued to preoccupy the Israelis for some months more. In Basel, Yoseph Ben-Gal and Otto Joklik were brought to trial, in the course of which they described the danger to Israel of the scientists' work in Egypt. Each was given a suspended sentence of two months in jail. The trial and the verdict thus were a moral victory for Israel.

The German government, however, did not do what was expected of it. It invoked no law to forbid the scientists to sell their services to a country in a state of war, or any other legal measure to force the return of the experts from Egypt. Bonn, nevertheless, in 1964 discreetly induced Pilz, Goerke, and some others to return to Germany by promising them higher salaries in a less explosive atmosphere.

The Knesset kept right on passing resolutions denouncing the German scientists until the outbreak of the Six Day War. After Iser's resignation a committee of ministers inquired into the affair and submitted its findings to the government, which issued an official release on the subject in September 1963:

The government has determined that it is necessary to firmly pursue the action against the German scientists working in Egypt, according to the indications given the Knesset by the Prime Minister and the Foreign Minister.

The government regrets the resignation of the head of the Secret Services, and hereby expresses its admiration and appreciation of his dedicated service, which has been crowned with great success in all the areas entrusted to him throughout his term in office.

It was, however, the minister of agriculture at that time, a retired general named Moshe Dayan, who at the climax of the crisis best kept his head about the rockets. In *Ma'ariv* he wrote:

Even if there has not been tangible evidence that the Egyptians were working on the production of nuclear weapons with the connivance of the German scientists and technicians, we may suppose

without too much risk of error that they are intending to do so . . .
We have to take cognizance of that eventuality. Perhaps some day
— perhaps even in the coming decade — Nasser will get his nuclear
weapons. I am in complete agreement with those who think we
should do our utmost to prevent German scientists and technicians
— and those of other countries — from helping with these "developments" in Egypt. We must take action through governmental channels and also by public condemnation.

But there is one thing I think must be strongly emphasized and
that is that the German people and their government ought not to
be confused with Pilz and his gang in Egypt. It is a false identification that can only do us harm. The best way to assure ourselves that
the Bonn government will take action against Pilz and company, and
that the German people will force it to do so, is to keep on friendly
terms with that government. A straw fire that goes out as soon as lit
will not settle that question.

Even if action against the Pilz crew got us everything obtainable,
it must not be believed that it would put an end to scientists and
technicians working for Nasser, whether German or of another nationality.

In the coming era, the rocket age, our own armaments and the
power of our own army are what will dissuade Nasser from starting
a war. We must devote our efforts to the strengthening and im-
provement of those armaments and that power.

On June 15, 1963, ten weeks after Iser Harel resigned, Ben-
Gurion submitted his own resignation "for personal reasons." It
is rather symbolic that those two men who had run the same
course together ever since the creation of the State of Israel
should leave their posts at almost the same moment. It puts a
conspicuous marker on the end of the Ben-Gurion era, the era
of Israel's rebirth.

Almost two and a half years went by before Iser Harel and
David Ben-Gurion met again. In early November 1965 Paula
Ben-Gurion invited Iser to pay the Old Man a visit. When he
arrived at their modest house on Keren-Kayemet Boulevard in
Tel Aviv, he was on the point of tears, and when he saw his old

boss again, he could restrain himself no longer. Ben-Gurion gave Iser his photograph, on which he had written:

To Iser Harel, faithful guardian of the State's security, its honor, and its secrets. With all my esteem and affection.